PSYCHOLOGY AS
A NATURAL AND
SOCIAL SCIENCE

BASIC CONCEPTS IN PSYCHOLOGY SERIES

Edward L. Walker, Editor

GENERAL

PSYCHOLOGY AS A NATURAL AND SOCIAL SCIENCE	Edward L. Walker
TEACHING THE BEGINNING COURSE IN PSYCHOLOGY	Edward L. Walker and Wilbert J. McKeachie
A LABORATORY MANUAL FOR THE CONTROL AND ANALYSIS OF BEHAVIOR	Harlan L. Lane and Daryl J. Bem
QUANTIFICATION IN PSYCHOLOGY	William L. Hays
BASIC STATISTICS	William L. Hays

PSYCHOLOGY: A NATURAL SCIENCE

NEUROPSYCHOLOGY: THE STUDY OF BRAIN AND BEHAVIOR	Charles M. Butter
SENSORY PROCESSES	Mathew Alpern, Merle Lawrence, and David Wolsk
PERCEPTION	Daniel J. Weintraub and Edward L. Walker
PERCEPTUAL DEMONSTRATION KIT	Daniel J. Weintraub and Edward L. Walker
HUMAN PERFORMANCE	Paul M. Fitts and Michael I. Posner
CONDITIONING AND INSTRUMENTAL LEARNING	Edward L. Walker

PSYCHOLOGY: A SOCIAL SCIENCE

MOTIVATION: A STUDY OF ACTION	David Birch and Joseph Veroff
THE CONCEPT OF HUMAN DEVELOPMENT	Elton B. McNeil
PSYCHODYNAMICS: THE SCIENCE OF UNCONSCIOUS MENTAL FORCES	Gerald S. Blum
ASSESSMENT OF HUMAN CHARACTERISTICS	E. Lowell Kelly
COGNITIVE PROCESSES	Melvin Manis
SOCIAL PSYCHOLOGY: AN EXPERIMENTAL APPROACH	Robert B. Zajonc
NON-FREUDIAN PERSONALITY THEORIES	P. James Geiwitz
BELIEFS, ATTITUDES, AND HUMAN AFFAIRS	Daryl J. Bem

PSYCHOLOGY AS A NATURAL AND SOCIAL SCIENCE

EDWARD L. WALKER

The University of Michigan

BROOKS/COLE PUBLISHING COMPANY
Belmont, California

A Division of Wadsworth Publishing Company, Inc.

To Alice and Bruce

L.C. Cat. Card No.: 74-89506

Printed in the United States of America

SERIES FOREWORD

Basic Concepts in Psychology was conceived as a series of brief paperback volumes constituting a beginning textbook in psychology. Several unique advantages arise from publishing individual chapters as separate volumes rather than under a single cover. Each book or chapter can be written by an author identified with the subject matter of the area. New chapters can be added, individual chapters can be revised independently, and, possibly, competitive chapters can be provided for controversial areas. Finally, to a degree, an instructor of the beginning course in psychology can choose a particular set of chapters to meet the needs of his students.

Probably the most important impetus for the series came from the fact that a suitable textbook did not exist for the beginning courses in psychology at the University of Michigan—Psychology 100 (Psychology as a Natural Science) and Psychology 101 (Psychology as a Social Science). In addition, no laboratory manual treated both the natural science and social science problems encountered in the first laboratory course, Psychology 110.

For practical rather than ideological reasons, the initial complement of authors comes from the staff of the University of Michigan. Coordination among geographically dispersed authors seems needlessly difficult, and the diversity of points of view in the Department of Psychology at Michigan makes the danger of parochialism quite small.

Each author in the Basic Concepts in Psychology Series has considerable freedom. He has been charged to devote approximately half of his resources to elementary concepts and half to topics of special interest and emphasis. In this way, each volume will reflect the personality and viewpoint of the author while presenting the subject matter usually found in a chapter of an elementary textbook.

PREFACE

This book, the "first chapter" of the Basic Concepts in Psychology Series, provides the student with several ways of organizing and integrating the contents of the series.

One organizational basis for any segment of knowledge is its place in relation to other segments. The first chapter of this book is therefore devoted to a discussion of psychology as a discipline among the other disciplines in modern universities.

Another organizational basis is the set of values and beliefs that are commonly held by scholars of a particular discipline. These are the discipline's articles of faith. Thus, the second and third chapters deal with some philosophical issues that are of concern to psychologists, to the academic community, and to society in general. In discussing these issues, Chapter 3 presents some empirical data concerning the views of a number of scholars on these issues. These data are presented in the form of mean ratings of the degree of agreement among certain groups of scholars on the various issues.

Two cross-indexes are provided for the books constituting the Basic Concepts in Psychology Series as of July 1, 1969. The first index is an alphabetical list of the authors cited in the series. The second is a conceptual index of the series; it is organized according to a conceptual outline of psychology. Two recent additions to the series (*Non-Freudian Personality Theories*, by P. James Geiwitz, and *Beliefs, Attitudes, and Human Affairs*, by Daryl J. Bem) are not included in these indexes.

Very special thanks are due to Charlotte L. Doyle, whose doctoral dissertation provided all of the material presented in Chapter 3. Her kind permission to use her ideas, her references, her quotations, her data, and, most of all, her insights, represents something more than simple generosity.

My thanks are also due to graduate students Joseph Mortenson, Jon Williams, and Linda Selzer for critical reading of the manuscript; and I thank Erasmus L. Hoch and Charlotte L. Doyle for a similar contribution. And, finally, I thank Camille Buda for her quick and accurate typing of the final manuscript and her invaluable aid in preparing the indexes.

CONTENTS

Series Foreword   v
Preface   vi
Chapter 1:   Psychology in Perspective   1
     The Perspective of Time   2
     Contemporary Perspective   4
       Divisional Structure in Liberal Arts Colleges   5
     Perspective within Psychology   6
       General Psychology   7
       Psychology as a Natural Science   7
       Psychology as a Social Science   8
       Interdisciplinary Psychology   8
Chapter 2:   Some Philosophical Issues in Contemporary Psychology   10
     Determinism in Contemporary Physics   10
     Determinism in Contemporary Psychology   12
Chapter 3:   An Empirical Study of the Attitudes of Some
     Contemporary Scholars   17
     Determinism in Science   18
     The Reality of Freedom   20
     Science as a Single Model of the Universe   24
     Determinism and Democracy   26
     Psychology and the "Two Cultures"   30
Chapter 4:   Psychology and the Language of Science   33
     The Languages of Psychology   33
     The Language of Experimental Proof   35
Chapter 5:   The Language of Theory   42
Chapter 6:   The Psychological Experiment   52
Chapter 7:   "Good" and "Bad" Theories   58
     References   62
     Author Index of the Basic Concepts in Psychology Series   65
     Conceptual Index of the Basic Concepts in Psychology Series   81

PSYCHOLOGY IN PERSPECTIVE

Psychology can be defined as the *scientific study of the activities of the individual man in interaction with his environment.* This definition is likely to be acceptable to psychologists as well as to scholars in related fields or disciplines, yet it can be challenged as being both too broad and too narrow. The definition is too broad because it encompasses the activities of scholars in other disciplines. For example, sociologists and anthropologists are concerned with problems that fall within this definition. The definition is too narrow because it excludes some activities carried on by psychologists. For example, comparative psychologists study the behavior of animals. Furthermore, many psychologists perform important functions that do not fit easily within a reasonable definition of science. The clinical psychologist may function as a scientist and may behave as an experimental psychologist, as we shall see later; but while he is helping a person to overcome a crippling emotional problem, he is exercising an art or skill.

An alternative to framing a short definition of psychology is simply *to describe psychology as the subject matter dealt with by those who are generally recognized as psychologists.* Such a description arises from the argument that psychology is not a single discipline that can be neatly clothed in a simple definition. Although there are certain seminal classes of behavior such as perception, learning, and motivation that are unambiguously and purely psychological, many psychologists work in subject matter that involves more than one disciplinary name, e.g., social psychology, educational psychology, engineering psychology, mathematical psychology, political behavior, psychoneurophysiology, the psychology of art and music, and others.

Both the short definition and the more pragmatic description are useful and meaningful. The first is an effort to place psychology within some framework, or schema, that systematizes all knowledge; and the second is an attempt to incorporate all the ferment of description, analysis, prediction, and control of all forms of the behavior of living organisms that is modern psychology.

THE PERSPECTIVE OF TIME

Psychology has a long past and a short history. Its past is as long as man's curiosity and speculation about human behavior. Its history extends back no further than the middle of the nineteenth century, when the beginnings of laboratory work on human behavior initiated the separation of psychology from philosophy. Some perspective on the nature of modern psychology can be gained by a brief survey of the evolution of four important ideas that characterize contemporary psychology: (1) empiricism, (2) experimentalism, (3) the recognition of individual differences in behavior, and (4) the effort to provide natural explanations of irrational behavior.

Psychology's most general characteristics today are a nearly universal faith in empiricism and a heavy dependence upon experimental methods as means of acquiring greater understanding of human behavior. Since both empiricism and experimentalism can be found in Greek philosophy, it becomes something of a problem to explain why nothing closely related to modern psychology developed between the Golden Age of Athens and the establishment of Wilhelm Wundt's laboratory in Germany late in the nineteenth century. Boring (1929, 1942) has shown clearly that the essence of experimental method was known and applied by the Greeks. Aristotle, despite an imperfect basis for separating fact from fiction, holds a place in history partly because he demonstrated the power that arises from the accumulation and systematization of factual knowledge, the essence of empiricism.

The explanation of this hiatus of at least twenty-three centuries is usually given in terms of the history of epistemology. Alternative bases for explaining human behavior, as well as the physical universe, were not only available but prevailed. Among major alternatives were Greek rationalism, theological explanations, and a belief in the supernatural. Greek rationalism suggested that knowledge was to be obtained exclusively by the process of human reasoning and that there was, by implication, little point in attempting to observe and record data. Theological explanations of the nature of man and the physical world clearly depended upon the interaction of the human intellect with the mind of God in varieties of religious experience. Belief in such evil and supernatural forces as demons, spirits, and the like precluded examination of social forces which might have played a contributing or causal role. Science, in the broad sense of the accumulation of systematic bodies of information and the experimental methods of acquiring new knowledge to add to the system, was simply a losing competitor in Western thought through most of this long period.

The great names of the beginnings of the Renaissance are those of men who began the return to the empirical and experimental philosophy and methods known to the Athenian Greeks. Thus in the thirteenth century, Roger Bacon believed that experimentation was the only avenue to truth that would lead man from the stupid and unprogressive debate that preoccupied contemporary intellectuals.

Descartes, early in the seventeenth century, enunciated a dualistic philosophy that separated the mechanical body from the soul. Since animals were believed not to have souls, an objective, scientific study of biological organisms could be conducted without evoking the fatal anger of the Church. It was a short step from Descartes's position to one that allowed scientific investigation of the physical body of man.

In the seventeenth and eighteenth centuries, German philosophers (as represented, for example, by Leibnitz) were strongly oriented toward explaining the character of the universe in terms of a rationally devised system. French and English philosophers of the same period were developing empirical and analytical approaches that stimulated objective investigation as a means of acquiring knowledge, thus laying the foundations of modern science.

Empiricism and experimentalism are characteristics basic to the development of all scientific disciplines. The idea that individual differences in behavior are normal and predictable and the idea that irrational behavior might have a natural and rational explanation are more closely identified with the development of psychology as a science.

It was not until the late nineteenth century that the work of Galton, in England, and Binet, in France, laid the foundations of the quantification of human characteristics. Galton was the first to bring the essence of Darwinism to bear on psychology and to apply the principles of variation, selection, and adaptation to the study of individuals and races. He is credited with inventing the psychological test (Boring, 1929). Binet's name is almost synonymous with the measurement of human intelligence. He developed the first practical intelligence test. It was devised to distinguish between those who failed to make normal progress in French schools by reason of stupidity and those who failed merely by reason of laziness. From Galton and Binet's work has grown the modern psychology of individual differences as well as the technical and applied aspects of statistical analysis and psychological measurement.

The predominance of Freudian thought in the twentieth century stems primarily from Freud's conception that irrational behavior in man does not require explanation in terms of the devil, demons, or an evil nature. Irrational behavior can be explained, instead, in terms of the normal functioning of aspects of character and personality of which the individual is not normally aware. Furthermore, Freud held that the character and organization of unconscious determinants of behavior can be studied through clinical methods, chiefly the free-association method. The scientific study of unconscious determinants of behavior is treated in another book of this series (Blum, *Psychodynamics: The Science of Unconscious Mental Forces,* 1966).

The preceding discussion has merely suggested four ideas as possible keystones of modern psychology: (1) empiricism, (2) experimentalism, (3) the normal, predictable variation in human behavior, and (4) the natural origins of irrational behavior. The two best secondary sources with which the student might begin to investigate the history of psychology are Boring (1929, 1942) and Murphy (1930, 1951). Boring has written a history of sensation and perception in psychology (1942) and a history of experimental psychology (1929), both of which are somewhat broader in conception and execution than their titles would suggest. Murphy's book, published in 1930 and again in revised form in 1951, is somewhat broader in scope than either of Boring's books. Students with a special interest in the past would do well to begin with these secondary sources and to proceed quickly to original sources. It is only in original material that one can attain the perspective of the present that arises from the momentary and fleeting impression of knowing and debating with a figure of the past.

CONTEMPORARY PERSPECTIVE

Contemporary perspective on the nature of psychology can be gained by a review of the place of psychology in the modern university and its place among academic disciplines. There is great variation among universities in the placement of psychology within the academic structure. Psychology is ubiquitous in the sense that there are few units of a modern university that might not have at least one psychologist teaching, participating in research, or carrying out a professional role. The place of psychology in the modern university is possibly best understood within the context of the development of universities themselves. Two patterns of growth are clearly apparent. One is the steady increase in the number of professional schools and colleges; the other is the differentiation of liberal arts colleges into increasing numbers of departments.

The more recent of the two growth patterns is the appearance of professional schools and colleges. As specialties became so sophisticated that substantial training was required to learn them, the institution of apprenticeship developed. With further growth of technical knowledge, the more efficient and concentrated training of a formal curriculum became necessary. The human and professional need for a liberal education to accompany the technical training resulted in the association of professional schools with liberal arts colleges to form the modern university. There are a great many kinds of professional schools in existence today, and new varieties may be anticipated.

The process of differentiation within philosophy is evident from the original meanings of the words *philosophy, mathematics,* and *doctor.* The literal meaning of the word *philosophy* was *love of wisdom. Mathematics* meant *things learned. Doctor* meant *teacher.* Some of the original meaning of these words is preserved in the academic degree, Doctor of Philosophy. As human knowledge grew in sheer quantity, specialties and subspecialties became differentiated. Within academic institutions there was a general tendency for specialties to develop within philosophy and to evolve into independent disciplines with distinctive labels. Generally, the nonprofessional liberal arts college contains the academic disciplines that have been differentiated from philosophy, and the curricular structure of such colleges tends to reflect the current state of evolution within human knowledge.

DIVISIONAL STRUCTURE IN LIBERAL ARTS COLLEGES

Most colleges of liberal arts contain divisional as well as departmental units. The most common divisions within the liberal arts are the *humanities,* the *natural sciences,* and the *social sciences.* None of the three admits to simple circumscription or to a simple definition that would be universally accepted, yet most academic disciplines find an uneasy home within one or more of them.

The humanities include the branches of cultural learning that emphasize the study of the ancient classics and of belles lettres. Historically, the term "humanities" applied chiefly to the renewed interest in Greek and Roman classics during the Renaissance. Today, the term also applies to a mode of thought centering on a set of interests and ideals that are distinctively humanistic. Typically, the division of humanities within a college of liberal arts contains departments teaching modern and ancient languages and literature, speech and drama, linguistics, music and art, archeology (especially classical archeology), and, perhaps, philosophy.

The natural sciences usually contain those branches of science that deal with objectively measured phenomena—with matter and energy and their interrelations and transformations. The natural sciences are frequently divided into the physical sciences, such as chemistry, physics, astronomy, and geology, and the biological sciences, such as botany, physiology, zoology, anthropology, and psychology. The natural sciences may also include mathematics and philosophy.

The social sciences can be defined as those branches of science that deal with institutions, the functioning of human society, and the interpersonal relationships of individuals as members of society. This division usually contains departments of economics, political science, history, sociology, anthropology, and psychology. Occasionally, the philosophy department may be included as well.

It is obvious that division of the liberal arts into humanities, natural sciences, and social sciences does not provide an unambiguous system of classification. It is not difficult to understand why philosophy is variously classified. If ancient philosophy is the source of all other disciplines, then it should not be classified simply within one of them. Nor is it easy to fit modern philosophy, which usually comprises logic, ethics, aesthetics, metaphysics and epistemology, into one division. Anthropology appears to belong (1) in the natural sciences insofar as it deals with physical anthropology, and (2) in the social sciences insofar as it deals with cultural anthropology. Psychology is clearly (1) a social science when it deals with interpersonal relations, and (2) a biological science when it deals with the brain and behavior.

The problem of placing psychology into a divisional niche is not materially aided by the invention of the term *behavioral sciences*. This is a new and not yet widely accepted name for a divisional structure generally intended to include psychology, anthropology, and sociology, leaving economics and political science in the social sciences. However, much of psychology tends to fall within the natural sciences as opposed to the behavioral sciences.

This discussion of the place of psychology in the divisional structure of the college of liberal arts of a modern university is included to aid the reader in comprehending the nature of psychology, its breadth, and its limits. Of the many differences which distinguish the humanities from the natural sciences and both from the social sciences, possibly the most important arise from the various meanings of the term *science* and the attitudes of individuals within the various disciplines toward science. For this reason, we will proceed to a discussion of the nature of science and of some issues of human value which are relevant to science.

PERSPECTIVE WITHIN PSYCHOLOGY

The diverse and heterogeneous character of psychology can be given some perspective through an examination of the subject matter included in the courses most frequently offered by psychology departments in modern universities. These courses can be divided into four categories: (1) general psychology, (2) psychology as a natural science, (3) psychology as a social science, and (4) interdisciplinary psychology.

GENERAL PSYCHOLOGY

There are a number of technical issues concerning the nature and methods of psychology that do not directly involve the subject matter or content of psychology. They are generally abstract rather than concrete and are thus *about* rather than *of* psychology. These matters give rise to courses or portions of courses in psychology that are devoted to general philosophical issues, the philosophy of science, experimental methodology and research design, the problems and techniques of measurement, and the problems of statistical analysis and inference. These subject matters are sometimes referred to as constituting metapsychology as opposed to psychology proper. They fit within general psychology. General psychology is sometimes used to include those aspects of psychology which are considered to be basic or elementary. Used in this broader sense, the term would include most of what is included in psychology as a natural science and psychology as a social science as well.

PSYCHOLOGY AS A NATURAL SCIENCE

In the history of psychology, laboratory methods were first applied to three general kinds of problem. They were (1) problems of the measurement of sensory experience, (2) problems of learning, and (3) problems of speed of reaction, first addressed primarily to the speed of transmission of neural impulses. For this reason, those subject matter areas most amenable to control through the experimental procedures developed in the physical and biological sciences are occasionally, although somewhat inaccurately, referred to as *experimental psychology*. Psychology as a natural science is essentially the product of laboratory work. The inaccuracy arises from the fact that social science aspects of psychology have also been subjected to laboratory investigation.

No other general characteristic of psychology as a natural science can be specified that clearly sets it apart from other aspects of psychology. There are matters of emphasis, however, that are worthy of note. While much work involving human subjects is carried out in the laboratory, many laboratory problems in natural science aspects of psychology, while relevant to human behavior and functioning, can be studied in animals. For example, most experimental work in psychoneurophysiology is carried out with animals as subjects, although the results are assumed to be applicable to the human nervous system. The units of measurement in natural science aspects of psychology tend to be metric—that is, translatable into terms of the equal-unit metric scale of grams, centimeters, and seconds. The variables of experimentation in psychology as a natural science tend to be nonverbal or non-symbolic in character. Finally, psychology as a natural science deals with those aspects of psychology most closely related to the other natural sciences.

PSYCHOLOGY AS A SOCIAL SCIENCE

Those aspects of psychology that fit best within the division of social science in the modern university are those which emphasize interpersonal relations. They tend to develop from studies that employ human subjects rather than animals, even though the social behavior of animals is often studied in the expectation that it will be relevant to human social organization. There is an emphasis on symbolic material and a tendency for measurement to be both more difficult than in natural science aspects and more nonmetric in character. There is a greater tendency to study social science problems in their natural setting, although many can be and are studied in the laboratory. Finally, these parts of psychology tend to be more closely related to social science disciplines such as anthropology and sociology than to natural science disciplines.

INTERDISCIPLINARY PSYCHOLOGY

The definitions of psychology given at the beginning of this chapter clearly include the interests of scholars who are not psychologists. If psychologists profess an interest in human and animal behavior, then they have joint interests with a great many other scientists. There is hardly an area of scholarly interest that does not involve psychological problems or share concerns with psychology. For this reason, most liberal arts colleges offer many interdisciplinary courses and, at the graduate level, interdisciplinary degree programs involving psychology and one or more other disciplines.

In the humanities there may be courses in experimental aesthetics, in personality theory as revealed in the novel, or about psychological factors in art, music, or drama. Cultural anthropology can be a major contributor to personality theory or the problems of perception. Psychological interpretations of historical events are becoming increasingly common. Psychological studies of political and economic behavior are becoming more frequent and are increasingly taken into account in applied politics and economics. Psycholinguistics has developed sufficiently to justify a doctoral degree program in some universities. Mathematical psychology has appeared as a rapidly developing field. No aspect of the basic medical sciences is without a psychological component, and terms such as neuropsychology, psychopharmacology, and the biochemistry of learning are becoming increasingly common. Thus, psychology has pervasive interest in nearly all parts of the differentiated body of philosophy.

There are few professional schools that are not involved with psychological problems. Educational psychology is usually an integral and important part of any school of education. Schools of medicine, psychiatry, and nursing, as well as other medical professional schools, usually include aspects of psychology in their training programs. The field that is now coming to be known as "human performance" within psychology was once called "human engineering." Professional schools of art, music, architecture, social work, and law all involve psychological problems and considerations. The involvement of psychology in other disciplines and professional training programs is so well established that it has produced two major forms of institutional bridges. (1) Many professional schools now contain within their own structures small psychology departments devoted to both service and research within the professional school. (2) Many doctoral degree programs now bear titles such as Education and Psychology, Psychology and Social Work, Engineering Psychology, etc.

Most of the subject matter involved in the interaction of professional training and academic psychology was once referred to as *applied psychology*. This term is disappearing because from these joint interests have emerged new problems and new knowledge—knowledge that goes far beyond the simple application of what is known in psychology to the problems of another field. It is for this reason that these aspects of psychology are labeled as interdisciplinary.

The Basic Concepts in Psychology Series is a survey of general psychology, psychology as a natural science, and psychology as a social science. It leaves interdisciplinary psychology for later courses.

SOME PHILOSOPHICAL ISSUES IN CONTEMPORARY PSYCHOLOGY 2

Contemporary psychology is an expression of positions on philosophical issues that distinguish it from the humanities and, to a lesser extent, from other disciplines within the natural and social sciences. Some of the issues are as old as the history of philosophy, and the debates on the basic issues continue without clear resolution. There are two reasons for introducing the student to some of the issues involved. It is difficult to evaluate the character and status of information such as that available in the Basic Concepts in Psychology Series without some appreciation of the value system that the information represents. Second, the social and political consequences that follow from the taking of a position on these issues is of utmost contemporary social importance.

Most psychologists make the fundamental assumption that human behavior is caused or determined. The goal of psychology is to describe, to predict, and to control human behavior. This manner of regarding human behavior follows from the assertion that the behavior of biological organisms, including man, is a natural phenomenon and from a faith in the deterministic element in the philosophical foundations of the physical sciences. There is little doubt that determinism characterizes the scientific revolution that has convulsed Western civilization. Whether determinism is basic to contemporary physical science is a question worth further examination.

DETERMINISM IN CONTEMPORARY PHYSICS

From the beginning of the scientific revolution until well into the twentieth century, the philosophy of determinism as applied to inanimate matter was almost completely universal and unquestioned. A clear statement expressing that philosophy is the following often-quoted passage from Laplace (1820, 1952 translation):

We ought to regard the present state of the universe as the effect of its antecedent state and the cause of the state that is to follow. An Intelligence, who for a given instant should be acquainted with all the forces by which Nature is animated and with the several positions of the entities composing it, if further this intellect were vast enough to submit these data to analysis, would include in the same formula the movements of the largest bodies in the universe and the lightest atom. Nothing would be uncertain for him . . . the past and the future would be present to the eyes.

The philosophical position expressed by Laplace fairly well represents both the popular view of physical science and the working assumptions of the physical scientist in his day-to-day activities. However, despite the enormous success of scientific enterprise based on this philosophical position, there have been points at which it appears to have broken down. Three of these have been sufficiently publicized to have come to the attention to the nonphysicist.

1. Physics provides two explanations for the transmission of light energy: the wave theory and the particle, or quantum, theory. These two theories are incompatible with each other; yet both can be proved to be valid.

2. A very fundamental form of uncertainty concerning physical events has been enunciated by the physicist Heisenberg (1958). He pointed out that the interaction of an event to be measured and the apparatus used in measurement is such that simultaneous determination of the position and velocity of a particle is not possible. Thus there is an inescapable indeterminateness at the very foundation of modern atomic physics. The problem is referred to as the Heisenberg uncertainty principle.

3. Physical theorists have had to rationalize simultaneous consideration of Newtonian physics, derived from the physical properties of large bodies, and quantum mechanics, derived from atomic physics. Both kinds of physical theory work wonderfully well, but they seem essentially incompatible. Newtonian physics seems deterministic and certain, but it is a limiting case of quantum mechanics, which is probabilistic, statistical, and therefore fundamentally uncertain.

Contemplation of these problems has led physicists to question physical determinism. Eddington (1935) said, "Ten years ago, practically every physicist was, or believed himself to be, a determinist, at any rate so far as inorganic phenomena were concerned. No serious doubt was entertained. . . . Then suddenly, determinism faded from physics." Bohr (1958) said, ". . . the renunciation of the very idea of determinism has given rise to doubts in the minds of many physicists and philosophers as to whether we are dealing here with a temporary expedient or confronted with an irrevocable step as regards objective description." Oppenheimer (1961) had little doubt on the issue. He said, ". . . the physical world is not completely determinant. There are predictions you can make about it, but they are statistical: and any event has in it the nature of the surprise, of the miracle, of something you cannot figure out. Physics is predictable, but within certain limits its world is ordered but not completely causal."

Thus, it is apparent that two models stand side by side within physics. The first is a deterministic model of the universe. Within it, every event is a causal product of previous events and is the cause of succeeding events, without doubt, uncertainty, or ambiguity. This model characterizes earlier, possibly outdated, physics. It is the model for much of the everyday activities in the physical sciences, and it is the conception of physics and science held by most modern nonphysicists. The second model of the universe is indeterminant, statistical, and probabilistic. It characterizes the more advanced physics of the mid-twentieth century.

DETERMINISM IN CONTEMPORARY PSYCHOLOGY

Determinism can be contemplated dispassionately, discussed rationally, and limited within narrow bounds when it is discussed with reference to inanimate objects. When it is discussed with reference to human behavior, the topic can cause heated and emotional arguments. While most people are willing to accept the idea of a determinant universe of nonliving materials, they reject the idea that human behavior is part of that universe and equally subject to general laws. Determinism applied to human behavior seems to conflict with the everyday subjective experience of freedom of choice and with the belief in individual self-determination.

The dominant characteristic of contemporary psychology is its dedication to the development of a *science* of human behavior. Within the context of this dominant attitude, a wide range of views exists. Probably the major polar issue in psychology is the incompatibility of positivism and existentialism. *Positivism* is a system of philosophy which excludes from consideration everything but natural phenomena or the properties of knowable things. It is concerned with positive facts and phenomena and excludes speculation concerning ultimate causes or origins. It spawned a philosophical movement called "logical positivism," which was dedicated to the rigorous definition of scientific terms in order to eliminate ambiguity, misunderstanding, and error. *Existentialism,* in some of its many manifestations, is an introspective and humanistic view of man which stresses the individual's intense awareness of his own contingency and his own freedom. It stresses the individual's responsibility for making himself what he is. It emphasizes the importance of personal freedom, personal decision, and personal commitment.

Among psychologists, Skinner (1953) has enunciated a consistent and unambiguous positivistic philosophy as applied to human behavior and affairs. For example, he says:

> Science . . . is an attempt to discover order, to show that certain events stand in lawful relation to other events. . . . But order is not only a possible end-product; it is a working assumption which must be adopted at the very start. We cannot apply the methods of science to a subject matter which is assumed to move about capriciously. . . . Science is not concerned just with "getting the facts," after which one may act with greater wisdom in an unscientific fashion. . . . If we are to enjoy the advantages of science in the field of human affairs, we must be prepared to adopt the working model of behavior to which a science will inevitably lead.

Following this philosophy with considerable faithfulness, Skinner has described an ideal society based on a scientific and positivistic approach to social organization in a book (1948) entitled *Walden II*.

A point of view which is in sharp contrast to Skinner's is evident in a quotation from Rogers (1961). He says, ". . . in the deepest moments of psychotherapy . . . I am in relationship with a person who is spontaneous, who is responsibly free, that is, aware of his freedom to choose who he will be, and aware also of the consequences of his choice. To believe, as Skinner holds, that all this is an illusion and that spontaneity, freedom, responsibility, and choice have no real existence, would be impossible for me." Elsewhere, Rogers (1962) says, "We are speaking, then, of a freedom which exists in the subjective person, a freedom which he courageously uses to live his potentialities. We are speaking of a freedom in which the individual chooses to fulfill himself by playing a responsible and voluntary part in bringing about the destined events of the world."

While the conflict represented by these two positions is broad and general and has many dimensions, much of the essence of the argument can be discussed by narrowing the problem to the single issue of the manner in which one is to regard the subjective experience of freedom of personal choice or free will.

One can hold to a positivistic position and deal with the problem of free will by assuming that it is an illusion of experience very similar to an optical illusion. For example, Immergluck (1964) says, "I propose that . . . our experienced subjective image of personal freedom represents a phenomelogical 'error,' a perceptual distortion which we are unable to shake, much as many of our surface impressions are literally trapped by perceptual illusion phenomena." In this statement, Immergluck has agreed with Skinner.

A somewhat less positive position is reflected in a statement made by Boring (1957) on the issue of whether human behavior is pre-determined. He says, ". . . I found out where lay the difference between us—McDougall, the voluntarist and me, the determinist. McDougall's freedom was my variance. McDougall hoped that variance would always be found in specifying the laws of behavior, for there freedom might still persist. . . . At any rate, a general fact emerges from this example: freedom, when you believe it is operating, always resides in an area of ignorance. If there is a known law, you do not have freedom." Thus free will, according to Boring, is to be tolerated as a matter of ignorance or as an element of an irreducible error term.

It is worthy of note that this position has elements that are similar to the modern view of physics. The psychologist who is a determinist is dedicated to the achievement of a degree of experimental control that will reduce or eliminate error in prediction. If that goal is unattainable, then modern physics and modern psychology would not differ in conception. Such a position has the virtue of permitting a single view of all behavior, animate and inanimate.

Numerous ways have been proposed for living with two incompatible conceptions of the universe. For example, Boring (1957) says:

> . . . fact and value . . . belong in two different worlds, each with its own language, and . . . the wise man must keep both in his repertoire if he is to get along in the culture in which he lives. . . . Causal determinism is the scientific model. It works enormously well. There are places in science where it breaks down, but they are not many. On the other hand, there are, in the process of living, all the situations in which values are called for and in which the scientific model itself fails. In such cases we get along best with the truncated model we call freedom. . . . causality is only the form of a model, and freedom is also a model, and we can use our models at will without letting them dominate us.

Implicit in this statement is a distinction that Boring makes explicit when he says, "The scientist's view is often different from the scientific view, for the scientist is a human being required to make value judgments if he is to survive in the milieu in which he lives." To this one can add a statement from Krutch (1954) in which he says, " . . . science, which can do so much, cannot decide what it ought to do, and that power which it confers must be guided by something outside it." This dualism posits an objective world of science, independent of the scientist, which is deterministic, amoral, and impersonal. If one is a psychologist, it is one's view of others. The contrast is a subjective world that is personal, involves free will, and contains issues of ethics and value.

A different view that tolerates both worlds is stated by Allport (1961). He says:

In this line of thought lies a possible reconciliation between the freedom claimed by existentialism and the determinism claimed by positivism. Precisely what do we mean when we say that the normal person is relatively free to program his own identity? Not that he is liberated from all of his drives. . . . Not that he is entirely free from his early learning. . . . All these pressures exist. But becoming is the process by which all these forces are employed to program a style of life for one's self. The basic existentialist urge to grow, pursue meaning, seek unity is also a given. . . . It is the desire for autonomy, for individuation, for selfhood, for existential uniqueness that also enters into the product. . . . The promise I see for myself is the essence of my freedom.

A similar assertion of the possibility of living simultaneously with both models comes from Rogers (1961). He says:

. . . behavior, when examined scientifically, is surely best understood in terms of prior causation. This is the great fact of science. But responsible personal choice, which is the most essential element in being a person, which is the core experience of psychotherapy, which exists prior to any scientific endeavor, is an equally prominent fact of our lives. . . . That these two important elements of our experience appear to be in contradiction has perhaps the same significance as the contradiction between the wave theory and corpuscular theory of light, both of which can be shown to be true, even though incompatible. We cannot profitably deny our subjective life, any more than we can deny the objective description of that life. . . . If we choose to utilize our scientific knowledge to free men, then it will demand that we live openly and frankly with the great paradox of the behavioral sciences.

While Rogers is apparently quite content to live with the paradox of positivism and existentialism, he has also stated a quite different solution to the problem, a solution in which the paradox is made to disappear. Rogers (1955) points out that science exists only in people and is therefore a subjective and humanistic product. There are not two views of the world but only one, which contains all of science within it. He says further, "It is at this point [where intersubjective verification has been achieved] that we are likely to think we have created a body of scientific knowledge. Actually there is no such body of knowledge. There are only tentative beliefs, existing subjectively in a number of different persons. If these beliefs are not tentative, then what exists is dogma, not science." Thus Skinner's "working assumption that must be adopted at the very start" is challenged as being an untestable proposition that, by its very inflexibility or immutability in the face of evidence or argument, is dogma and therefore unworthy of science.

Those familiar with metaphysics will recognize that Skinner's argument is a monism, a single view of the world that accepts the physical world to be precisely what it appears to be and nothing more. The views of Boring, Allport, and Krutch, for example, are dualisms in which two views of the world are entertained seriously and simultaneously. Rogers's final view is a monism which is not very different from subjective idealism, in which mind is the only reality and the physical world is viewed as a construction from human intellect.

This brief review of aspects of positivism and existentialism is written in the form of a "battle of quotations" to make clear that the issues are contemporary and real and that the differences are ones that divide contemporary writers. It remains to be seen whether the issues actually divide academic disciplines and subdivisions within psychology.

AN EMPIRICAL STUDY OF THE ATTITUDES OF SOME CONTEMPORARY SCHOLARS

3

Contemporary scholars do not all hold the same attitudes toward the nature of science and the implications that the scientific model holds for the affairs of men. Psychologists hold views that are somewhat different from those of other academic disciplines, and psychologists associated with the natural science aspects of psychology diverge from psychologists more closely allied with the social sciences.

Data on the attitudes of scholars toward problems associated with the status of science were collected by Doyle (1965) at the University of Michigan. She first collected quotations from a variety of writers with respect to four issues: (1) the extent to which science is based upon determinism, (2) the extent to which human freedom is an illusion based on ignorance, (3) the extent to which the scientific model is regarded as the single best view or only as one of several ways of viewing the world, and (4) the extent to which the scientific model is regarded as being in conflict with democratic society. A large number of scholars were asked to indicate the degree to which they agreed or disagreed with each of the quotations, which were presented without an indication of their origin.

The results reported here were obtained from a relatively small number of scholars at a single institution. The task of rating the extent of agreement was difficult, and many scholars found the statements to be ambiguous when taken out of context. Of 625 forms sent out, only 196 (31%) are represented in the results below. The humanities are represented by 22 scholars, mostly from the English Department. The natural sciences are represented by 14 scholars from the physical sciences (physics, chemistry, and mathematics) and 17 from the biological sciences (microbiology, pharmacology, physiology, and zoology). Answers were obtained from 34 social scientists (anthropology, economics, political science, and sociology). Natural science aspects of psychology are represented by 47 people, and social science aspects by 62. While the numbers are small and represent only one university, they constitute differences that are probably not too unrepresentative.

DETERMINISM IN SCIENCE

The quotations concerning the extent to which determinism is a nuclear element of science are these:

1. The ultimate fact about the universe is not that everything in it obeys a law but that the random, or at least the unpredictable, is always present and effective. (Krutch, 1954)[1]

2. No mechanist [determinist] claims that he can either foresee or determine what an individual man will do. At most he asserts that he can determine and foresee in terms of an average. (Krutch, 1954)

3. Science . . . is an attempt to discover order, to show that certain events stand in lawful relations to other events. But order is not only a possible end product; it is a working assumption which must be adopted at the very start. We cannot apply the methods of science to a subject which we assume to move about capriciously. (Skinner, 1953)

4. Uncertainty [in science] is the result of partial ignorance. (Krutch, 1954)[2,3]

5. All the real evidence in favor of mechanistic [deterministic] assumptions are partial. . . . He [the scientist] has not presented evidence to prove that all human actions are determined. The possible reasons for believing that some realm of freedom does exist cannot be ruled out. (Krutch, 1954)

6. The unpredictable and the indeterminant [in science] are part of [its] ultimate reality. (Krutch, 1954)

7. Reluctantly, perhaps, but step by step nevertheless, the concept of strict determinism is abandoned by the physicists. Most of them now admit that when we can predict only average, not individual behavior,

[1] The quotations from *The Measure of Man*, copyright 1954 by Joseph Wood Krutch, are reprinted by permission of the publisher, Bobbs-Merrill Company, Inc.

[2] The quotations are given here as they appeared in the questionnaire in Doyle (1965). In many instances they are slightly modified from the original. The references indicate the source of the quotation. In several instances, this one in particular, the quotation does not represent the view of the author cited. Similar cases are marked with an asterisk subsequently.

[3] Of the 43 quotations which appeared in the questionnaire, 29 were used in the quantitative analysis, and 14 were dropped because not all participants were willing to express an opinion or because they indicated that the expressed opinion was too ambiguous. This quotation and the ones subsequently marked with a dagger were not used in the analysis.

it is, sometimes at least, because of the factors introduced by either free or random elements, not simply because our data or our formulae are incomplete. (Krutch, 1954)

8. A scientist operates under the tacit assumption that there is order underlying all phenomena that he studies. Otherwise his work would be pointless. He hopes to find the nature of this order. He also assumes that all forms of order are determined—that is to say, caused—and his job is to discover these determinants or causes. (Hoagland, 1964)

The quotations were rated by the scholars on an 8-point scale with a value of 8 representing "Very Strong Agreement" with a particular statement and a value of 1 representing "Very Strong Disagreement." Ratings of the seven statements (note that statement 4 was not used in the analysis) were combined in such a manner that values above 4.5 represented some degree of agreement that determinism is an essential aspect of science, while ratings below the midpoint, 4.5, indicate some degree of disagreement. This was done by reversing the orientation of the scales on some of the items. If one believed in absolute determinism, one would agree very strongly with statements 3 and 8 and disagree very strongly with statements 1, 2, 5, 6, and 7. Therefore, the numerical values for the ratings of the latter five statements were reoriented. The reader might enjoy rating his own degree of agreement or disagreement on each of the statements and calculating a mean value before reading the results. He can then calculate his own position on the issues for comparative purposes.

It will be noted that, in the results that follow, most of the mean values fall below the midpoint (4.5) and generally represent degrees of disagreement on each of the issues.

The results with respect to the seven statements on determinism in science are shown in Figure 1. In that figure, it is clear that natural scientists and humanists are in near accord in the extent of their disagreement with the proposition that science necessarily implies determinism. Social scientists are nearly neutral, while psychologists in general tend to agree with the proposition in comparison with the others. Among psychologists, the experimental psychologists, who would be classified as belonging to the natural sciences, represent the extreme position. Psychologists allied with the social sciences, at 4.4 on the scale, tend to disagree with the proposition and do not differ greatly in their attitudes from other social scientists.

SCIENCE AND DETERMINISM

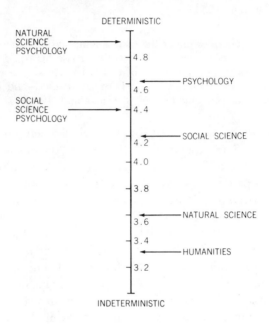

Figure 1

The figure illustrates differences among groups of scholars in the extent to which they regard science as being characterized by determinism. The upper portion of the scale (over 4.5) indicates a tendency to agree with statements asserting determinism in science, while the lower portion (below 4.5) indicates a tendency to disagree (Doyle, 1965). In this and in subsequent similar figures, the larger groups are plotted on the right and subdivisions of some of them are plotted on the left.

THE REALITY OF FREEDOM

The deterministic view of the world that arises from science is incompatible with the feeling each of us has of being free to choose, of being a free agent. If one adopts the scientific model as deterministic, then the subjective experience of free will must be regarded as an illusory phenomenon, a figment of the imagination. Free will can also be regarded as being in question because science has not proceeded far enough to settle the issue. Thus the question of the reality of free will lies in the realm of ignorance, just outside what we know. A further alternative is to regard the determinism of science as an incomplete picture of the universe, a universe in which free will is and will remain a reality.

In Doyle's study, scholars were asked to indicate the extent to which they regarded freedom of human choice to be real or illusory. They did so by stating their degree of agreement with each of the following quotations:

1. The free will character of our action is an illusion. (Immergluck, 1964)

2. The hypothesis that man is free is not essential to the application of scientific method to human affairs. The free inner man who is held responsible for his behavior is only a prescientific substitute for the kinds of causes which are discovered in the course of a scientific analysis. (Skinner, 1953)

3. Freedom, when you believe it is operating, always resides in an area of ignorance. If there is a known law, you do not have freedom. (Boring, 1957)

4. Behind the ancient and possibly quite unsatisfactory concepts of free will, individual responsibility, and the validity of value judgments lie some realities without which it is not possible to manage a world in which human beings will be either successful or happy. (Krutch, 1954)

5. Our experienced image of personal freedom represents a phenomenological error, a perceptual distortion we are unable to shake, much as many of our surface impressions are literally trapped by perceptual illusion phenomena. (Immergluck, 1964)

6. Man is, in his barest essence, a free agent, propelled by self-initiated inner forces, that by their very nature deny prediction and scientifically ordered description customarily applied to inanimate objects. (Immergluck, 1964)*

7. Man's vaunted creative powers, his capacity to choose, and our right to hold him responsible for his choice—none of these is conspicuous in this new self-portrait [provided by science]. Man, we once believed, was free to express himself in art, music, and literature, to inquire into his nature, to seek salvation in his own way. He could initiate action and make spontaneous and capricious changes. . . . But science insists that action is initiated by forces impinging upon the individual and caprice is only another name for behavior for which we have not yet found a cause. (Skinner, 1955)†

8. Thought, consciousness, and the power to choose are realities no matter how difficult they are to reconcile with those other realities the mechanists stress. (Krutch, 1954)†

9. The belief in freedom of action is . . . a superstition, one that is, however, justified biologically by the fact that it is woven into the fine

structure of society. Language itself would have to be eviscerated were this conception to be extirpated from it. . . . It is a useful superstition. (Boring, 1957)

10. Freedom is the individual's capacity to know that he is the determined one, to pause between stimulus and response and thus to throw his weight, however slight it may be, on the side of one particular response among several possible ones. (May, 1962)

11. To some students of behavior, free will is an epiphenomenon—an illusion—since all behavior may be regarded as the resultant of our phylogenetic development and the individual's day to day experiences. However, the fact is that we can never hope to know the meaning to an individual of his plethora of past experiences, nor can we know the details of his genetic makeup and its impact on his brain function; for all practical purposes, much of his behavior must remain relatively undetermined both to himself and to others. Thus man may be considered to have free will. (Hoagland, 1964)†

12. Behavior, when examined scientifically, is surely best understood in terms of prior causation. . . . But responsible personal choice, which is the most essential element in being a person . . . is an equally prominent fact in our lives. That these two elements of our experience appear to be contradictory has, perhaps, the same significance as the contradiction between the wave and the corpuscular theory of light, both of which can be shown to be true. We cannot profitably deny the freedom which exists in our subjective life, any more than we can deny the determinism which is evident in the objective description of that life. We have to live with the paradox. (Rogers, 1961)

If one believes in the reality of free will, one will agree with statements 4, 6, 10, and 12 and disagree with statements 1, 2, 3, 5, and 9. Therefore the scale values of statements 4, 6, 10, and 12 were reoriented to yield the mean responses of various groups on this issue, as shown in Figure 2. Humanists were found to express a degree of belief in the reality of free choice that is at the far end of the scale in an absolute sense and divergent from other groups in a relative sense.

When the attitudes of the total groups of natural scientists, social scientists, and psychologists are considered (the right-hand side of Figure 2) little difference can be shown between them. However, this is an issue that separates subgroups of psychologists and subgroups of natural scientists, as shown on the left-hand side of the figure. The physical scientists express a much firmer faith in the reality of free will than do the biological scientists. Among psychologists, the psychologists who are allied with the social sciences show far more faith in the reality of free will than do psychologists allied with the natural sciences.

It is worthy of note, however, that the extreme view expressed

REALITY OF FREEDOM

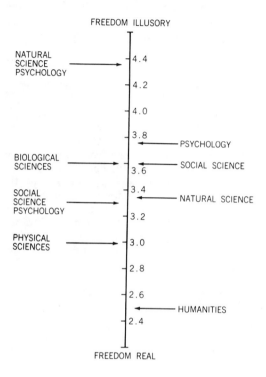

Figure 2

Differences among groups of scholars with respect to the extent to which they regard free will as an illusion or a reality (Doyle, 1965).

by the experimental psychologists in "Natural Science Psychology" is one of near neutrality on the issue. They rank below 4.4 and a value of 4.5 represents the middle of the scale. Thus all groups express opinions supporting the reality of free will and differing only in the degree of their support. A comparison of Figures 1 and 2 shows that when the opinion to be considered is concerned with an abstraction, namely science, the values are higher than is true when the issue concerns the individual. All values in Figure 1 are higher than the corresponding values in Figure 2. It is apparently easier to accept determinism as an abstraction than to accept it as applying to oneself.

SCIENCE AS A SINGLE MODEL OF THE UNIVERSE

The deterministic, scientific model may be regarded as the only view of the universe (including man) or it may be regarded as only one of several models of the universe. In Doyle's study, scholars were asked to indicate the extent to which they agreed with the following quotations:

1. Science must be something less than the one way to truth. (Boring, 1957)

2. A scientific conception of human behavior dictates one practice, a philosophy of personal freedom another. Confusion in theory means confusion in practice. The present unhappy condition of the world may in large measure be traced to our vacillation. The principal issues in dispute between nations . . . are intimately concerned with the problem of human freedom and control. Totalitarianism or democracy . . . planned society or laissez faire, the impression of cultures on alien peoples, economic determinism, individual initiative, propaganda, education, ideological warfare—all concern the fundamental nature of behavior. We shall almost certainly remain ineffective in solving these problems until we adopt a consistent point of view. (Skinner, 1953)

3. . . . science, which can do so much, cannot decide what it ought to do, and that power which it confers must be guided by something outside it. (Krutch, 1954)

4. A science of ethics . . . will supersede the erratic intuitions of the artist. (Cattell, 1948)

5. As the use of science increases, we are forced to accept the theoretical structure with which science represents its facts. (Skinner, 1955)†

6. Causal determinism is the scientific model. It works enormously well. There are places where it breaks down, but there are not many. On the other hand, there are, in the process of living, all the situations in which values are called for and in which the scientific model itself fails. In such cases we get along best with the truncated causality model we call freedom. You can have as many models as you want and use them when you will. (Boring, 1957)†

7. Determinism and free will represent two basically different and divergent views in modern psychology, which cannot simply be dealt with through the fiat notion that "both are somehow right" within their own limited framework or that they really complement one another in jointly reflecting the total realities of psychological life. (Immergluck, 1964)†

8. Fact and value belong in two different worlds, each with its own language, and the wise man must keep both in his repertoire if he is to get along in the culture in which he lives. (Boring, 1957)†

9. . . . the widely held views as to the disparate and mutually exclusive domains of science on the one hand and values and ethics on the other is the result of the failure to recognize certain unspoken premises always implicit in "ought" or "should" statements, that when these premises are recognized, such statements become identical with scientific statements, all of which can be put into a conditional statement of the if-then type. (Lundberg, 1948)

10. The scientist's view is often different from the scientific view, for the scientist is a human being required to make value judgments if he is to survive in the milieu in which he lives. (Boring, 1957)†

11. It is not true that statements containing "should" or "ought" have no place in scientific discourse. (Skinner, 1953)

12. Science is not just concerned with "getting the facts" after which we may act with greater wisdom in a non-scientific fashion. If we are to enjoy the advantages of science in the field of human affairs, we must be prepared to adopt the working model for behavior to which science will inevitably lead. (Skinner, 1953)

13. What a Shakespeare has to say about human nature and human conduct is likely to be as true as, and rather more important than, what the summarizer of ten thousand questionnaires tells us. (Krutch, 1954)

These statements can be ordered with belief in science as the best or only model on one end of the scale, and with belief in the simultaneous value of other views of the world on the other. Persons who believe science is the best or only model should agree with items 2, 4, 9, 11, and 12 and disagree with items 1, 3, and 13. In this manner, a single value can be obtained expressing the extent of agreement or disagreement that the science model is the single best view.

Figure 3 represents the mean attitudes expressed by the various groups, obtained by reversing the scale values of items 1, 3, and 13. The humanists again stand apart in the extent of their disagreement with science as the single view of the universe. This is also the only one of the four issues on which the social scientists stand between the humanities and the natural scientists. Psychologists and natural scientists, when taken as groups, express identical attitudes. However, when these two groups are subdivided, large differences do appear. The biological scientists express the most extreme view and go farthest toward acceptance of science as the best or only world view, while the physical scientists appear allied with the humanities in the extent to which they reject science as the one view of the universe. The views of psychologists allied with the natural sciences do not differ greatly from the views of the biological scientists, while the views of psychologists allied with the social sciences approach the degree of rejection of science as a world view expressed by other social scientists. Again it should

STATUS OF SCIENCE AS A MODEL

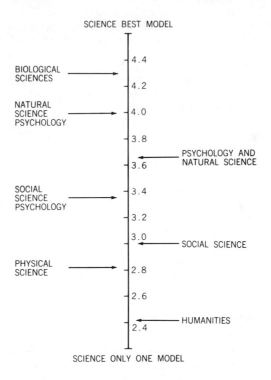

Figure 3

*Differences among groups of scholars with respect
to the extent to which they regard the scientific
model as the one model of reality or only as one of
several models (Doyle, 1965).*

be noted that all groups produced mean values that are below 4.5 and
are thus on the "disagreement" end of the scale. They, for the most
part, identify themselves as scientists, yet they reject science as the
only approach to the universe (including man).

DETERMINISM AND DEMOCRACY

One of the most troublesome aspects of a scientific view of the
universe is the conflict that it produces with the fundamental tenets of
democracy. A hardheaded, objective approach to human behavior leads

to the inevitable conclusion that socially pathological behavior, whether it be a senseless crime against a person or a senseless riot against boredom, arises from pathology in the social system. When people riot instead of channeling their energy into socially useful and constructive paths, it is clearly social conditions that have shaped their behavior toward senseless destruction and away from socially useful behavior. A person who grows up in a ghetto or in a rural poverty area without benefit of either education or opportunity cannot rationally be expected to become a productive and constructive member of society.

The democratic tradition, on the other hand, demands that the individual person be a creature who is self-determined, that he have free choice, that he be able to make individual decisions and abide by the consequences of his decisions. If he transgresses the common law, he is to be punished for his freely chosen path of wrongdoing. Thus, a rioting mob is held to be freely choosing destructiveness rather than choosing conformity or constructiveness. Therefore, it is deemed proper to punish it rather than simply to constrain it.

This fundamental conflict in our society is reflected in the following series of quotations on which scholars were asked to indicate their degree of agreement. The issue is the extent to which democracy and determinism, as implied by a science of human behavior, are in conflict.

1. "Democracy" as the West defines it . . . is meaningless except on the assumption that the individual man's thoughts and desires are to some extent uncontrollable and unpredictable. (Krutch, 1954)

2. Determinism with its intrinsic lack of freedom need not alarm those of us who are ideologically committed to a democratic way of life. . . . In both a totalitarian and democratic setting, the individual is not really free in the basic philosophic meaning of that term, but his behavior may be regarded as being determined to varying degrees by two different sets of factors: external in one instance, internal in the other. (Immergluck, 1964)

3. The behavioral sciences proceed from premises directly opposed to the moral premises of the law [jurisprudence]. (Sachar, 1963)†

4. The novels and dramas of every age have based their depiction of characters upon the assumption that human beings have the capacity of self-determination. Any other assumption would destroy art. (Niebuhr, 1955)†

5. There need be no contradiction between political freedom and philosophic determinism; such a contradiction exists only if we insist on basing our notions of political and social freedom on free-will metaphysics. (Immergluck, 1964)

6. The ideal of a "free society" is absurd unless individuals are somehow free. (Krutch, 1954)

7. Despite all modern scientific or metaphysical deterministic theories, the jurisprudence of the world has almost never varied in assuming responsible freedom of self. (Niebuhr, 1955)†

8. The theory of democracy requires that man possess a measure of rationality, a portion of freedom, a generic conscience, . . . ideals, and unique value. (Allport, 1955)

9. The so-called democratic philosophy of human behavior . . . is increasingly in conflict with the application of the methods of science to human affairs. (Skinner, 1955)†

10. Criminal law appears . . . as an instrument for reinforcing and celebrating the moral principles of society. . . . The philosophy underlying this approach considers each man to be operating as if he had complete freedom of the will. Since he can choose the path of moral right or moral wrong, his commission of a criminal act constitutes a free choice of evil. . . . (Sachar, 1963)†

The ratings of agreement and disagreement with these statements can be oriented to form a single scale of degree of agreement with the proposition that determinism and democratic philosophy are compatible. If one believes they are in conflict, one will disagree with 2 and 5 and agree with 1, 6, and 8 of the above quotations. The mean values for the various groups on this issue are shown in Figure 4. Again the humanists express a rather strong position. They see determinism in human affairs as inconsistent with Western democracy. Natural scientists express attitudes that place them exactly in the middle of the scale, indicating precise neutrality. Psychologists express a very mild degree of agreement with the proposition that determinism and democracy are consistent. Furthermore, there is very little difference between the two groups of psychologists.

COMPATIBILITY OF DETERMINISM AND DEMOCRACY

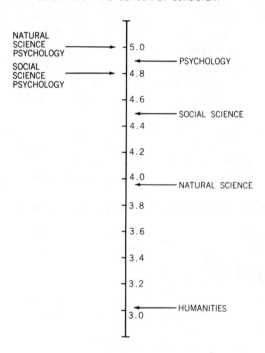

DETERMINISM AND DEMOCRACY CONSISTENT

DETERMINISM AND DEMOCRACY INCONSISTENT

Figure 4

Differences in the extent to which groups of scholars view the determinism of science as being consistent or compatible with democratic principles (Doyle, 1965).

PSYCHOLOGY AND THE "TWO CULTURES"

C. P. Snow (1959, 1964) has explored a schism in the intellectual life of our times between science and the humanities. He says, ". . . I believe that intellectual life of the whole of Western society is increasingly being split into two polar groups. . . . Literary intellectuals at the one pole—at the other the physical sciences. Between the two, a gulf of mutual incomprehension, hostility and dislike, but most of all, lack of understanding. . . . Their attitudes are so different that even on the level of emotion, they can't find much common ground." While Snow's thesis is based on many aspects of human value, four must be basic to the schism: (1) determinism in human affairs, (2) the reality of free choice, (3) the extent to which the scientific model is regarded as the best view of the universe including man, and (4) the degree of consistency of science and democracy. When the attitudes of scholars on these issues are combined into a single scale reflecting a generalized

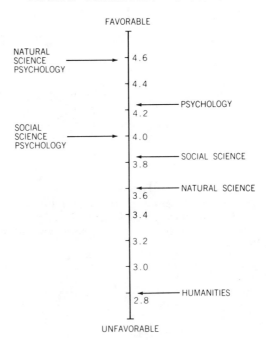

GENERAL COMMITMENT TO SCIENCE

Figure 5

Differences in the extent to which groups of scholars have a commitment favorable to a scientific view of the world as represented by mean agreement on all four of the relevant issues (Doyle, 1965).

attitude toward science, the extent of the schism should be apparent. Figure 5 reflects a combination of the data in the previous four figures.

As Snow has said, there is a difference in the positions taken by the humanists and the natural scientists. Humanists do tend to express a consistent antiscientific point of view. However, the difference between the humanists and the natural scientists is not so great as Snow's position might lead us to suspect. Furthermore, the natural sciences include both the biological sciences and the physical sciences; of these two, it is the physical scientists who express attitudes toward science that lie closer to the humanities. Snow's argument places the physical sciences at one pole.

Snow also expresses the hope that psychology and the social sciences might serve to bridge the chasm of understanding. To the extent to which the data of Figure 5 are relevant, it is clear that psychology and the social sciences have adopted attitudes toward science and determinism which make them poor candidates to play the role of mediator.

It is also clear in Figure 5 that, among identifiable subgroups of scholars, it is the psychologists who identify themselves with the natural sciences and who occupy an anchor position on a scale of scientific determinism. These are chiefly psychologists who work in the laboratory—the experimental, physiological, and comparative psychologists. They are psychologists who are responsible for our knowledge and understanding of the processes of sensation, perception, learning, motivation, performance, and the physiological mechanisms underlying these processes. Among them are the psychologists who wrote the volumes in the Basic Concepts in Psychology Series that are classified under the natural sciences.

Psychologists who identify themselves more closely with the social sciences express attitudes toward science that are very similar to those expressed by social scientists. Among them are individuals whose opinions range from those of the experimental psychologists to opinions much closer to those expressed by scholars from the humanities. These are the psychologists interested in the development of the individual, the adult personality, the assessment of human characteristics, cognitive processes, and man's social characteristics. If we had comparable data on the attitudes of the particular individuals who wrote the volumes treating of psychology as a social science in the Basic Concepts in Psychology Series, their attitudes toward science would probably be more typical of experimental psychologists than of social scientists in general.

While all degrees of commitment to science and determinism are represented among psychologists, psychologists as a group are probably more strongly committed to a deterministic view of human behavior

than any other group of scholars. Advancement in psychological knowledge has occurred almost exclusively through the assumption that human
behavior is orderly and predictable. This assumption, however repug-
nant it may seem to a given person, has proved a profitable strategy.
It is the assumption that underlies the application to human behavior
of all logic and procedure that can be categorized as belonging to
scientific methods. Because science appears to most people to have
quite different implications when it is applied to human behavior than
it does when applied to inanimate objects, we will now turn to a brief
review of some of the essential characteristics of science in its application to psychology.

PSYCHOLOGY AND THE LANGUAGE OF SCIENCE

4

The word *science* has many meanings. A standard dictionary definition of science is likely to be as unrestricted as "any department of systematized . . . knowledge obtained by study and practice . . . a branch of study concerned with observation and classification of facts. . . ." By this definition, it is quite possible to be an existentialist and scientist simultaneously. It is by this definition that history is sometimes classified as a social science. It is more common, however, to restrict the word to refer to facts and theory obtained through precise observation and experimentation yielding quantitative data that is treated with maximum rigor. In this sense, science is characterized by positivism.

Psychology as a systematic body of knowledge began to burgeon as it began to change from a purely speculative aspect of philosophy to a more rigorous, positivistic, and experimentally oriented subject matter. It was thus positivism and experimentalism that initiated psychology's separation from philosophy in the latter half of the nineteenth century. Today, in the latter half of the twentieth century, psychology is accumulating information at a rate that has produced major problems for those who would systematize the field. Much of this new information arises from experimental developments.

This chapter will be devoted to some aspects of psychology as a positivistic and experimental science with a special emphasis on the special languages involved.

THE LANGUAGES OF PSYCHOLOGY

Many terms in any realm of knowledge are technical terms coined specifically for and used exclusively in talking about the subject matter —for example, "electron," "libido," "parthenogenesis," and "dactyl." On the other hand, many of the terms in a particular field either have been borrowed from the common language or have found a use in common language even though they originally had only a technical meaning— for example, "evolution," "motivation," "mass," "acid," and "projection."

Psychology, more than any other discipline, poses difficulties arising from the uncommon use of common words. When a learning theorist uses the word "habit," he is likely to have specified a very strict definition of the word based on the procedures he uses in carrying out his experiments. Thus, habit, for him, is strictly a product of his training procedures and is identified by a limited aspect of the organism's performance. His use of the term is very different from the meaning one might have for it when one says, "I have a habit of writing awkward sentences." When a psychologist, writing in the context of psychoanalytic theory, uses the word "anxiety," he means something very different from the meaning of the word as it is used in everyday conversation.

There are limits to the degree to which common words can be used with restricted meaning. You may recall a conversation between Alice and Humpty Dumpty. He has just been explaining to Alice why it is better to celebrate 364 unbirthdays each year rather than one birthday.

"There's glory for you!" [he said, referring to one birthday and one present a year].

"I don't know what you mean by 'glory,'" Alice said.

Humpty Dumpty smiled contemptuously. "Of course you don't—till I tell you. I meant 'there's a nice knock-down argument for you!'"

"But 'glory' doesn't mean 'a nice knock-down argument,'" Alice objected.

"When *I* use a word," Humpty Dumpty said, in rather a scornful tone, "it means just what I choose it to mean—neither more nor less."

"The question is," said Alice, "whether you *can* make words mean so many different things."

"The question is," said Humpty Dumpty, "which is to be master—that's all."

While it may sometimes seem that psychologists pose unnecessary difficulties in making uncommon use of common words, the practice arises from a Hobson's choice. Is it easier to invent an entirely new word and ask the reader to learn both the word and its meaning, or is it easier to use a word the reader already knows and ask him to learn a specialized and restricted meaning of it? The history of psychology reveals many instances of the coining of words that either never found widespread acceptance or disappeared after a brief period of use. The more common occurrence has been the use of common words that have been given specialized and sometimes highly precise meanings. The student's task is to learn to discriminate such special meanings. The close relations between psychology and other disciplines result in a frequent borrowing of terms. For example, a discussion of the neural basis for learning is likely to involve terms from physiology, neural anatomy, genetics, and biochemistry; social psychology makes use of terms from sociology and anthropology; principles of human performance are often dealt with in language that is common to engineering. Thus each of the volumes in this series is likely to require the student to learn new technical terms, new meanings for familiar old terms, and the meanings of terms borrowed from other fields of knowledge.

There are at least three sources of borrowed language that psychologists use in many, if not all, subareas of psychology. The universal language of mathematics is one. In this series, *Quantification in Psychology* and *Basic Statistics* are an introduction to general applications of mathematics to psychology. Other volumes, such as *Human Performance*, *Social Psychology: An Experimental Approach*, and *Conditioning and Instrumental Learning*, introduce the reader to applications of mathematics to special problems.

Two other sources of language generally used in psychology merit further discussion. One is the language of experimentation developed in the natural sciences. This language describes the procedures of experimental proof. In the broadest sense of the word "experimental," the language of experimental proof applies to the manner in which questions are answered objectively with a minimum of human bias. The other source is the language of theory that arises from philosophy and particularly from the philosophy of science. This is a language used in discussing the procedures and rules for arriving at precise meanings for psychological terms.

THE LANGUAGE OF EXPERIMENTAL PROOF

The acts of conceiving and executing an experiment and observing its results hold a potentiality for intellectual pleasure that is unsurpassed. An experiment can be conducted with the expenditure of no more time and effort than that spent by a person sitting idly in the park devising hypotheses concerning the origin of a birdcall or the slight quaking of a bush. The experimenter may sit passively watching the bush and waiting for the emergence of a bird, a stray dog, or a young couple. At the other extreme, a single experiment may be the product of the consorted brainpower of the world community of physicists and engineers supported by several federal gigabucks.[1] It costs considerably more to take a close look at Venus than to look under a bush. The difference between the two experiments is one of magnitude, not one of kind.

---

[1] A "federal gigabuck" is $1,000,000,000 in tax money appropriated from the U. S. Treasury. It represents an escalation from the "megabuck," which had a brief period of primacy in the world of research. A research project in the "megabuck" class can no longer command extensive coverage in leading newspapers. For the curious, the next level of escalation will be "terabuck."

The essence of an experiment involves three steps. The first step is contemplation of a body of information. The second is the induction of a hypothesis. The third is arrangement of conditions of observation so that deductions from the hypothesis can be tested and thus be verified or disproved. C. S. Peirce, the nineteenth-century American philosopher, defined an experiment in this manner: Peirce said that (1) all information concerning the world comes to us through our senses, (2) much information concerning the world is available to immediate experience, (3) some information is not ordinarily available to the senses and thus to immediate experience, and (4) an experiment consists of an arrangement of conditions that makes available to immediate experience information that would not have been available without the conduct of the experiment. Peirce's sequence is one of *induction, deduction,* and *verification.*

It should be clear that when the essence of an experiment is described in this manner life itself becomes a succession of experiments. While driving your car, your senses are suddenly assaulted by a series of rhythmic bumps. You quickly assess the condition of the road, ascertain that it is smooth, and generate the hypothesis that you have a flat tire. You pull off to the side, get out and look, and find the tire flat. You have surveyed the relevant information, deduced a hypothesis, and verified your conclusion. You have performed an experiment. Of course, such experiments—experiments verifying flat tires on automobiles, or the presence of white-throated vireos, or lovers in a quaking bush—lack elegance. Such experiments also lack other general characteristics of scientific endeavor.

Scientific observation has objectives and hallmarks that set it apart from the everyday experiment. Thus, scientific observation is sometimes distinguished from ordinary observation as being systematic, purposeful, and objective. Other hallmarks of scientific observation are that the body of information being contemplated is large enough to require intellectual effort, that the problem is both important and directed to a specific objective, and that the observations are available to more than one observer.

Another set of terms frequently employed state the aims of science as an effort to describe, to predict, and to control phenomena. Control can have a range of meanings. As a minimum, only intellectual control is implied. That is, if your scientific efforts are of sufficient quality, then your intellectual efforts to deal with the phenomena can be rigorous and productive. You have intellectual control of the phenomena under scrutiny. If you have intellectual control, you may, for either scientific or other human purposes, undertake deliberate control of the phenomena. If the phenomena are electrical and you undertake deliberate control to supply the world with cheap power, you may become both honored and rich. If the phenomena are aspects of human behavior and you undertake deliberate control to relieve human suffering, you may be honored as a humanitarian. If you undertake deliberate control to further political ends, you may invoke the nightmare of George Orwell's *1984*. Thus, the control implied is one of capacity; and the control abhorred is an objectionable use of that capacity.

Psychologists engaged in efforts to describe, predict and control human behavior (and thus to contribute to the science of psychology) employ a variety of methods that have been shaped by the special characteristics of the rich variety of problems psychologists meet and by the special limitations resulting from the fact that it is the human animal that attracts their interest. Most of these methods, however, are general methods in the sense that they are applicable to, or may have arisen from, other disciplines.

The "case history method" is often employed in an effort to determine the probable cause of some particular class of behavior—often, but not always, a class of abnormal behavior. For example, suppose that a community is having difficulties with vandalism perpetrated by a sizable group of school children in the seventh and eighth grades. One might assign a number of investigators to prepare a case history of each of the children involved. Someone might then review this set of case histories, trying to find a common cause for the delinquent behavior. If a common cause is found, the community might then deal with the immediate problem more effectively and might also be able to correct the conditions which produced the behavior in order to prevent its occurrence in subsequent crops of seventh-grade students. The case history method, though primitive, is often the best available, and it is frequently effective and fruitful. The emphasis in the case history method is on the immediate problem, and the relevant information to be collected usually concerns events in the remote past, events for which there are no useful records. Human memory is fallible in reproducing events which were not considered noteworthy at the time they happened. The primitive character of the case history method is due to difficulty in performing the first step in the scientific process —the systematic assembly of relevant facts in the search for testable hypotheses.

The term "clinical methods" applies largely to the techniques of a single investigator dealing with a single subject. Most clinical methods are applied to troublesome or pathological conditions, in a context of treatment. Clearly, a clinical psychologist dealing with human behavior can be experimental in his orientation. The intensive exploration of the personality of one person, as it may be conducted by a psychotherapist, can yield a systematic and purposeful body of information concerning that person. From that body of information, the therapist can, through the process of induction, generate fruitful hypotheses concerning the behavior of the individual in question. Many such hypotheses can be tested through experiment. If the hypothesis is that the patient is made anxious by any reference to authority figures, the therapist may proceed through a long series of tests in which he mentions both authority figures and figures that do not represent authority positions and observes the presence or absence of signs of anxiety in response to each class of stimuli. The therapist, in other words, performs a series of experiments.

There are generally three limitations on clinical methods: (1) they are usually applied to the problems of one individual, and the experiments described may thus yield a general principle applicable only to one person; (2) the nature of the one-to-one relationship of the therapist and client precludes the possibility of another investigator reviewing the same body of facts to determine the extent to which the process of induction, hypothesis, and verification is objective or is idiosyncratic and subjective; and (3) events dealt with clinically usually involve a malfunction of some kind. None of these three limitations prevent the incorporation of clinical evidence into the science of human behavior, but all three do pose difficulties.

A great many advances in science have occurred through the use of what has been called "naturalistic observation." The term implies little more than what it seems to imply—the observation of materials or organisms in their normal state in nature behaving as they normally do. To be useful in science such naturalistic observation must be systematic, purposeful, and objective. Thus, bird-watching would not be classified as naturalistic observation. The careful and repeated observation and recording of natural behavior can, however, yield information obtainable in no other way. Many scientists who have chosen to devote their lives to naturalistic observation argue that laboratory studies are often meaningless because the conditions in a laboratory are so unnatural that findings there are not greatly relevant to behavior in natural settings. On the other hand, laboratory psychologists argue that causal or lawful relationships are exceedingly difficult to establish in natural settings, given the complexity of the situation and the investigator's limited ability to control the environment.

The essence of naturalistic observation is the accumulation of a systematic body of knowledge (the first of the three stages in the scientific process). However, induction, hypothesis, and verification can also occur in the natural setting. Astronomers test their predictions even though they cannot directly manipulate variables. Other natural scientists, such as fish ecologists, are sometimes able to intervene in the events they are studying.

While the essence of an experiment is a simple arrangement and a single instance, what is usually meant by "experimental psychology" is that aspect of psychology that is carried on in the laboratory. Even this designation is relatively fuzzy. The essence of experimental psychology is not a matter of where the experiment is conducted (in the laboratory or in the field) but a matter of the degree of control exercised by the experimenter over relevant variables.

In the classic laboratory experiment, all variables save one are under the control of the experimenter. The value of that one variable is changed to some degree, and the effect of that change on the behavior is noted. The variable that is changed by the experimenter is referred to as the *independent variable*. The behavior that is observed is called the *dependent variable*. In a good experiment, all other variables that might produce changes in the value of the dependent variable are controlled in some manner.

There are several general characteristics of the classic laboratory experiment that are worthy of note. You may recall that in our original definition of an experiment, the term is applied to a single test. The laboratory experiment, by that definition, is not a single experiment but is usually a large number of experiments. Where it is possible to do so, the same experiment is conducted repeatedly on the same organism and consistent results tend to bolster the truth of the hypothesis in reference to that single organism. Where it is possible to do so, the same experiment is carried out on a number of organisms, and consistent results tend to bolster the truth of the hypothesis when applied to the whole population of similar organisms. Thus, the classic laboratory experiment is actually a multiplicity of experiments performed repeatedly to test the universality of the result.

A second general characteristic of the classic laboratory experiment is that it tends to involve variables that can be measured and quantified. In one of the illustrative experiments early in this chapter, the simple shaking of a bush was the independent variable, and the presence or absence of a young couple was the dependent variable. By contrast, a standard laboratory experiment may involve ten values of the independent variable, equally spaced on a linear metric scale, a number of controlled variables quantitatively specified, and a dependent variable that is read in metric units that can be plotted into a complex function of the independent variable.

In many instances, the experimenter can produce any value of the independent variable he wishes to study. For example, if he is interested in the effect of the amount of reward on the speed of an animal's running behavior, he may measure food reward in milligrams and manipulate the amount of reward over a large range. Because he was free to perform an experimental manipulation with such a variable, it can be called a *manipulable variable*.

On the other hand, the variable in question may not be subject to manipulation but may be subject to assessment. For example, if your hypothesis says that individuals who are high in need for achievement will solve more problems in a given period of time than individuals who are low in need for achievement, there is little that you can do to manipulate need for achievement, the independent variable. You can, however, measure need for achievement and relate this measurement to the number of problems solved in a given period of time. Such an independent variable can be referred to as an *assessment variable*.

Control variables or control operations are of at least two general classes. You may find that the exploratory behavior of the rat, a variable in which you are interested, is affected by the temperature, the humidity, and the amount of light present. Your hypothesis, however, is about the relation between certain characteristics of the animals' early experience and the animals' later exploratory behavior. In such a case, you would exert *experimental control* over the uninteresting variables, setting the temperature, humidity, and light levels at constant values throughout the experiment.

On the other hand, you may have a hypothesis concerning the effect of test anxiety on the quality of performance on an academic task. You may be fairly certain that there are a number of other variables, such as a variety of early childhood experiences, that might also influence academic performance. You may not be interested in such variables at the moment, and they certainly aren't amenable to experimental control. In this case, you might very carefully draw two groups from a single population of subjects in such a manner that you can be reasonably certain that the variables in which you are not interested are equally likely to be represented in the two groups. You would then be exerting *statistical* control rather than manipulative control.

Psychologists tend to use the terms "stimulus variable" or "stimulus situation" or "situational variable" in reference to most of the independent variables that they use. They also tend to refer to dependent variables as "response," "response variables," or "behavioral variables."

In summary, the language of experimentation has as its basic terms:

    independent variable or "stimulus" or "situational variable," which may be either a

        manipulable variable or an

        assessment variable, operating in the presence of

    control variables, the nature of which may be either

        experimental control or

        statistical control, in order to permit observation of the

    dependent variable or "response" or "behavioral variable."

These terms are frequently used almost interchangeably with the set of terms arising from the language of theory, a topic to be discussed in Chapter 5. Before leaving the topic of experimentation, the reader should realize that three sets of problems have barely been touched upon in the foregoing discussion. These topics are: (1) the issues and problems of measurement that are fundamental to any discussion of experimental variables, (2) the elements of experimental design which must be understood and can become quite elegant, and (3) the problems of statistical analysis and control. These three issues are discussed in three other volumes in this series. *Quantification in Psychology, Basic Statistics,* and *Assessment of Human Characteristics.*

THE LANGUAGE OF THEORY

The first word in the language of theory, and the object of all experimentation, is the Latin word *data*. The rarely used singular form, *datum,* is nearly equivalent to the English word "fact." Unfortunately, some facts are more factual than others. Contrary to popular usage, facts actually vary in their degree of ambiguity. When ambiguity is reduced to a minimum, a fact becomes a datum and a collection of facts becomes data.

There is a vast difference between an event and a fact, or datum. An event is an occurrence in the real world; a datum is a symbolic record of an event. An event and its record are assumed to be in close correspondence, but the nature of the correspondence is not a simple matter and has been a controversial issue in centuries of scholarly argument.

Rather than debate the nature of the relationship between an event and a datum, let us adopt one position with the understanding that it is arbitrary and debatable. This solution to the problem of obtaining agreement on the correspondence between a set of events and a set of data involves the use of *ostensive definitions*. Suppose you wish to establish a clear dividing line between a class of things that you wish to label as "soft" and a class that you wish to label as "hard." Furthermore, suppose that you wish to obtain agreement between yourself and others so that when any one of you labels an object as "hard," it is reasonably certain that you will all label it as "hard." You might undertake to achieve agreement by pointing to or showing others a series of objects and indicating in each case whether the object is "hard" or "soft." Assuming that everyone agrees on the task, and that your judgment is taken as the standard, it would be possible finally to reach agreement on the meaning of "hard" and "soft." The act of pointing or showing is the fundamental operation that gives the ostensive definition its name.

However, the physical act of showing or pointing is not always possible, nor is it always reasonable even if it is possible. How would you perform the task of definition if the concept were pain? You could neither show nor point discriminatively. Pointing, then, is only a symbolic representation of the act of designating the particular class of event you wish to label as pain. Something more than an ostensive definition is needed. The something more can be operational definitions.

Pointing is an *operation* that can be involved in the making of an ostensive definition. Other operations can serve as well. Operational definitions can be regarded as sets of unambiguous directions designed to make sure that what you mean by pain is what someone else means by pain. For example, you might stick yourself with a pin and stick someone else with a pin and make clear that the resulting experience is what you mean by pain. Both the thing that is defined ostensively and the operational arrangements that constitute the operational definition are fundamentally subjective experiences, yet we are most confident that we can agree on operations even when there is great difficulty in being sure of agreement with respect to the thing operated on.

If we can agree that a set of operations are all the same and that the event ostensively defined is the same event, then a number of such events can be collected into a class and given a class name. This name and the events it represents constitute an *empirical construct* and *concept*. It is called a "construct" because it is created by setting events and operations in order and is thus constructed of them. It is called a "concept" because it is a generalization from particulars. It is called an "empirical" construct because it is available to immediate experience. Thus, "stimulus intensity" is an empirical construct. The operations involved in varying the intensity of a sound in a particular instance would constitute the operational definition; the many similar operations for varying the physical intensity of stimuli combine to form the general concept; the experience of stimulus intensity is thus identified by the operations even though it is a subjective experience. In science, an empirical construct is one that is measured directly; the operations of measurement constitute the operational definition of the construct.

Constructs that are not directly measurable, and therefore not empirical, are higher-level or *theoretical constructs*. Such constructs may bear no relation to the real world, as is frequently true of theoretical constructs in mathematics. However, to be useful in an empirical science a theoretical construct must bear some relation to empirical constructs and thus to the real world.

The statement of relationship between a theoretical construct and one or more empirical constructs can be referred to as a *coordinating definition*. For example, changes in skin resistance can be measured directly, and the galvanic skin response (GSR, a change in skin resistance) is an empirical construct that represents a class of easily specifiable operations. Anxiety is a theoretical construct that is not directly measurable. Yet one can establish a relation between the GSR and anxiety by stating the nature of the relationship. If you say, "The greater the change in skin resistance produced by the presentation of a stimulus, the greater the anxiety produced by that stimulus," this statement of relationship is a coordinating definition.

Statements defining the relationship between two or more theoretical variables can be called *implicit definitions*. For example, the theoretical construct "habit" may be coordinated to an empirical variable, "number of trials." An implicit definition of the relationship between habit and anxiety may be desired. In attempting to construct such an implicit definition, you may discover that a third theoretical variable is necessary, and you may therefore invent the concept of "excitatory potential" to represent, on a theoretical level, a value that is some combination of habit and anxiety. You then establish a coordinating definition relating excitatory potential to an empirical construct that you can measure. It may take the form "The greater the excitatory

TYPES OF CONSTRUCTS AND DEFINITIONS

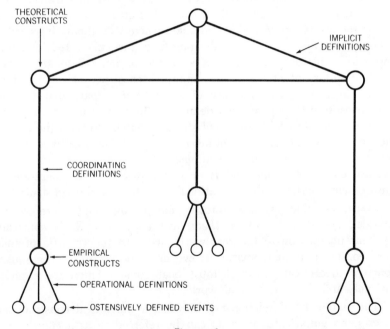

Figure 6

Visual analogy of the relations of theoretical or higher-level constructs (at the top) to empirical constructs and, ultimately, to actual events. The various kinds of definitions are represented by connecting lines.

potential, the fewer the errors in performance of a problem task." At this point, you may be able to write implicit definitions relating the three theoretical constructs. For example, you might say, "As anxiety increases from a low level, its interaction with habit will be of such a nature that excitatory potential will increase through middle values of anxiety and then decrease with further increases in anxiety."

This theory is stated in a relatively crude form, but it is now clearly enough organized so that it can be tested. Figure 6 is similar to a diagram in Koch (1941) that organizes the various classes of events, constructs, and definitions in visual form. This arrangement arises from the logical status of constructs. In discussing the language of experimentation, a distinction is made between two classes of empirical constructs, or variables: independent and dependent. Since an independent variable is controlled by the experimenter in order to observe the effect on the dependent variable, independent variables are usually segregated on the left and dependent variables on the right to indicate the order of consideration. When this is done, as in Figure 7, "higher-level" theoretical constructs are seen as falling in the middle, between

INTEGRATION OF THE LANGUAGES OF EXPERIMENTATION AND THEORY

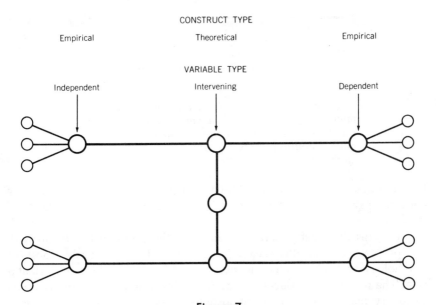

Figure 7
Visual analogy of the unfolding of theory structure to accommodate the logical sequence of experimentation.

independent and dependent variables. It is this arrangement that gives rise to the name *intervening variable,* which is frequently used in psychology to refer to a theoretical construct that intervenes between the experimental manipulations and the results.

Figure 8 is a convenient representation of (1) the distinction between independent, intervening, and dependent variables, and (2) the distinction between empirical (outside the box) and theoretical (inside the box) variables. There is little argument concerning empirical constructs, since ostensive and operational definitions reduce the ambiguity

STRUCTURE OF PSYCHOLOGICAL THEORY

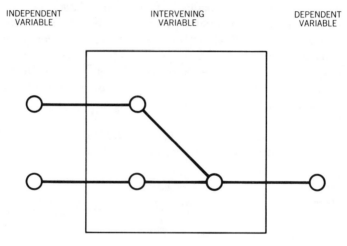

Figure 8

Visual representation of the relation of independent, intervening, and dependent variables in psychological theory. The square box is intended to distinguish empirical (outside) from theoretical (inside) variables.

to a minimum in these cases. Much of the controversy in psychology concerns psychological theory—that is, it concerns what is "in the box" in Figure 8.

Perhaps the most general statement of the problem has to do with the problem of "surplus meaning." As indicated previously, most of psychology and all of scientific psychology is positivistic in its orientation. The material introduced briefly in the last few pages is an approach to theory borrowed from the philosophical school of logical positivism. Positivism is an attempt to define terms unambiguously and to eliminate anything that cannot be related directly to observable, objective events. Strictly interpreted, no concept means anything more than the operations specified and the definitions provided. Anything else is surplus meaning and should be eliminated. The distinction is very similar to the distinction between what a word denotes and what it connotes. The denotative meaning of a word is precisely what its definition says. The connotative meaning includes all of what it suggests. In poetry or literature, words are sometimes chosen precisely because they are rich in connotative meaning. In science, precision in meaning can come only from clear and unambiguous definitions and a conscious effort to eliminate surplus connotations. Thus, in scientific writing the reader is able to substitute the definition of a term for the term itself, whenever it is used, without changing the writer's meaning.

One kind of surplus meaning is commonly unrecognized by beginning students and by a few advanced ones as well. It is the tendency to think of psychological concepts as entities, as real things. For example, the "unconscious" is often visualized as a sack filled with primitive urges. Of course, neither the "unconscious" nor the "urges" are things. They are processes rather than entities, and the names probably should not be used as substantive nouns. Often, however, it is awkward to avoid a substantive noun, so psychologists persist in using many such nouns to stand for ongoing processes. However, whether the issue is dealt with explicitly or not, psychological terms are abstract concepts, empirical and theoretical. They are never entities, whatever other kinds of surplus meaning may be attached to them.

Another, more subtle, issue having to do with surplus meaning and intervening variables is the question of whether intervening variables should have any surplus meaning of any kind. A strict logical positivist would say that they should not—that the entire meaning of a concept should be exhausted by the definitional structure of Figure 6. Arguments have been raised in favor of surplus meaning. Theories are frequently a source of hypotheses for new research in psychology, and few hypotheses would arise from a theoretical formulation in which there is no surplus meaning. Hypotheses can be arrived at in mathematics, or in a mathematical formulation, strictly by deduction, and the process of deduction is facilitated by a complete absence of surplus meaning; in contrast, there are few, if any, theories in psychology that permit a purely deductive approach. Hypotheses arise from deductions that have something less than mathematical rigor and from inductive reasoning made possible by the surplus meaning resident in the concepts. In practice, then, positivistic rigor is an ideal rarely met: it is not a question of whether there is surplus meaning in a concept, but a question of how much.

One final term of theory language is occasionally used to refer to a class of intervening variables in which there is a specific kind of surplus meaning. A *hypothetical construct* is an intervening variable described or defined in such a manner that it specifies clearly that a new, different, and as yet unrealized coordination to the empirical level may be found for it. For example, one might create a psychological concept such as "arousal," defined in terms of a set of operationally defined empirical constructs such as "stimulus change," "novelty," "surprisingness," and the like. One might include in one's definition the expectation that arousal will be found to be related to some aspect of activity in the excitatory portion of the reticular system in the brain. "Arousal," so defined, would be a hypothetical construct. The hypothetical relation between (1) the operations of stimulus change, novelty, and surprisingness and (2) a set of operations, as yet unspecified, involving neurophysiological variables, is surplus meaning far beyond the first meaning for arousal.

One of the difficulties facing the reader of psychological material is the fact that a single word is frequently used in several different ways, often within the same text, and that each way in which it is used has a different status within the logical structure we have been discussing. Let us use the term "perception" as an example.

Figure 9, a diagram patterned after Figure 8, shows three different

THREE MEANINGS OF "PERCEPTION"

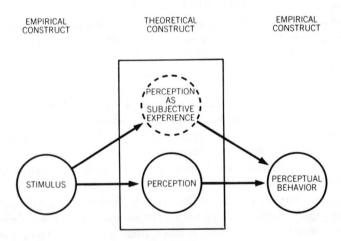

EMPIRICAL
CONSTRUCT

THEORETICAL
CONSTRUCT

EMPIRICAL
CONSTRUCT

PERCEPTION
AS
SUBJECTIVE
EXPERIENCE

STIMULUS PERCEPTION PERCEPTUAL BEHAVIOR

Figure 9

Three different uses of the term are involved in creating the theoretical construct "perception" from the empirical constructs of "stimulus" and "perceptual behavior."

uses of the term "perception." A stimulus, representative of an operationally defined empirical construct, is presented and gives rise to "perception," a subjective experience. The individual describes his experience, and his description constitutes "perceptual behavior," also an empirical construct. The perceptual behavior is used to make inferences about "perception in general," a theoretical construct. While "perception as a subjective experience" and "perception as a theoretical construct" may seem the same, they are not. The theoretical construct has a role as a tool in scientific development, while the subjective experience remains as a source of delight or dismay to the individual who has it, depending on the nature of the stimulus and the esthetic sensibilities of the perceiver. Thus perception as a subjective experience, perception as a class of behavior, and perception as a theoretical construct are very different.

The role assigned to perception as a theoretical construct in psychological theory can be quite varied. Figure 10 portrays a role for perception in a simple behavior theory. A change in a stimulus is assumed to make a change in perception (a theoretical construct) and to

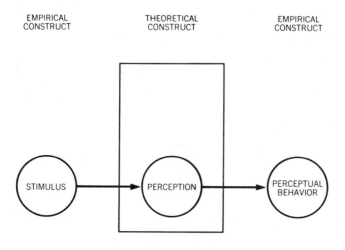

"PERCEPTION" IN A SIMPLE BEHAVIOR THEORY

EMPIRICAL CONSTRUCT	THEORETICAL CONSTRUCT	EMPIRICAL CONSTRUCT

STIMULUS → PERCEPTION → PERCEPTUAL BEHAVIOR

Figure 10
The diagram is that of the construct "perception" with a central role in a simple behavior theory.

produce measurable perceptual behavior as a result. For the most part, but not in all cases, Figure 10 would serve as the basic pattern of classical theories of perception. The interest in the classical field of perception is in perception alone, and the only kind of behavior that is of interest is perceptual behavior. Figure 9 would do as well for some general behavior theories. Such theories are based on the assumptions that all of the multitude of variables that are of interest to psychology have an impact on perception and that we behave in accordance with the way in which we see the world. In such a perceptual, or cognitive, theory, all behavior is perceptual behavior.

There are few such purely perceptual behavior theories in psychology. However, there are many theories in which perception is assigned some important functional role. Suppose behavior is divided into two classes, one of them determined by perception and the other determined by some other theoretical construct, X. Figure 11 is a diagram of one possible role assigned to perception in such a case.

TYPICAL ROLE OF "PERCEPTION" IN THEORY

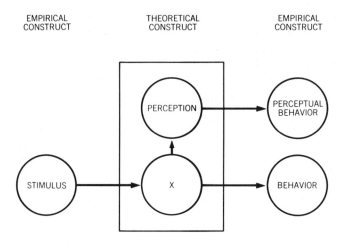

Figure 11

The diagram shows the most common, or typical, role of the construct "perception" in general theories of behavior.

The nature of the stimulus determines the value of X. The value of X determines the nature of perception, as implicitly defined. Perception, in turn, determines the character of perceptual behavior. The value of X also determines the properties of nonperceptual behavior. The extent to which the two classes of behavior are correlated is a question to be determined empirically, and the empirical facts will become the basis for theoretical statements concerning the four possible relations (three coordinating definitions and one implicit definition) indicated by the four interconnecting lines in Figure 11. Note that perception as a subjective experience does not appear in the figure.

It would be necessary to add a number of concepts to the diagram in order to represent any existing theory. Nevertheless, the functional role assigned to perception in Figure 11 corresponds to the manner in which perception is treated in most general behavior theories in psychology—and in many miniature theories which do not undertake to account for all forms of behavior.

What is meant by the assertion that psychology poses problems because of the uncommon use of common words should be clear from the foregoing discussion. It should be equally clear that a single word can have a variety of meanings depending on the context and the specific meaning a writer has provided for it. Understanding psychology consists largely of understanding the language of psychology with all of its difficulties and complexities.

A student today is not likely to proceed very far in psychology before he will have the opportunity to take a laboratory course. The main objective of such a course is to introduce the student to some of the important methods of psychology. Laboratory courses are often designed to bring the student as close as possible to becoming an independent investigator, capable of carrying out experiments on his own.

What is involved in performing an independent experiment or investigation? The answer to this question depends, of course, on the subject matter of the experiment and the competence of the experimenter, but the answer also depends on the way in which the continuous process of experimentation is broken down into exploratory steps.

The following set of "instructions" covers an arbitrary series of fifteen steps in which theory and action interact to produce a representative psychological experiment. (Note that the nineteen terms and concepts introduced in the last two chapters have been italicized on first appearance in this series of steps.)

1. Learn enough about an area to perceive a gap in knowledge. This step covers so much ground that it can mean as little as a few days of intensive study in a limited area or as much as a lifetime of effort. It can refer to a subset of information that is fairly circumscribed, or it can refer to efforts to systematize and classify knowledge of human behavior that spans the history of psychology. Whatever the size of the body of knowledge or the length of the period of study, a student has not carried out an independent investigation until he has independently fulfilled this step in the process.

2. Formulate a general problem statement. The process is one of inductive reasoning, and its nature is something of a mystery. *Induction* is an aspect of logic on which logicians have much less to say than they have on deductive processes. Nor have psychologists made great headway in analyzing the process of induction. Yet if a student is searching for a problem area and a problem statement, the procedure is clear. One reads and studies. One cogitates and contemplates. Suddenly an idea emerges, or seems to emerge. A problem statement is formulated, and the formulator has the clear experience of having found a problem worth more of his time and effort.

3. Develop a variety of forms of the problem statement. The first form of the problem statement is rarely one that can be used directly. While the statement may seem clear when it first emerges, it usually proves to be intractable. The terms in which it is formulated may leave something to be desired, and usually a new search of the literature must be made. The search may be long or short, depending in part on the extent (1) that one is able to find a suitable set of *theoretical concepts,* already developed, in the sense that the concepts provide all of the meaning that is required by the experimenter, (2) that the *implicit definitions* relating the concepts to one another already exist, and (3) that *coordinating definitions* to *empirical constructs* are established. If any of these conditions cannot be met through a search of the literature, then it is necessary, if the study is to be a good study, for the experimenter to develop the missing parts. When this task is accomplished, the problem statement can usually be made in a number of different forms.

4. Select the form of the problem statement that seems to be most suitable for research. Not all forms of the problem statement will prove equally amenable to experimentation. A choice must often be made on the basis of a number of aspects of the situation that cannot be combined into a simple formula. The form of the problem statement that seems most important or most interesting may not be the most practical. The most practical may appear trivial. Whatever the basis, a choice must be made.

5. Refine the problem statement to hypothesis form. The problem statement itself is usually not directly testable. It is usually necessary to extract from it a testable hypothesis. The problem statement usually takes the form of a statement of relations between variables. A hypothesis is usually in the classic "if, then" form: if one changes the value of x, then the value of y will be changed in a predicted direction. Furthermore, hypotheses are frequently phrased in the null rather than the positive form. Thus, even though one thinks a change in x will necessarily be followed by a change in y, the hypothesis is likely to be stated in the form "a change in x will not be followed by a change in y." This is the "null hypothesis," and if the experimental results are of the kind and direction one expected, then statistical tests will allow one to reject the null hypothesis and accept the finding as being a true difference within certain "confidence limits." A hypothesis is stated in the null form because of the logic of statistical inference. This problem, along with the meaning of "confidence limits," is discussed by Hays (*Basic Statistics,* 1967, in this series).

It is worth noting at this point that the intellectual processes involved so far have been a blend of induction and *deduction.* The process of formulation is largely inductive, while the drawing of conclusions is largely a matter of deduction. The hypothesis is in deductive form: if *x*, then *y*. It is also worthy of note that, if one has proceeded as indicated, the experiment that follows will consist of *verification*. If, on the other hand, some of the process described has been omitted, and if one proceeds directly to the experiment, then the result will not have the status of verification. The result will instead be something one might call an experimental induction. Experiments in which steps are missing are commonly called exploratory, or pilot, experiments. If one has carried out exploratory research, it is then usually necessary to carry out another experiment to verify the conclusion one has come to on the basis of the first one.

6. Explore a range of coordinations to the empirical level. The most precise and exact statement of a hypothesis offers a broad range of coordinations to the empirical level and a choice of empirical constructs. For example, the hypothesis may involve the theoretical concept "anxiety." Shall we choose groups of subjects who are either anxious or not anxious according to some test, or shall we undertake to make some subjects anxious by devising an anxiety-producing situation? At this stage, it is usually important to weigh the ease and quality of particular *operational definitions* and the certainty that particular *ostensive definitions* point unambiguously to the class of event that is relevant to the empirical and thus the theoretical construct.

7. Select the variables for study. Step six has narrowed the range of variables on the basis of the nature of the problem to be studied, but at this stage one is faced with a set of practical problems. Which variables are feasible to study? There are a plethora of bases for choice, and a choice must now be made on the basis of the amount of the experimenter's time that will be involved, the amount of money he has, specific equipment that is available or that can be borrowed or purchased, the presence of useful space, the availability of suitable experimental subjects, the ethical values of our society that may be involved, and any number of other mundane aspects of the situation.

8. Plan procedures. The first step in this stage is to choose which *independent variables* to *manipulate*, which variables might be of interest that cannot be manipulated but can become *assessment variables*, which variables to *control experimentally* and which to *control statistically*, and, finally, which *dependent variable* or variables to use. Having made these decisions, one must then proceed to plan the actual physical procedure in sufficient detail so that someone else could duplicate the experiment and reproduce the conditions under which your results are to be obtained. The variables at this level, the procedures, and the measurements of independent, dependent, and control variables constitute the operational and, implicitly, the ostensive definitions involved.

Since our theory is now unfolded into experimentally testable form, our theoretical constructs have become *intervening variables.* Whether they are *hypothetical constructs* as well depends upon the vision we have for their future and the future experiments we may have in mind.

9. Execute the experiment. This stage can be dull, often in the extreme; also, it is often frustrating. Most experiments involve repetitious execution of the same acts over and over. Boredom can become astonishingly acute, especially when months of work are involved. Frustration arises from the fact that very few experiments can be carried out exactly as planned the first time—subjects fail to show up, animals become ill and die, power failures interfere with the functioning of electrical equipment. The human animal has an unlimited capacity for unintentional intervention, and the experimental plan, laid out so meticulously, is likely to prove to have been faulty. There is an endless number of unanticipated problems that can arise. The typical experiment, even one that arrives at a successful conclusion, is likely to involve at least one step backward for every two steps forward, and the frequency of two steps backward is greater than one might imagine.

10. Assemble and organize the *data.* If we succeed in completing the experiment in a satisfactory manner, it will have produced data; and sometimes the amount of data is prodigious. It then becomes necessary to assemble this data in some workable form. This is often a set of calculations that are both simple and numerous and result finally in long lists of numbers or check marks in tabular form. This phase is also dull and time-consuming.

11. Analyze the data. In this phase, one reduces the information on large sheets of tabulations or numbers to a much smaller set of tabulations or numbers which can be more easily understood. This is the exciting part, the moment one has been waiting for—did it happen as your theory says it should happen? Since the variety of next steps, if the results are not what one expected them to be, are nearly endless, we shall skip that possibility and assume that the results appear just as they should have. One then needs to find out whether one was simply lucky or whether the deduction involved in producing the hypothesis was probably sound.

12. Test for statistical significance. In this step, a variety of procedures may be used, depending on the character and quality of the measurement operations and on the form in which the results are stated. Results are occasionally so obvious that statistics are not necessary. Usually, however, a quantitative judgment must be rendered. Nearly all statistical tests involve a comparison of the size of the difference or correlation that one found with some estimate of the range of findings one might have expected to obtain by chance. If the difference is large compared to this chance range, then the null hypothesis is rejected

and one confidently asserts the finding to be positive—that is, one accepts a positive statement of the hypothesis to be true. At this point the deduction is verified. One might also stop here to ponder the question of the application of some form of the uncertainty principle to human behavior.

13. Draw suitable conclusions. It is a remarkable fact that no matter how long we stop to ponder the question of deterministic as contrasted with statistical conceptions of human behavior, the probability is exceedingly high that the conclusions we draw from our results will not be justified. There is an irresistible tendency to generalize our results far beyond the particular situation in which they were tested. A statement of the results that does not go beyond the findings is likely to be a dull, dry statement. Casting it in general terms gives it body and meaning. The meaning, however, is clearly surplus meaning. Any generalization goes beyond the findings, so it is not a question of whether the results will be stated in generalized terms, but a question of how general the statement can be and still be tolerated.

14. Write up the experiment. The processes of induction, deduction, and verification are complete in themselves, internally. However, they will have provided nothing more than a highly personal period of toil, travail, and possibly pleasure unless a fourth element is added. Research is not research until it is communicated and can become a part of the body of empirical information available to all. This usually requires that the results of the experiment be put into written form— often a painful process. The experimenter has worked long and hard to devise an interesting question; he has put great time and effort into convincing himself that the results are a matter of fact. He has a feeling of pleasure when he reaches the end of his journey and discovers a small quantity of truth. He is convinced. Now he must convince the world. Not all good experimenters are good writers. Furthermore, the process of writing up the experiment—the logic behind it, the procedure used, and the results and conclusions—frequently leads to exposure of flaws and gaps in reasoning, to procedures which might have been a bit better than those used, and to a nagging feeling that the broad sweeping conclusion the experimenter has in mind had better be redrawn in a somewhat less sweeping form.

15. Rewrite the paper to conform to some set of external standards. No matter how good the first draft of a research paper is, it is not likely to be the last draft. Nearly every avenue to the body of empirical results available to all has a specific set of requirements that are imposed on the paper. If the paper is to be a thesis and is to be submitted as a part of degree requirements, there are numerous rules and regulations concerning its form. Furthermore, there is likely to be at least one faculty member who will read the paper and suggest changes. If a

paper is to be submitted to a journal, the journal is likely to have rigid requirements. Furthermore, the journal has an editor and a set of referees to whom he may send the paper to be criticized. The version that appears in hard covers on the thesis shelf in a library, or the version that is eventually published several years after the experiment was finished, is usually vastly different than the first version.

This set of fifteen steps in doing an experiment was referred to at the beginning of this section as the description of a cycle. It is an exceedingly rare event when the fifteen steps are accomplished in sequence without reversal. It is much more common that one lands on a penalty square and is required to "go back to GO without collecting $200." These backward regressions in a general progression from the beginning of the process imply that the process has an end. It does not. The sequence was described as a cycle because when one reaches the end one finds oneself back at the beginning. More often than not, one finds that when he has completed a research project successfully he is aware of more unsolved problems than he imagined at the beginning. It seems that the more one learns, the more one realizes he doesn't know. For this reason, research can become an absorbing, tantalizing, satisfying, frustrating, and thoroughly delightful lifework. That it becomes such for many probably accounts for the virtual explosion of scientific knowledge in our times and for the overwhelming mass of information concerning human behavior on the one hand and the perception that there is vastly more to be learned on the other. The human social problems demanding answers are infinite in comparison to the solutions available. The procedures introduced in this chapter offer not merely an avenue for solutions, but a promising one.

A necessary element of scientific development is freedom of debate. Ordinarily, debates are won by the debater with the greatest persuasive skill. In science, however, it should be the argument, not the debater, that is given the nod.

To call an argument meritorious implies that there are good arguments and bad ones, or good theories and bad ones. The difficulty arises when one undertakes to specify the criteria against which one is to judge the relative merits of a theory. There is no simple solution to the problem and no set of criteria on which there is extensive agreement. For that reason no effort will be made to espouse a set of criteria here. What follows is merely a listing of some of the issues and problems associated with judgments of "goodness" and "badness" in psychological theories.

Let us first distinguish the quality of the theory from the quality of the use that is made of it. A good psychological theory can be used equally well for good and bad ends. Intensive psychotherapy and behavioral therapy can salvage people who are psychologically crippled and make them relatively happy and functional members of the community. The same techniques when employed for political ends can become "brainwashing" and subject to worldwide censure. Thus, the use of a theory is not a basis for deciding if the theory itself is good or bad. The physicists responsible for the development of atomic theory are not to be judged on the basis of the uses to which governments put atomic power, and those uses, be they good or bad, are not a basis for judging the goodness or badness of developing theory.

There are sets of terms used occasionally to distinguish good and bad or better and worse among theories. These terms refer strictly to internal characteristics. Three of these terms are "internal consistency," "comprehensiveness," and "simplicity." It is occasionally possible to show that a theory can be used to deduce consequences that are mutually incompatible. Such a theory would usually be regarded as poorer than one that did not permit such an error. Judged on this basis alone, this evaluation would be justified. In actual cases, however, internal inconsistency usually occurs only in complex and comprehensive theories.

Comprehensiveness refers to the extent or range of phenomena to which a theory is applicable. If a comprehensive theory is found to be internally inconsistent (a characteristic which can be corrected), who is to say that it is a poorer theory than a less comprehensive theory that is internally consistent? In psychology, the theories least troubled with the problem of internal inconsistency are miniature theories developed to account for behavior in a very limited range. Everything else being equal, a simple theory is to be preferred over a complex one. However, everything else is rarely equal.

Another criterion occasionally applied to theories is the degree of "elegance." In mathematics some solutions to classical problems are regarded as elegant in contrast to other solutions which are equally correct or exact but which require a greater number of steps through somewhat more devious routes. Even if the criterion of elegance could be quantified and applied, it is doubtful if such an elegant term could be applied to any existing psychological theories. Elegance is probably a property that belongs to pure mathematics, if it belongs anywhere. Thus the properties of internal consistency, comprehensiveness, simplicity, and even elegance are better regarded as goals for theory than as criteria for comparative judgments of good and bad.

Other qualities sometimes mentioned in judging the value of theories are related more to what the theories do than to what they are. Thus a theory that is able to offer prediction and control of behavior is sometimes considered to be better than a theory that appears to have less ability in this respect. Correlated with this is the quality of being heuristic. A heuristic theory is one that stimulates investigation, research, and discovery. A heuristic theory is a productive theory. These two criteria are themselves internally inconsistent. A theory that provides the ultimate in prediction and control would be one that had solved the problem. It would not generate further research because there would not be further problems to be investigated. Thus, a maximum in prediction and control would represent a minimum in heuristic value. These properties of theories are certainly suitable as descriptive terms to apply to theories, but they involve serious problems when used as a basis for judging value.

Theories in psychology are occasionally judged on the basis of the humanistic importance of the problems they attack. For example, Koch (1961) has said that psychology's "history has been largely a matter of emulating the methods, forms, symbols of the established sciences, especially physics. In doing so, there have been inevitable tendencies to retreat from broad and intensively significant ranges of its subject matter and to form rationales for doing so which could invite further retreat."

It is likely that Koch's statement was intentionally exaggerated and motivated to goad psychology into further effort and toward a reassessment of its own position and directions. It is not difficult to frame a counterargument. It is rare that an immediate problem is solved by attacking it directly. Often, there are many trivial problems that must be solved first, even without a clear understanding of their eventual exact applications. Science in most areas has advanced fastest in a combination of pure and applied research. Robert Glazer is reported to have suddenly developed the idea of the bubble chamber while sitting in the "Pretzel Bell" in Ann Arbor, Michigan, watching bubbles form and rise to the top of a glass of beer. A research proposal to develop a bubble chamber was rejected by a number of national fund-granting agencies because their panels of experts could not see in a glass of beer, as Glazer did, the possibility of solutions to broad and intensely significant problems. A small grant was made by the university, the bubble chamber was developed, a Nobel prize was won, and no self-respecting physics department is now without a bubble chamber as a tool for tracing the paths of atomic and subatomic particles! Not all psychological research is addressed to problems that appear intensely significant to a humanist, but much psychological research, and psychology as a whole, is addressed to problems of humanistic significance.

Koch accuses psychology of patterning itself after the established sciences, especially physics. While that argument can be and has been made, a case can be made for reversing the positions of psychology and physics on the issue. The physical sciences have proceeded, until recently, as if science existed apart from the scientist. A number of fundamental problems that are seen dimly and lately by physical scientists have been faced directly, of necessity, by social scientists for a much longer time. Three examples will suffice to indicate the argument.

1. There has never been a time in which psychologists have been able to ignore the fact that psychological properties cannot be measured without the measuring operation determining the character of the result in part or even in large measure. Even the act of asking a person a question is likely to change the state that is being asked about. Psychology has developed elaborate and highly sophisticated methods of coping with this problem. The Heisenberg uncertainty principle was a late realization of a fundamental fact of scientific investigation.

2. The statistics that are being applied in quantum mechanics were not developed in physics. The first steps were probably those taken to deal with problems of gambling. Further development was initiated in the biological sciences, chiefly in agriculture to permit the testing of the effects of fertilizers, and in psychology because of the persistent necessity of dealing with individual differences. Thus a challenging

argument can be made that physics is borrowing methods from psychology.

3. A final argument can be made that psychology is attacking socially significant problems and producing knowledge that carries the potential for solving them at a far greater rate than that at which our society is developing social institutions and mechanisms for applying the psychological knowledge that is available. If this argument holds, then Koch is attacking the wrong people. The readers of the volumes in this series may be the judge.

REFERENCES

Allport, G. W. *Becoming: Basic considerations for a psychology of personality.* New Haven, Conn.: Yale University Press, 1955.

Allport, G. W. *Pattern and growth in personality.* New York: Holt, Rinehart and Winston, 1961.

Alpern, M., Lawrence, M., & Wolsk, D. *Sensory processes.* Belmont, Calif.: Brooks/Cole, 1967.

Birch, D., & Veroff, J. *Motivation: A study of action.* Belmont, Calif.: Brooks/Cole, 1966.

Blum, G. S. *Psychodynamics: The science of unconscious mental forces.* Belmont, Calif.: Brooks/Cole, 1966.

Bohr, N. *Atomic physics and human knowledge.* New York: Wiley, 1958.

Boring, E. G. *A history of experimental psychology.* New York: Appleton-Century, 1929.

Boring, E. G. *Sensation and perception in the history of experimental psychology.* New York: Appleton-Century, 1942.

Boring, E. G. Is human behavior predetermined? *Scientific Monthly,* 1957, **84**, 189–196.

Butter, C. M. *Neuropsychology: The study of brain and behavior.* Belmont, Calif.: Brooks/Cole, 1968.

Cattell, R. B. Ethics and the social sciences. *American Psychologist,* 1948, **3**, 193–198.

Doyle, C. L. Psychology, science, and the western democratic tradition. Unpublished doctoral dissertation, University of Michigan, 1965.

Eddington, A. S. *New pathways in science.* Cambridge, England: Cambridge University Press, 1935.

Fitts, P. M., & Posner, M. I. *Human performance.* Belmont, Calif.: Brooks/Cole, 1967.

Hays, W. L. *Basic statistics.* Belmont, Calif.: Brooks/Cole, 1967.

Hays, W. L. *Quantification in psychology.* Belmont, Calif.: Brooks/Cole, 1967.

Heisenberg, W. *Physics and philosophy: The revolution in modern physics.* New York: Harper & Row, 1958.

Hoagland, H. Science and the new humanism. *Science,* 1964, **143**, 111–114.

Immergluck, L. Determinism-freedom in contemporary psychology: An ancient problem revisited. *American Psychologist,* 1964, **4**, 270–281.

Kelly, E. L. *Assessment of human characteristics.* Belmont, Calif.: Brooks/ Cole, 1967.

Koch, S. The logical character of the motivational concept, I and II. *Psychol. Rev.,* 1941, **48**, 15–38 and 127–154.

Koch, S. Psychological science versus the science-humanism antinomy: Intimations of a significant science of man. *American Psychologist,* 1961, **10**, 629–639.

Krutch, J. W. *The measure of man: On freedom, human values, survival, and the modern temper.* Indianapolis: Bobbs-Merrill, 1954.

Lane, H. L., & Bem, D. *A laboratory manual for the control and analysis of behavior.* Belmont, Calif.: Brooks/Cole, 1965.

Laplace, P. S. de. *A philosophical essay on probabilities,* 1820. Translation by F. W. Truscott and F. L. Emory. New York: Dover, 1952.

Lundberg, G. Semantics and value problems. *Social Forces,* 1948, **27**, 114–117.

Manis, M. *Cognitive processes.* Belmont, Calif.: Brooks/Cole, 1966.

May, R. The psychological basis of freedom. *Pastoral Psych.,* 1962, **13**, 47–54.

McNeil, E. B. *The concept of human development.* Belmont, Calif.: Brooks/ Cole, 1966.

Murphy, G. *An historical introduction to modern psychology.* (Rev. ed.) New York: Harcourt, Brace & World, 1951.

Niebuhr, R. *The self and the dramas of history.* New York: Scribner's, 1955.

Oppenheimer, J. R. Aanalogy in science. *American Psychologist,* 1961, **11**, 127–135.

Rogers, C. R. Persons or science: A philosophical question. *American Psychologist,* 1955, **10**, 267–278.

Rogers, C. R. *On becoming a person: A therapist's view of psychotherapy.* Boston: Houghton Mifflin, 1961.

Rogers, C. R. *Learning to be free.* Paper given to a session on "Conformity and Diversity" in the conference on "Man and Civilization," sponsored by the University of California School of Medicine. San Francisco, January 28, 1962.

Sachar, E. J. Behavioral science and the law. *Scientific American,* 1963, **209**, 39–45.

Snow, C. P. *Two cultures and the scientific revolution: The Rede lecture.* New York: Cambridge University Press, 1959.

Snow, C. P. *Two cultures: And a second look.* New York: Cambridge University Press, 1964.

Skinner, B. F. *Walden II.* New York: Macmillan, 1948.

Skinner, B. F. *Science and human behavior.* New York: Macmillan, 1953.

Skinner, B. F. Freedom and the control of man. *Amer. Schol.,* 1955, **25**, 47–65.

Walker, E. L. *Conditioning and instrumental learning.* Belmont, Calif.: Brooks/Cole, 1967.

Walker, E. L., & McKeachie, W. J. *Some thoughts about teaching the beginning course in psychology.* Belmont, Calif.: Brooks/Cole, 1967.

Weintraub, D. J., & Walker, E. L. *Perception.* Belmont, Calif.: Brooks/Cole, 1966.

Zajonc, R. B. *Social psychology: An experimental approach.* Belmont, Calif.: Brooks/Cole, 1966.

Each of the fourteen volumes included in the index is referred to by a set of code letters chosen because of their discriminability and mnemonic value. The code letters are:

ALW-SP	Alpern, Lawrence, and Wolsk, *Sensory Processes*
B-NP	Butter, *Neuropsychology*
B-PD	Blum, *Psychodynamics*
BV-MSA	Birch and Veroff, *Motivation: A Study of Action*
FP-HP	Fitts and Posner, *Human Performance*
H-BS	Hays, *Basic Statistics*
H-QP	Hays, *Quantification in Psychology*
K-AHC	Kelly, *Assessment of Human Characteristics*
M-CP	Manis, *Cognitive Processes*
M-HD	McNeil, *Human Development*
W-CL	Walker, *Conditioning and Instrumental Learning*
W-PNSS	Walker, *Psychology as a Natural and Social Science*
WW-P	Weintraub and Walker, *Perception*
Z-SP	Zajonc, *Social Psychology*

AUTHOR INDEX OF THE
BASIC CONCEPTS IN PSYCHOLOGY SERIES

Adams, J. K., WW-P, 80
Adams, J. S., Z-SP, 44
Adams, P. A., M-CP, 10, 116
Ader, R., Z-SP, 25-27
Ades, H. W., B-NP, 55, 111, 182, 185
Adey, W. R., B-NP, 83, 184
Adkins, R. J., B-NP, 83, 183
Adler, A., B-PD, 13-14; BV-MSA, 76; M-HD, 21
Adolph, F., B-NP, 146
Adrian, E. D., B-NP, 77, 90, 183
Ager, J. W., M-CP, 77, 113
Agranoff, B. W., B-NP, 178, 190
Ajmone-Marsan, C., B-NP, 56, 182
Alfrey, V. G., B-NP, 179
Allee, W. C., Z-SP, 18-19
Allen, M. B., B-NP, 129, 186
Allen, W. F., B-NP, 90, 184
Allison, J., BV-MSA, 12, 31-32
Allport, F. H., Z-SP, 16, 19, 21, 87-88
Allport, G. A., WW-P, 51
Allport, G. W., BV-MSA, 65; K-AHC, 2, 29, 103; W-PNSS, 14-16, 28
Allyn, J., Z-SP, 65
Alpern, M., ALW-SP, 37, 59, 62; B-NP, 39; FP-HP, 5, 47; M-HD, 13; WW-P, 56, 63, 69, 79, 82
Alter, M., M-CP, 14, 114
Amassian, V. E., B-NP, 123, 186
Ames, A., Jr., WW-P, 50-51
Ammons, R. B., M-CP, 9, 113
Amore, J. E., ALW-SP, 123
Amsel, A., W-CL, 74
Anand, B. K., B-NP, 147-148, 188
Anastasi, A., H-QP, 68; K-AHC, 5, 103
Anderson, J. E., M-HD, 6
Anderson, N. S., FP-HP, 68, 148
Andersson, B., B-NP, 146, 188
Appley, M. H., FP-HP, 27, 37
Applezweig, D. W., K-AHC, 33, 103
Applezweig (Appley), M. H., W-CL, 72
Arago, N. F. J., ALW-SP, 22
Arana-Iniquez, R., B-NP, 122, 187
Arden, G. B., B-NP, 56, 181
Aries, P., M-HD, 66

Aristotle, W-PNSS, 2
Asch, S. E., WW-P, 91; Z-SP, 37-40, 88-89
Aserinsky, E., B-NP, 133, 186
Ashida, S., W-CL, 34-35
Atkinson, J. W., BV-MSA, 20-22, 25, 28-31, 60, 67, 78; K-AHC, 46, 104; WW-P, 84-86
Attneave, F., FP-HP, 48-49, 86
Austin, G. A., M-CP, 56, 113
Averbach, E., FP-HP, 62
Axelrod, J., B-NP, 155

Babich, F. R., B-NP, 178, 190
Backer, R., B-NP, 152, 189; W-CL, 69
Bacon, Roger, W-PNSS, 3
Baerends, G. P., W-CL, 9
Bafett, H. C., B-NP, 74, 183
Bagshaw, M., B-NP, 154, 189
Bahrick, H. P., FP-HP, 14, 73, 132
Bakan, P., WW-P, 48
Baker, C. H., FP-HP, 147
Bandura, A., BV-MSA, 76; W-CL, 115-117; Z-SP, 40, 48-50
Banks, J. H., Jr., Z-SP, 55-58, 64-65, 67, 73
Bard, P., B-NP, 154, 188
Barker, C. T., BV-MSA, 62
Barker, R. G., M-HD, 39
Barlow, H. B., ALW-SP, 62
Barnes, G. W., W-CL, 79
Baron, A., W-CL, 80
Barron, F., M-CP, 106, 113; WW-P, 80
Bartlett, F. C., FP-HP, 123, 136; M-CP, 24, 93, 113
Bates, C., FP-HP, 98
Batini, C., B-NP, 129, 186
Battig, K., B-NP, 111, 185
Bayley, N., M-HD, 39
Beach, F. A., B-NP, 149, 151, 188; BV-MSA, 44, 47-48
Beck, E. C., W-CL, 85
Beidler, L. M., ALW-SP, 115, 123; B-NP, 93, 184

Békésy, G. von, ALW-SP, 92-98, 101; B-NP, 62, 97
Bell, C., ALW-SP, 124
Bell, R. Q., BV-MSA, 47
Belloni, M., BV-MSA, 40
Bem, D. J., ALW-SP, 74; M-CP, 13, 21, 115; W-CL, 122
Bender, L., K-AHC, 57
Benjamin, R. M., B-NP, 95, 184
Bennett, E., FP-HP, 146
Bentham, J., BV-MSA, 3
Benzinger, T. H., B-NP, 155
Berger, H., B-NP, 119
Berger, S. M., Z-SP, 35-37
Bergmann, G., W-CL, 84
Bergum, B. O., Z-SP, 11-13
Berkeley, G., WW-P, 21-22, 29
Berkowitz, L., BV-MSA, 69; M-CP, 76, 113
Berkun, M. M., BV-MSA, 33; W-CL, 77-78
Berlyne, D. E., B-PD, 65; BV-MSA, 35, 53; W-CL, 75; WW-P, 92
Berman, A. J., B-NP, 114, 186
Berman, E., BV-MSA, 68
Bernard, C., ALW-SP, 140, 145
Bersh, P. J., W-CL, 55, 57
Biddulph, R., ALW-SP, 83, 101
Bieber, I., BV-MSA, 64
Biederman, I., FP-HP, 128
Binet, A., W-PNSS, 3
Birch, D., BV-MSA, 38-40; W-CL, 38, 88; Z-SP, 14
Birch, H. G., M-CP, 83, 113
Birmingham, H. P., FP-HP, 118
Bixenstine, V. E., Z-SP, 76-78
Black, A. H., W-CL, 85
Blackwell, H. R., ALW-SP, 37-38, 62; W-CL, 64; WW-P, 77
Blackwell, O. M., ALW-SP, 37-38, 62
Blake, L., B-NP, 52, 181
Blake, R. R., Z-SP, 38
Blodgett, H. C., BV-MSA, 15-16; M-CP, 7-8,113
Blum, G. S., K-AHC, 57; W-CL, 12; W-PNSS, 4
Bodian, D., B-NP, 13-14, 181
Bohr, N., W-PNSS, 11
Boller, W. R., M-HD, 69
Bolles, R., BV-MSA, 39
Bonnet, C., FP-HP, 61
Bonvallet, M., B-NP, 126, 128-129, 186-187

Boring, E. G., ALW-SP, 124-125; FP-HP, 55; W-PNSS, 2-4, 14, 16, 21-22, 24-25; WW-P, 41-43
Bower, G. H., BV-MSA, 23; M-CP, 49, 113; W-CL, 43-44, 46, 80
Bowlby, J., M-HD, 60-61
Boycott, B. B., B-NP, 179
Boynton, R., FP-HP, 79
Brady, J. V., ALW-SP, 10-11; B-NP, 155, 188; Z-SP, 14
Brainard, R. W., FP-HP, 105
Braun, H. W., W-CL, 21
Bray, C. W., ALW-SP, 92, 98, 101
Brazier, M. A. B., ALW-SP, 145; B-NP, 12, 17, 24, 135
Breen, R. A., W-CL, 61
Brehm, J., M-CP, 103, 113
Brewer, F., B-NP, 119-124, 126, 186
Bright, P. J., B-NP, 78, 190
Brillat-Savarin, Jean Anthelme, ALW-SP, 121
Brindley, G. S., ALW-SP, 37-38, 62; B-NP, 56, 181
Brink, J. J., B-NP, 178, 190
Broadbent, D. E., FP-HP, 36, 58, 65, 132
Brobeck, J. R., ALW-SP, 142-43, 145; B-NP, 142, 147, 188-189
Brodel, M., ALW-SP, 86-87
Brogden, W. J., W-CL, 23, 82-83
Bronfenbrenner, U., BV-MSA, 60
Brown, I. D., FP-HP, 148
Brown, J. S., BV-MSA, 36, 40; W-CL, 81
Brown, P. K., ALW-SP, 28, 34, 36, 64; B-NP, 44, 81
Brown, R. W., M-CP, 88-89, 113; Z-SP, 44
Brown, T. C., B-NP, 90, 184
Bruce, H. M., ALW-SP, 102, 123
Bruce, R. H., Z-SP, 100, 102
Bruce, R. S., Z-SP, 25
Bruner, J. S., FP-HP, 130; M-CP, 54, 113; WW-P, 9, 85
Brunswik, E., WW-P, 8, 40
Brush, E. S., W-CL, 53-54
Brush, F. R., W-CL, 53-54
Bryan, W. L., FP-HP, 8-9, 71
Bucy, P. C., B-NP, 96, 152-153, 184, 188
Buddenbrock, W. von, ALW-SP, 12
Bunnell, S., Jr., WW-P, 80
Burke, B. S., M-HD, 17
Burnstein, E., BV-MSA, 38-39; W-CL, 38; Z-SP, 98
Buros, O. K., K-AHC, 79, 103

Burtt, H. E., M-CP, 19, 113
Buschke, H., FP-HP, 66
Bush, R. B., Z-SP, 108
Buswell, G. T., FP-HP, 71
Butler, R. A., B-NP, 66, 182; W-CL, 79-80
Bubash, S., B-NP, 178, 190
Butsch, R. L. C., FP-HP, 71
Butter, C. M., ALW-SP, 98, 140;
    BV-MSA, ix; FP-HP, 35; M-HD, 13;
    W-CL, 41-43, 49, 79
Bykov, K. M., ALW-SP, 143, 145

Campbell, A. A., W-CL, 23
Campbell, B. A., B-NP, 147, 189;
    BV-MSA, 23; W-CL, 37, 41-43, 80
Campbell, D. T., Z-SP, 89-91
Campbell, F. W., ALW-SP, 58, 63
Cantril, H., M-HD, 69; Z-SP, 45
Capehart, J., W-CL, 76
Carlisle, H. J., B-NP, 144, 188
Carmichael, L., M-CP, 25, 113
Carter, L. F., WW-P, 85
Carterette, T. S., W-CL, 87
Cartwright, D., Z-SP, 97
Casey, K. L., B-NP, 86, 183
Cattell, J. M., K-AHC, 88
Cattell, R. B., K-AHC, 26, 103;
    W-PNSS, 24
Centers, R., Z-SP, 43-45
Chambers, R. M., W-CL, 78
Chambers, W. W., B-NP, 122, 187
Champion, R. A., W-CL, 52
Chapanis, A., FP-HP, 146
Chapman, D. W., BV-MSA, 57
Charles, D. C., M-HD, 69
Charles, L. P., WW-P, 49
Chase, A. M., ALW-SP, 63
Chase, W. G., FP-HP, 59-60
Cheatham, P. G., FP-HP, 77-78
Chen, S. C., Z-SP, 16-18, 84-86
Cherry, E. C., FP-HP, 57-58
Chhina, G. S., B-NP, 148, 188
Chorover, S. L., B-NP, 161, 190
Chow, K. L., B-NP, 65, 160, 182;
    WW-P, 50
Church, R. M., W-CL, 53; Z-SP, 31-33
Cimabue, WW-P, 24
Clark, B., WW-P, 71
Clark, R. A., BV-MSA, 29, 38-39; K-AHC,
    104; W-CL, 38
Clark, S. L., B-NP, 33, 36
Clark, W. H., M-CP, 23-24, 114

Cleghorn, R. A., ALW-SP, 12
Cliff, N., M-CP, 63, 113
Clifford, L. T., BV-MSA, 25-26
Cofer, C. N., FP-HP, 27, 37; M-CP,
    101, 115
Cohen, A. R., M-CP, 103, 113
Cohen, B. B., M-CP, 56, 113
Cohen, B. D., WW-P, 78
Cohen, E., M-CP, 56, 113
Cohen, I., M-CP, 14, 114
Cohen, J., WW-P, 63, 65
Cohen, S. M., B-NP, 161, 190
Coleman, E. B., FP-HP, 139
Collias, N. E., B-NP, 59
Condillac, E. B. de, WW-P, 22
Conover, D. W., FP-HP, 48
Conrad, R., FP-HP, 68, 106
Coombs, C. H., H-QP, 23, 75; K-AHC,
    27, 103
Coons, E. E., W-CL, 61
Coppock, W. J., W-CL, 78, 83
Corti, A., ALW-SP, 86, 101
Costello, R. D., B-NP, 125
Cotton, J., W-CL, 43
Craik, K. J. W., FP-HP, 118
Crawford, B. H., ALW-SP, 26-27, 64
Creamer, L. R., FP-HP, 80-81
Crespi, L. P., W-CL, 46
Criswell, J., Z-SP, 108
Critchley, M., B-NP, 83, 85, 183
Crocker, E. C., ALW-SP, 108, 123
Cronbach, L. J., H-QP, 68; K-AHC, 37,
    86, 88, 103
Crook, M. N., FP-HP, 36
Crosby, E. C., B-NP, 36, 108
Cross, H. A., W-CL, 83
Crossman, E. R. F. W., FP-HP, 16, 66,
    111, 119-120
Crowder, R. G., FP-HP, 134
Crutchfield, R. S., Z-SP, 39
Culler, E. A., B-NP, 111, 170, 185, 190
Cutler, R. L., M-HD, ix, 24; WW-P, 80

Dallenbach, K. M., FP-HP, 62; M-CP,
    27-28, 115
Dalton, J., ALW-SP, 68
Danielson, F. H., M-HD, vii
Darby, C. L., Z-SP, 34
Dartnall, H. J. A., ALW-SP, 62
Darwin, Charles, H-QP, 8; Z-SP, 7
Dashiell, J. F., W-CL, 37; Z-SP, 12-13, 102
Davenport, C. B., M-HD, vii
Davidson, J. M., B-NP, 151, 188

da Vinci, Leonardo, see Vinci
Davis, H., ALW-SP, 115, 123; B-NP, 60, 64, 182
Davis, R., FP-HP, 80
Davis, R. C., M-HD, 44; W-CL, 85
Davis, R. E., B-NP, 178, 190
Davson, H., ALW-SP, 62-63
Dawes, R. M., FP-HP, 143-144; M-CP, 62, 77, 113, 116
Deese, J., M-CP, 7, 29, 114
Degan, J., FP-HP, 146
Deininger, R. L., FP-HP, 22
Delafresnaye, J. F., B-NP, 122
De Lange, H., ALW-SP, 62
Delgado, J. M. R., B-NP, 84, 110, 183, 185
De Lorenzo, A. J., ALW-SP, 104, 123
Dember, W., BV-MSA, 62; WW-P, 91-92
Dement, W., B-NP, 133-134, 186-187
Dennis, W., M-HD, 20
Denny-Brown, D., B-NP, 112, 185
Descartes, Rene, B-NP, 1; W-PNSS, 3
Desmedt, J. E., B-NP, 70, 182
De Soto, C. B., Z-SP, 96-98
Dethier, B. G., ALW-SP, 8, 12
Deutsch, M., Z-SP, 39
De Valois, R. L., ALW-SP, 46-47, 63; WW-P, 65
De Vries, H., ALW-SP, 106, 123; B-NP, 87-88, 184
Dewson, J. H. III, B-NP, 70, 182
Diamond, I. T., B-NP, 66-67, 69, 182-183
Diderot, D., WW-P, 24
Dill, D. B., ALW-SP, 145
Di Lollo, V., BV-MSA, 17-18
Dingman, W., B-NP, 178, 190
Dinsmoor, J. A., W-CL, 50
Doane, B., B-NP, 114, 185
Dobelle, W. H., ALW-SP, 36, 63; B-NP, 44, 181
Dobzhansky, T., Z-SP, 85
Dollard, J., M-CP, 94-95, 114; M-HD, 50; W-CL, 110-116; Z-SP, 29-34, 40
Donhoffer, H., B-NP, 172-173, 190
Donner, K. O., B-NP, 47
Doty, P., M-HD, 12
Doty, R. W., W-CL, 85
Dowling, J. E., ALW-SP, 51, 63
Doyle, C., W-PNSS, 17, 20-21, 23-24, 26, 29-30
Dreger, R. M., K-AHC, 4, 103
Dufort, R. H., W-CL, 84
Dugdale, R. L., M-HD, vii
Duncan, C. P., W-CL, 101-103; WW-P, 49

Duncker, K., M-CP, 100, 104, 114; WW-P, 58
Durfort, R. H., BV-MSA, 18-19
DuVerney, J. G., ALW-SP, 90-91, 101

Earl, R., BV-MSA, 54; W-CL, 33; WW-P, 91-92
Ebbinghaus, H., M-CP, 18-20, 30, 33, 114
Eccles, J., B-NP, 21-22, 24
Eddington, A. S., W-PNSS, 11
Edwards, A. L., K-AHC, 29, 46, 103; M-CP, 32, 114
Edwards, W., FP-HP, 148-149; WW-P, 43
Ehrenfreund, D., W-CL, 48
Egger, M., B-NP, 155, 188
Egyhazi, H., B-NP, 177, 190
Eisenman, J. S., ALW-SP, 141-142, 145; B-NP, 143, 189
Eldred, E., B-NP, 110, 185
Elkin, F., M-HD, 64-65
Elkind, J. I., FP-HP, 118-119
Ellen, P., W-CL, 81
Elliott, D. N., K-AHC, 64, 104
Ellson, D. G., W-CL, 72
Enroth-Cugell, C., ALW-SP, 58
Epstein, A. N., B-NP, 147, 189
Eratosthenes, Z-SP, 2
Erickson, R. P., B-NP, 94, 185
Erickson, T. C., B-NP, 120
Eriksen, C. W., WW-P, 76
Erikson, E., B-PD, 20; BV-MSA, 46; M-HD, 27
Eron, L. D., BV-MSA, 76
Esakov, A. I., B-NP, 94, 184
Espinas, A., Z-SP, 8
Estabrook, A. H., M-HD, vii
Estes, W. K., W-CL, 24, 49, 87, 128-129, 133
Etkin, W., Z-SP, 30
Evans, R. M., WW-P, 28
Evarts, E. V., B-NP, 134, 186
Ewald, J. R., ALW-SP, 92, 97, 101
Eysenck, H. J., Z-SP, 100-102

Farber, I. E., BV-MSA, 36
Feather, N. T., BV-MSA, 60
Fechner, G. T., B-PD, 1; H-QP, 25-29

Feld, S. C., BV-MSA, 78
Feldinger, I., BV-MSA, 54
Feldman, R. S., W-CL, 81
Fenichel, O., B-PD, 65
Fenn, W. O., FP-HP, 79
Ferster, C. B., W-CL, 101-103
Feshbach, S., BV-MSA, 75
Festinger, L., BV-MSA, 65; M-CP, 102-104, 114; Z-SP, 58-60, 65-66
Ficks, L., FP-HP, 50
Field, J., ALW-SP, 146; B-NP, 45, 60, 129
Finch, C., B-NP, 170, 190
Fink, J. B., W-CL, 35
Fisher, A. E., B-NP, 155
Fiske, D. W., K-AHC, 57, 84, 104
Fitts, P. M., B-NP, 156, 190; FP-HP, 11, 14, 22-24, 100, 102-103, 105-106, 110, 113, 114-115, 128, 132; W-CL, 4; Z-SP, 13
Fivel, H. W., M-CP, 48, 116
Fjeld, H. A., Z-SP, 34
Fleming, W. H., M-CP, 103, 113
Flesch, R., M-CP, 70, 114
Fletcher, H., ALW-SP, 78-79, 101
Flexner, J. B., B-NP, 178, 190
Flexner, S. B., B-NP, 178, 190
Flynn, J. P., B-NP, 148, 155, 188-189
Forer, B. R., K-AHC, 85, 103
Forgays, D. G., W-CL, 79
Fowler, H., BV-MSA, 23; W-CL, 43-44, 46, 80, 82
Fox, S. S., BV-MSA, 20
Fraenkel, S., ALW-SP, 145
Frank, L. K., B-NP, 116
Franklin, M., M-CP, 33, 115
Freeman, F. N., FP-HP, 112
French, E. G., BV-MSA, 30, 64
French, J. D., ALW-SP, 10, 12; B-NP, 122-123, 126, 135, 186-187
French, J. R. P., BV-MSA, 79, 81
French, N. R., B-NP, 59
Freud, A., B-PD, 5
Freud, S., B-PD, ix, 2, 2-13; BV-MSA, 3, 43-46, 48-49, 73, 76; K-AHC, 88, 90; M-CP, 30, 31; M-HD, 21, 27, 32; W-PNSS, 3
Frick, F. C., FP-HP, 50
Frisch, K. von, Z-SP, 55
Fromm, E., B-PD, 17-18; M-HD, 69
Frommer, G. P., B-NP, 94, 185
Fuller, J. L., K-AHC, 4, 103
Funkenstein, D. H., B-NP, 155

Furth, J. J., B-NP, 179
Fuster, J. M., B-NP, 126, 186

Galambos, R., B-NP, 64, 67, 70, 117, 182
Galanter, E., ALW-SP, 12; Z-SP, 108
Galton, Francis, ALW-SP, 72; K-AHC, 3-4, 88, 103; W-PNSS, 3
Gardner, E., B-NP, 11, 23, 26, 28, 37, 60, 117, 141
Garner, W. R., FP-HP, 86, 88
Gasser, H., B-NP, 18
Gastaut, H., B-NP, 171,190
Gates, M. G., Z-SP, 18-19
Geiselhart, R., W-CL, 21
Geiwitz, P. J., B-PD, 65
Gelb, A., WW-P, 57
Geldard, F. A., ALW-SP, 136, 145
Gellhorn, E., ALW-SP, 145
Gerall, A. A., W-CL, 52
Gerard, H. B., Z-SP, 39
Gernandt, B. E., ALW-SP, 128, 145
Gesteland, H. C., ALW-SP, 109, 123; B-NP, 89, 184
Gibson, E. J., WW-P, 83
Gibson, J. J., ALW-SP, 139, 145; B-NP, 40, 71, 181, 183; WW-P, 8, 28, 36-37, 47, 83
Girden, E., B-NP, 170, 190
Glanville, A. D., FP-HP, 62
Glanzer, M., M-CP, 23-24, 114
Glanzer, R., W-PNSS, 60
Gleason, T. G., M-CP, 62, 116
Gleitman, H., BV-MSA, 23
Gleser, G., K-AHC, 86, 103
Glickman, S. E., W-CL, 61
Glucksberg, S., M-CP, 97-98, 114
Glunzer, M., BV-MSA, 61
Goddard, Henry, M-HD, viii
Goldberg, L., K-AHC, 84, 103
Goldfarb, W., M-HD, 62
Goldman-Eisler, E., FP-HP, 131
Goldstein, L. S., M-CP, 14, 114
Goldstein, M. L., W-CL, 47
Goodenough, F., M-HD, 52
Goodman, C. C.,WW-P, 85
Goodnow, J. J., M-CP, 54, 113
Goodrich, K. P., W-CL, 84
Gordon, D. A., WW-P, 63
Gordon, K. H., Z-SP, 99-102
Gormezano, I., M-CP, 50, 114; W-CL, 24
Goranson, R. E., M-CP, 76, 113
Gotkin, L. G., M-CP, 14, 114

Gough, H. G., K-AHC, 104
Gould, J. D., FP-HP, 30
Graham, ALW-SP, 42
Granit, R., ALW-SP, 12, 63; B-NP, 46-47, 56, 110, 125, 181, 185
Grant, D. A., FP-HP, 22; M-CP, 50, 114; W-CL, 38-39, 52
Grastyan, E., B-NP, 172-173, 190
Gray, J. A. B., B-NP, 76, 183
Graybiel, A., WW-P, 71
Green, H. C., ALW-SP, 140, 145
Greene, W. A., W-CL, 35
Greenspoon, J., M-CP, 11-12, 114; WW-P, 78
Greenspoon, T., Z-SP, 43
Gregg, L. W., W-CL, 135
Grice, G. R., W-CL, 55-56
Griffin, D. R., ALW-SP, 9, 12
Gross, C. G., B-NP, 161, 190
Grossman, M. I., B-NP, 149, 188
Gruender, A., W-CL, 52
Guedry, F. E., Jr., WW-P, 73
Guidi, T., WW-P, 28
Guilford, J. P., H-QP, 23, 34, 55; K-AHC, 15, 67, 104
Gunn, D. L., ALW-SP, 145
Gurin, G., BV-MSA, 78
Gurnee, H., Z-SP, 22-23, 29
Guthrie, E. R., M-CP, 39, 114; W-CL, 26; Z-SP, 29
Guttman, L., H-QP, 70, 75
Guttman, N., BV-MSA, 34; W-CL, 64

Haagen-Smit, A. J., B-NP, 97
Hagins, ALW-SP, 31
Haider, M., B-NP, 126, 187
Haig, C., ALW-SP, 63
Hall, J. F., W-CL, 37
Halpern, B. P., ALW-SP, 123; B-NP, 94, 185
Hamburger, U., M-HD, 6
Hamilton, W., FP-HP, 61
Hammel, H. T., B-NP, 143, 189
Hammer, E. R., WW-P, 48
Haney, W. V., Z-SP, 61-62
Hanford, P., W-CL, 37
Harary, F., Z-SP, 97
Hardy, J. D., ALW-SP, 141-142, 145; B-NP, 143, 189
Hardy, M., B-NP, 108
Harlow, H. F., ALW-SP, 11; B-NP, 97, 179; BV-MSA, 64; M-CP, 83-85, 103, 114; W-CL, 79, 91; Z-SP, 25

Harlow, M. K., W-CL, 91
Harpman, J. A., B-NP, 73
Harris, D. B., M-HD, 4, 17
Harris, G. W., B-NP, 150, 188
Harris, P., W-CL, 32, 67
Harrison, F., B-NP, 142, 188
Harsh, C. H., Z-SP, 34
Harter, N., FP-HP, 8-9, 71
Hartline, H. K., ALW-SP, 44-45, 63; B-NP, 23, 97
Hartman, E. B., FP-HP, 49
Hartman, T. F., W-CL, 52
Hartmann, E. von, B-PD, 2
Hartmann, H., B-PD, 19-20
Harvey, J., Z-SP, 39, 112
Harvey, O. J., M-CP, 72, 115
Hassler, R., B-NP, 110-111, 185
Hathaway, S. R., K-AHC, 30
Hays, W. L., K-AHC, 3, 20, 32, 44, 104; W-CL, 96; W-PNSS, 53; WW-P, 78
Hebb, D. O., B-NP, 127, 187; B-PD, 65; BV-MSA, 53; FP-HP, 25; W-CL, 12-14; WW-P, 6, 12, 17, 22, 75
Hecht, S., ALW-SP, 25-26, 63
Heider, F., Z-SP, 97
Heilbrun, A. B., K-AHC, 104
Heise, G. A., FP-HP, 51; M-CP, 68, 116
Helmholtz, Hermann L. F. von, ALW-SP, 36, 43-44, 91-92, 101; B-NP 44, 47; B-PD, 2; FP-HP, 93-94; Z-SP, 2
Helson, H., FP-HP, 26, 73; WW-P, 7, 64; Z-SP, 38
Helvetius, C. A., Z-SP, 7-8
Henning, H., ALW-SP, 108, 123; B-NP, 88, 184
Hensel, H., B-NP, 183
Herbart, J. F., B-PD, 1
Herbert, M. J., Z-SP, 34
Hering, E., ALW-SP, 36, 43-45, 47; B-NP, 48
Hernandez-Peon, R., B-NP, 125-126, 133, 135, 186, 187
Heron, W., M-HD, 15; W-CL, 14
Hess, E. H., W-CL, 8-12; Z-SP, 30
Hess, W. R., ALW-SP, 145; B-NP, 110-111, 127, 185, 187
Heyns, R. W., BV-MSA, 64; WW-P, 86, 88, 90
Hick, W., FP-HP, 99, 105, 116
Highes, R. H., M-CP, 39, 117
Hildum, D. C., Z-SP, 44
Hilgard, E. R., M-CP, 108, 114; M-HD, 45-46, 48; W-CL, 23-24
Hillman, B., W-CL, 24

Hinsey, J. C., B-NP, 107
Hippocrates, K-AHC, 13
Hirsch, I. J., FP-HP, 75-76
Hoagland, H., W-PNSS, 19, 22
Hobson, W-PNSS, 34
Hochberg, J. E., WW-P, 64
Hodgson, E. S., B-NP, 97
Hoebel, B. G., B-NP, 147, 188
Hoffeld, D. R., W-CL, 83
Hoffman, D., Z-SP, 44
Hoffman, L. R., M-CP, 110, 114
Hoffman, L., M-HD, 70
Hogan, H. P., M-CP, 25, 113
Holmes, Oliver Wendell, M-HD, viii
Holmgren, B., B-NP, 110, 185
Holst, E. von, B-NP, 155, 181
Holway, A. H., WW-P, 41-42
Horney, K., B-PD, 17; BV-MSA, 69
Horowitz, M., BV-MSA, 69
Horton, H. P., M-CP, 39, 114
Horwitz, M., Z-SP, 52
House, E. L., B-NP, 145
Hovland, C. I., FP-HP, 127; M-CP, 72,
    114; W-CL, 30-32, 62-64, 66; Z-SP, 66
Howe, E. S., M-CP, 63, 115
Hubel, D. H., B-NP, 48, 51, 53, 55, 96,
    181-182; WW-P, 18-19
Hugelin, A., B-NP, 126, 128, 187
Hulicka, I. M., W-CL, 76
Hull, C. L., BV-MSA, 3-6, 28, 36-37;
    M-CP, 46, 115; W-CL, 24, 27, 31, 62,
    65, 68, 75
Humphrey, T., B-NP, 36, 108
Humphreys, L. G., W-CL, 24
Hunt, F. R. W., ALW-SP, 63
Hunt, E. L., W-CL, 21
Hunt, J. M., W-CL, 35
Hunt, R. W. G., ALW-SP, 63
Hunter, J., B-NP, 185
Hunter, W. S., M-CP, 92-93, 115; W-CL,
    24
Hurvitz, J., B-NP, 179
Husband, R. W., Z-SP, 13
Hutchinson, G. E., B-NP, 116
Huxley, H. E., B-NP, 23
Hyden, H., B-NP, 177, 190
Hyman, R., FP-HP, 100-102, 106

Iggo, A., B-NP, 77, 183
Immergluck, W-PNSS, 13, 21, 24, 27
Isaacson, R. L., B-NP, 155, 188
Iscoe, I., Z-SP, 39
Ison, J. R., W-CL, 68-69, 88

Jacobovits, L. A., M-CP, 64, 115
Jacobs, B., Jr., W-CL, 88
Jacobs, R. C., Z-SP, 89-91
Jacobsen, C. F., B-NP, 160
Jacobson, A., B-NP, 179, 190
Jacobson, A. L., B-NP, 178; W-CL, 21
Jahoda, Marie, H-QP, 68
James, W., BV-MSA, 3; K-AHC, 14
James, W. T., Z-SP, 25
Jane, J. A., B-NP, 67, 69, 183
Janis, I. L., Z-SP, 66
Janowitz, H. D., B-NP, 149, 188
Jarvik, M. E., WW-P, 80
Jasper, H. H., B-NP, 83, 114, 120, 123,
    125, 129, 169-170, 184-185, 187,
    190-191
Jastrow, J., WW-P, 77, 95
Jenkins, H. M., FP-HP, 127
Jenkins, J. G., M-CP, 27-28, 115
Jenkins, W. O., W-CL, 56, 103
Jennings, H. H., BV-MSA, 70; Z-SP,
    93-95
Jensen, G. D., BV-MSA, 13
Jersild, A., M-HD, 67-68
John, E. R., B-NP, 166-172, 190
Johnson, L. D., FP-HP, 70
Johnson, W., M-CP, 66, 115
Johnston, J. W., ALW-SP, 123
Jones, E. E., Z-SP, 39
Jones, H. E., M-HD, 48
Jones, J. E., W-CL, 52
Jones, M. C., M-HD, 39, 48
Jonvet, M., B-NP, 125, 131-133, 135, 187
Jordan, L., BV-MSA, 47-48
Jordan, N., Z-SP, 98
Judd, C. H., WW-P, 45, 95
Judd, D. B., WW-P, 67, 95
Judson, A. I., M-CP, 101, 115
Jung, R., B-NP, 110-111, 185
Jung, C. G., B-PD, 14-16; K-AHC, 14-15;
    M-HD, 1-2

Kaada, B. R., B-NP, 90, 95, 184
Kagen, J., BV-MSA, 62
Kalish, H. I., BV-MSA, 36; M-CP, 56,
    115; W-CL, 64
Kamin, L. J., W-CL, 52-54, 58-59
Kanno, Y., B-NP, 64, 182
Kare, M. R., ALW-SP, 123
Karlin, J. E., FP-HP, 109
Kasl, S., BV-MSA, 81
Katona, G., M-CP, 41, 115
Katsuki, Y., B-NP, 63-64, 66, 69, 182-183

Katz, B., B-NP, 19, 24
Katz, Daniel, Z-SP, 45
Katz, David, Z-SP, 25
Katz, L., Z-SP, 95
Kaufman, L., WW-P, 42
Kawakami, M., B-NP, 149, 189
Keen, R., Z-SP, 48
Keller, A. D., B-NP, 143-144, 188
Keller, F. S., FP-HP, 9; W-CL, 103
Kelley, H. H., Z-SP, 66, 68-72
Kellogg, W. N., W-CL, 23, 85
Kelly, E. L., K-AHC, 31, 57, 78, 80, 84, 96, 104
Kendall, S. B., W-CL, 83
Kendler, H. H., M-CP, 28, 52, 115
Kendler, T. S., M-CP, 52, 115
Kendrick, D. C., W-CL, 35
Kennedy, D., B-NP, 96
Kenshalo, D. R., ALW-SP, 146
Keppel, G., FP-HP, 69, 154
Kessen, M. L., BV-MSA, 19, 33; W-CL, 77-78
Kibler, A. W., FP-HP, 98
Killam, K. F., B-NP, 166-169, 171-172, 190
Kimble, G. A., BV-MSA, 18, 19; W-CL, 20, 24, 30, 41, 65-66, 68, 84, 103
Kimmel, H. D., W-CL, 35, 52
Kimura, K., B-NP, 93, 184
King, R. A., W-CL, 59-61
Kinsey, A. C., BV-MSA, 47
Kish, G. B., W-CL, 79-80
Kite, E. A., M-HD, vii
Kleitman, N., B-NP, 133-135, 186
Klemmer, E. T., FP-HP, 50, 97-98
Klopfer, P. H., Z-SP, 18
Kluever, H., B-NP, 96, 152-153, 184, 188
Knaff, R. P., FP-HP, 70
Knighton, R. S., B-NP, 125
Knights, R. M., Z-SP, 48
Knowles, W. B., B-NP, 122, 187
Koch, A. M., Z-SP, 34
Koch, H. L., FP-HP, 13-14
Koch, S., ALW-SP, 123; W-PNSS, 45, 59-61
Koenig, K., BV-MSA, 58, 82
Koffka, K., WW-P, 84
Kohler, I., WW-P, 18
Köhler, W., M-CP, 81-82, 103, 115; WW-P, 5, 47
Kohn, M., W-CL, 77-78
Korzybski, A., M-CP, 65, 115
Kostir, Mary S., M-HD, vii
Kraeling, D., BV-MSA, 23

Kretschmer, E., K-AHC, 13-14, 55, 104
Kris, E., B-PD, 19-20
Kruger, L., B-NP, 83, 114, 183, 186
Krutch, J. W., W-PNSS, 14, 16, 18-19, 21, 24-25, 27-28
Kuethe, J. L., Z-SP, 97
Kuffler, S. W., B-NP, 181
Künnapas, T. M., WW-P, 45-46

Lambert, W. E., M-CP, 64, 115
Land, E. H., WW-P, 66-67
Landauer, T. K., B-NP, 179
Landis, C., K-AHC, 60, 104
Lane, H., ALW-SP, 74; W-CL, 104-105, 122
Langford, T. L., B-NP, 68
Lantz, D., M-CP, 89, 115
LaPlace, P. S. de, W-PNSS, 10-11
Larson, K., B-NP, 188
Lashley, K. S., B-NP, 159, 161, 179, 190; WW-P, 50
Lauer, D. W., W-CL, 85, 87
Lauer, E. W., B-NP, 36, 108
Lawless, R. H., M-CP, 26, 114
Lawrence, D., B-NP, 39
Lawrence, M., ALW-SP, 73, 78, 101; FP-HP, 5, 47; WW-P, 56, 63, 69, 79, 82
Lazarus, R. S., WW-P, 76-77
Leacock, S., K-AHC, 23
Le Bon, G., Z-SP, 89
Lee, G. B., ALW-SP, 37, 62
Le Grand, Y., ALW-SP, 63
Lehman, H. C., M-CP, 107-108, 115
Lehr, D. J., Z-SP, 11-13
Leibnitz, G. W. von, B-PD, 1; W-PNSS, 3; WW-P, 22
Lele, P. P., B-NP, 75, 183
Lenneberg, E. H., M-CP, 88-89, 113
Leonars, J. A., FP-HP, 105
Lesser, G., BV-MSA, 64
Lettvin, J. Y., B-NP, 49, 51, 89, 97, 181, 184
Levin, H., BV-MSA, 76; M-HD, 51; W-CL, 79
Levine, S., B-NP, 155
Levy, N., W-CL, 85
Lewin, K., BV-MSA, 3, 21, 57; M-HD, 24
Lewis, D. J., W-CL, 61, 101-103
Lewis, H. B., M-CP, 33, 115; Z-SP, 52
Li, C. H., B-NP, 155
Lichten, W., FP-HP, 51
Lichter, W., M CP, 68, 116

Lindman, H., FP-HP, 148
Lindsay, D. B., K-AHC, 29, 103
Lindsley, D. B., B-NP, 122, 125-126, 187
Lipetz, M., Z-SP, 74-76
Lipman, E., B-NP, 111, 185
Lippitt, R., M-HD, 70; W-CL, 84
Lissak, K., B-NP, 172-173, 190
Litwin, G., BV-MSA, 21-22, 30
Livingston, R. B., B-NP, 126, 186
Livingston, W. K., B-NP, 97, 116
Lloyd, K. E., FP-HP, 70
Locke, J., BV-MSA, 3; M-HD, 2-3
Loevinger, J., K-AHC, 101, 104
Loofbourrow, G. N., ALW-SP, 145
Lorenz, K., W-CL, 7, 12; Z-SP, 91-92
Lorge, I., WW-P, 83
Low, H. I., W-CL, 53
Low, L., W-CL, 37, 53
Lowell, E. L., K-AHC, 104
Lowenfeld, B., M-HD, 14
Lowenstein, R., B-PD, 19-20
Lowenstein, W. R., ALW-SP, 134, 145;
    B-NP, 76, 97, 183
Luce, R. D., Z-SP, 108
Luchins, E. S., M-CP, 99, 115
Luchins, S. A., M-CP, 99-100, 115
Lufkin, M. H., B-NP, 74, 183
Lundberg, G., W-PNSS, 25
Luria, A. R., B-NP, 69, 182

Maccoby, E., BV-MSA, 76; M-HD, 51
Maccoby, N., Z-SP, 65-66
Mace, C. A., FP-HP, 27
Machiavelli, N., Z-SP, 4
Mackintosh, N. J., W-CL, 68, 87-88, 90
Mackworth, J., FP-HP, 38-39, 62
MacLean, P. D., ALW-SP, 10, 12
MacNichol, E. F., Jr., ALW-SP, 36, 63;
    B-NP, 44, 47-48, 97, 181-182
Madarasz, I., B-NP, 172-173, 190
Maddi, S., BV-MSA, 54
Magnes, J., B-NP, 129-130, 187
Magni, I., B-NP, 129, 187
Magoun, H. W., B-NP, 120-123, 142,
    186-187, 189
Maher, B. A., W-CL, 61
Mahone, C., BV-MSA, 60
Maier, N. R. F., M-CP, 83, 101, 110,
    114-116; W-CL, 81
Malcolm, E., K-AHC, 84, 104
Malis, L. I., B-NP, 83, 183
Maltzman, I., M-CP, 110, 116

Malzberg, B., M-HD, 17
Mandler, G., BV-MSA, 30, 60
Manis, M., M-CP, 62, 72, 75, 116;
    W-CL, 4; Z-SP, 96
Mann, L. I., W-CL, 84
Margules, D. L., B-NP, 152, 189
Marks, W. B., ALW-SP, 35-36, 63;
    B-NP, 44, 181
Marler, P., Z-SP, 92
Marlowe, D., Z-SP, 76
Marnhashi, J., B-NP, 77, 183
Maroney, R. J., Z-SP, 79-81, 93
Marquis, D. P., W-CL, 21
Marriott, F. H. C., ALW-SP, 63
Marrow, A. J., BV-MSA, 61-62
Marshall, R. W., M-CP, 26, 114
Martin, R. C., W-CL, 81
Marx, M. H., W-CL, 44-46
Maslow, A. H., M-HD, 45-46
Mason, E., ALW-SP, 145
Mason, J. W., Z-SP, 14
Masterson, B., B-NP, 67, 69, 183
Masure, R. H., Z-SP, 18
Maturana, H. R., B-NP, 49, 51, 97, 181
Max, L. W., M-CP, 85-86
Maxwell, J. C., ALW-SP, 17, 36
May, M. A., W-CL, 47
May, R., W-PNSS, 22
Mayer, C. L., ALW-SP, 12
Mayer, J., B-NP, 148, 188
McAllister, D. E., W-CL, 84
McAllister, W. R., W-CL, 84
McBurney, D. H., ALW-SP, 119-120, 123
McCann, S. M., B-NP, 146, 188
McCleary, R. A., B-NP, 155, 179; WW-P,
    76-77
McClelland, D. C., BV-MSA, 28-29, 60;
    K-AHC, 46, 104; WW-P, 84
McConnell, J. V., W-CL, 21; WW-P, 80
McCulloch, W. S., B-NP, 49, 51, 97,
    116, 181
McDonald, F. J., W-CL, 115; Z-SP, 40,
    48-50
McDougall, W., M-HD, 2; W-PNSS, 14;
    Z-SP, 2
McGaugh, J. L., W-CL, 61
McGlone, B., B-NP, 74, 183
McGonigle, B., W-CL, 88
McHale, T. J., WW-P, 70
McKean, K., FP-HP, 139, 141
McKinley, J. C., K-AHC, 30
McNeil, E. B., BV-MSA, 42; M-HD, 31,
    49; W-CL, 2, 12; WW-P, 80

Mead, Margaret, K-AHC, 4, 104; M-HD, 62
Mednick, S. A., M-CP, 111-112, 116
Medow, H., Z-SP, 52
Meehl, P. E., K-AHC, 70, 74, 104
Meikle, T. H., Jr., B-NP, 52, 165, 182, 190
Melton, A. W., FP-HP, 67
Melzack, R., W-CL, 13-14, 16
Mendelson, M., B-NP, 76, 183
Meredith, H. V., M-HD, 5
Merkel, J., FP-HP, 99-100
Merton, P. A., B-NP, 56, 110, 181, 185
Mettler, C. C., B-NP, 185
Mettler, F. A., B-NP, 111, 170, 185, 190
Meumann, E., Z-SP, 10
Meyer, D. K., W-CL, 79
Michael, R. P., B-NP, 150, 188
Milbrook, B., BV-MSA, 62
Miles, R. C., W-CL, 48, 79
Milgram, S., BV-MSA, 75; Z-SP, 39
Miller, A. J., FP-HP, 149
Miller, E. A., FP-HP, 51, 54
Miller, G. A., FP-HP, 66, 67, 138, 139, 140, 141; M-CP, 21-22, 67-68, 70, 116
Miller, J. G., FP-HP, 10, 34-35, 133; WW-P, 78
Miller, K. S., K-AHC, 4, 103
Miller, N., Z-SP, 29-34, 40
Miller, N. C., M-HD, 50
Miller, N. E., B-NP, 146-147, 155, 189; BV-MSA, 19, 24, 33, 46, 72-73; M-CP, 94-95, 114; W-CL, 50, 56, 61, 77-78, 80, 82, 110-111, 114, 116
Miller, R. E., Z-SP, 55-58, 64-65, 67, 73
Miller, W. H., B-NP, 23, 97
Mills, A. W., ALW-SP, 100-101
Mills, J., M-CP, 102, 116
Milne, L., ALW-SP, 12
Milne, M., ALW-SP, 12
Milner, B., B-NP, 69, 162, 183, 191
Milner, P., BV-MSA, 20; W-CL, 79
Minas, J. S., Z-SP, 74-76
Miner, N., B-NP, 164
Mira, L. R., K-AHC, 57
Mirsky, Alfred E., B-NP, 179
Mirsky, Allan F., B-NP, 154-155, 189
Mirsky, I. A., Z-SP, 55
Mischel, W., M-CP, 93, 116
Mishkin, M., B-NP, 55, 111, 160-162, 182, 184-185, 191
Mittelstaedt, H., B-NP, 56-57, 181
Miyadi, D., Z-SP, 92

Mizuguchi, K., B-NP, 77, 183
Montagu, A., M-HD, 16
Montague, E. K., WW-P, 73
Montgomery, K., BV-MSA, 61
Montgomery, K. C., W-CL, 79
Moore, J. W., W-CL, 24, 79
Moreno, J. L., Z-SP, 93-94
Morin, R. E., FP-HP, 22
Morrell, F., B-NP, 169, 170, 191
Morrow, M. W., W-CL, 81
Morse, R. W., B-NP, 83, 183
Moruzzi, G., B-NP, 116, 121, 123, 129-130, 185
Mountcastle, V. B., ALW-SP, 138-39, 145-46; B-NP, 77, 79, 81-82, 84, 154, 183-184, 188
Moushegian, G., B-NP, 68
Mouton, J. S., Z-SP, 38
Mowbray, G. H., FP-HP, 105-106
Mowrer, C. H., M-CP, 63-64
Mowrer, O. H., BV-MSA, 24, 27; W-CL, 41
Mundy, D., Z-SP, 68-72
Munson, W. A., ALW-SP, 78-79, 101
Murdock, B. B., FP-HP, 67
Murphy, G., W-PNSS, 4
Murphy, J. V., Z-SP, 55
Murray, E. J., B-NP, 118, 187
Murray, H. A., BV-MSA, 28; K-AHC, 46, 104; M-HD, 45-46
Mussen, P., M-HD, 39
Muzio, T. N., B-NP, 134, 187
Myers, L. B., WW-P, 48
Myers, R. E., B-NP, 164-165, 191

Nafe, J. P., ALW-SP, 146
Nakayama, T., ALW-SP, 141-142, 145; B-NP, 143, 189
Nauta, W. J. H., B-NP, 155, 188
Neff, W. D., B-NP, 66-67, 69, 182-183
Neisser, U., FP-HP, 59-60, 104
Nelson, V. L., BV-MSA, 61
Netter, F., B-NP, 30, 33, 35
Newcomb, T. M., Z-SP, 97
Newton, Isaac, ALW-SP, 15
Niebuhr, R., W-PNSS, 27-28
Nirenberg, M. W., B-NP, 177, 179
Nobel, K. W., B-NP, 70, 182
Noble, M., FP-HP, 14, 132; W-CL, 52
Noshay, W. C., B-NP, 125, 190
Norris, E. B., W-CL, 57-58
North, A. J., W-CL, 88, 90

Nuthmann, A. M., Z-SP, 48
Nygaard, J. E., W-CL, 32, 67

Oakley, B., B-NP, 95, 184
Oberly, H. S., Z-SP, 107-108
O'Connell, D. C., WW-P, 70
O'Connor, C. M., B-NP, 21-22, 132-133
Odbert, H. S., K-AHC, 2, 103
Ogawa, N., Z-SP, 55-58, 64-65, 67, 73
Ogle, K. N., ALW-SP, 63
Olds, J., ALW-SP, 11-12; B-NP, 90,
    151-153, 155, 185, 189; BV-MSA, 20;
    W-CL, 79
Oppenheimer, J. R., W-PNSS, 11-12
Oonishi, T., B-NP, 69, 183
Orwell, George, W-PNSS, 37
Osborn, A. F., M-CP, 109, 116
Osgood, C. E., M-CP, 59-65, 116;
    WW-P, 15, 50
Osler, S. F., M-CP, 48, 116
Oswald, I., B-NP, 70, 136, 183
Ottoson, D., ALW-SP, 108, 112, 123;
    B-NP, 88, 185
Oyama, T., WW-P, 49

Paillard, J., FP-HP, 72
Palestini, M., B-NP, 129, 186
Pallie, W., B-NP, 75, 184
Palmer, E., B-NP, 75, 184
Pansky, B., B-NP, 145
Panum, P. L., WW-P, 33-34, 36-37
Parinaud, ALW-SP, 21
Parkes, A. S., ALW-SP, 102, 123
Parkes, R. D., BV-MSA, 66
Patton, H. D., B-NP, 41, 91, 102, 164
Patton, R. M., W-CL, 35
Pavlov, I. P., W-CL, 29, 34-35, 68, 70, 77
Pearson, K., K-AHC, 3
Peele, T., B-NP, 95
Peirce, C. S., W-PNSS, 36; WW-P, 77
Pelkwijk, J. J. Ter, W-CL, 5
Penfield, W., B-NP, 83, 179, 184
Pennypacker, H. S., W-CL, 52
Perin, C. T., W-CL, 55
Perlman, C. A., W-CL, 61
Perky, C. W., WW-P, 78
Pessin, J., Z-SP, 12-14, 21
Peterson, C. R., FP-HP, 149
Peterson, J. R., FP-HP, 100, 102-103,
    114-115
Peterson, L. R., FP-HP, 67

Peterson, M., FP-HP, 67
Petrie, A., WW-P, 49
Pettigrew, T. F., WW-P, 51
Pew, R., FP-HP, 74, 118
Pfaffmann, C., ALW-SP, 10, 12, 119-120,
    123; B-NP, 91, 93-94, 96, 185
Phillips, L., FP-HP, 148
Piaget, J., Z-SP, 49
Pierce, J. R., FP-HP, 109
Pirene, M., ALW-SP, 63
Pitts, W. H., B-NP, 49, 51, 97, 181, 184
Plant, J. S., M-HD, 69
Plateau, T., ALW-SP, 15, 53
Plato, K-AHC, 2
Poggio, G. F., B-NP, 79, 184
Pollack, I., FP-HP, 48, 50, 70, 106
Polyak, S. L., B-NP, 9, 43, 52
Pompeiano, O., B-NP, 129-130, 187
Posner, M. I., B-NP, 190; FP-HP, 53-55,
    59, 69, 125, 129, 134-135, 149; W-CL, 4;
    Z-SP, 13
Postman, L., M-CP, 10, 116; WW-P, 8, 83
Potash, H. M., Z-SP, 76
Poulton, E. C., FP-HP, 68, 71, 118,
    141-142, 148
Prentice, W. C. H., WW-P, 5
Prescott, P. A., M-HD, 69
Pressey, S. L., M-CP, 12
Pribram, K. H., B-NP, 55, 70, 83, 114,
    154, 179, 182-183, 186, 189
Proctor, L. D., B-NP, 125
Propst, B., BV-MSA, 54
Pruvot, P., B-NP, 171
Pubols, B. H., Jr., W-CL, 79
Purkinje, J. E., ALW-SP, 24

Quastler, H., FP-HP, 108, 109

Radloff, R., Z-SP, 68-72
Rank, O., B-PD, 16
Rapaport, D., B-PD, 72
Raphael, WW-P, 23, 27
Rapoport, A., Z-SP, 52, 95, 113
Rasmussen, E. W., Z-SP, 24-27
Ratliff, F., ALW-SP, 45, 63; B-NP, 23, 97
Ratoosh, P., Z-SP, 74-76
Rauson, S. W., B-NP, 33, 36, 107, 142,
    147, 188-189
Raven, B., BV-MSA, 79
Rawson, H., Z-SP, 76
Remmers, H. H., K-AHC, 64, 104

Reynolds, B., W-CL, 51
Rhoades, M. U., FP-HP, 106
Ricci, G. F., B-NP, 114, 185
Richter, C. P., ALW-SP, 118, 123
Riesen, A. H., W-CL, 2; WW-P, 18
Riesz, R. R., ALW-SP, 84, 101
Riopelle, A. J., B-NP, 55, 182; Z-SP, 34
Robinovitz, W-CL, 135
Robinson, F., B-NP, 114, 186
Robinson, J. S., W-CL, 79
Robson, J. G., ALW-SP, 58, 63
Roby, T. B., B-NP, 91, 152, 185, 189;
    BV-MSA, 19, 29; W-CL, 79
Rock, I., WW-P, 42
Rodger, R. S., W-CL, 88
Roffwarg, H. P., B-NP, 134, 187
Rogers, C. R., W-PNSS, 13, 15, 22
Rojas, A., B-NP, 184
Romer, O., Z-SP, 2
Rorschach, H., K-AHC, 27
Rose, J. E., ALW-SP, 146
Rosenblith, W. A., ALW-SP, 12, 123, 145;
    B-NP, 63, 82, 135
Rosenzweig, M. R., B-NP, 97; WW-P, 83
Rosenzweig, S., M-CP, 33, 117
Ross, L. E., W-CL, 52
Rossi, G. F., B-NP, 129, 186-187
Rossman, E., FP-HP, 134-135
Rosvold, H. E., B-NP, 111, 154, 185, 189
Rousseau, J. J., M-HD, 2; Z-SP, 42, 83
Roussel, J., W-CL, 74
Rubenstein, H. S., B-NP, 87
Rubin, ALW-SP, 123
Rubin, E., WW-P, 11
Ruch, T. C., B-NP, 41, 91, 102, 163
Ruebush, B., BV-MSA, 63
Ruff, G. E., M-HD, 15, 77
Runkel, P. J., Z-SP, 62-64
Runquist, W. N., FP-HP, 12
Rupert, A. L., B-NP, 68
Rushton, W. A. H., ALW-SP, 32-35,
    38-39, 50-52, 63
Rutherford, ALW-SP, 91-92, 97

Sachar, E. J., W-PNSS, 27, 28
Sagara, M., WW-P, 49
Saint Paul, U. von, B-NP, 155
Sampson, E., BV-MSA, 81
Sanford, R. N., WW-P, 84
Sapir, E., M-CP, 71, 117
Sarason, S., BV-MSA, 30, 60, 68, 83

Satinoff, E., B-NP, 144, 189
Sato, M., B-NP, 76, 183
Sauer, E. G. F., ALW-SP, 9, 12
Savin, H. B., FP-HP, 18, 21
Sawyer, C. H., B-NP, 149-151, 188-189
Sawyer, J., K-AHC, 22, 74-75, 104
Schachtel, E. G., M-HD, 34
Schachter, S., BV-MSA, 65; Z-SP, 60
Schlag-Rey, M., Z-SP, 39
Schlosberg, H., FP-HP, 12, 71, 74;
    W-CL, 64; WW-P, 57
Schneider, D., ALW-SP, 113, 123
Schneider, D. E., W-CL, 38-39
Schneider, R. J., FP-HP, 149
Schoenfeld, W. N., W-CL, 103
Schooler, K., WW-P, 85
Schoonard, J., WW-P, 48
Schreiner, L. H., B-NP, 122, 187
Schultz, R. W., FP-HP, 12
Schultze, M., ALW-SP, 21
Schwartz, M., W-CL, 53
Scodel, A., Z-SP, 74-76
Scott, J. P., W-CL, 13
Scott, P. P., B-NP, 150, 188
Scott, T. H., W-CL, 13
Scott, V. B., W-CL, 85
Seaman, G., WW-P, 64
Sears, R. R., BV-MSA, 76; M-HD, 51
Sechzer, J. A., B-NP, 165, 190
Seeger, C. M., FP-HP, 23-24
Segundo, J. P., B-NP, 122, 187
Seibel, R., FP-HP, 17-18, 106
Seidman, D., BV-MSA, 49; Z-SP, 24
Selfridge, J. A., FP-HP, 138; M-CP,
    21, 116
Seligman, M. E. P., W-CL, 72, 80
Semmes, J., WW-P, 50
Seward, J. P., W-CL, 85
Shagass, C., B-NP, 169, 190
Shannon, C., FP-HP, 86, 90-92
Sharpless, S. K., B-NP, 123, 187; W-CL,
    61
Sheenan, M. M., FP-HP, 147
Sheffield, F. D., B-NP, 91, 152, 185,
    189; W-CL, 37, 79
Sheffield, V. F., BV-MSA, 19
Sheldon, W. H., K-AHC, 14, 55, 104
Shepard, R. N., FP-HP, 68-69, 127, 130,
    147; W-CL, 64
Sherif, M., M-CP, 72, 114; M-HD, 3;
    WW-P, 91; Z-SP, 88
Sherrick, C. E., FP-HP, 75-76
Shibuya, T., B-NP, 88, 185

Shlaer, S., ALW-SP, 63
Shower, E. G., ALW-SP, 83, 101
Sickles, W. R., WW-P, 45
Sidowski, J. B., Z-SP, 67-70, 72
Silver, C. A., W-CL, 83
Silverman, R. E., M-CP, 14, 114
Simon, H. A., W-CL, 135
Singer, R. D., Z-SP, 45-48
Singh, B., B-NP, 148, 188
Sivian, L. J., ALW-SP, 78
Skinner, B. F., BV-MSA, 37; M-CP, 12,
    14, 17, 56-59, 78, 117; W-CL, 24, 80,
    94-96, 99, 101, 103, 107, 109, 116;
    W-PNSS, 12-13, 15, 18, 21, 24-25, 28
Smith, C. G., B-NP, 29
Smith, K. U., FP-HP, 29
Smith, M., Z-SP, 100, 102
Smith, O. A., B-NP, 147, 189
Smith, W. M., FP-HP, 29
Smock, C., BV-MSA, 62
Smode, A., FP-HP, 31, 33
Smoke, W., Z-SP, 103-108
Snider, R. S., B-NP, 117
Snoddy, G. S., FP-HP, 15-16
Snow, C. P., W-PNSS, 30-31
Soderberg, V., B-NP, 56, 181
Solomon, H., Z-SP, 108
Solomon, P., ALW-SP, 10, 12
Solomon, R. L., BV-MSA, 22, 24;
    W-CL, 53-54
Sontag, L. W., BV-MSA, 62
Sparrock, J. M. B., ALW-SP, 62
Spelt, D. K., W-CL, 21
Spence, K. W., W-CL, 31, 39-41, 57-58,
    66, 84; Z-SP, 14
Sperling, G., FP-HP, 63-65
Sperling, S. E., W-CL, 88
Sperry, R., B-NP, 114, 163-165, 179,
    186, 191
Spiegel, J., FP-HP, 146
Spielberger, C. D., M-CP, 57, 117
Spitz, R., M-HD, 59-60, 61
Spivey, B. E., ALW-SP, 37, 62
Spong, P., B-NP, 126, 187
Sporn, M. B., B-NP, 178, 190
Sprague, J. M., B-NP, 52, 122, 182, 187
Sprague, L. T., FP-HP, 118-119
Spranger, E., K-AHC, 29
Stagner, R., M-CP, 117
Stamm, J. S., B-NP, 164-165, 190
Stanley, J. C., Jr., W-CL, 103
Stefflre, V., M-CP, 89, 115
Steinberg, J. C., B-NP, 59

Stellar, E., B-NP, 122, 155, 178, 187, 190
Stern, C., M-HD, 11
Stevens, C. F., B-NP, 23-24
Stevens, J. C., FP-HP, 18, 21
Stevens, S. S., K-AHC, 104
Stevenson, H. W., Z-SP, 48
Stiles, W. S., ALW-SP, 26-27, 37-39, 63
Stone, C. P., M-HD, 39
Stoupel, N., B-NP, 124
Stratton, G. M., FP-HP, 29; WW-P, 18
Stretch, R. G., W-CL, 88
Strodtbeck, F., BV-MSA, 63-64
Strong, E. K., K-AHC, 31, 104
Stroop, J. B., Z-SP, 100, 102
Stuiver, M., ALW-SP, 107, 123; B-NP,
    87-88, 184
Suci, G., M-CP, 61, 116
Suga, N., B-NP, 64, 182
Sullivan, H. S., B-PD, 18-19
Suppes, P., Z-SP, 39, 108
Svaetichin, G., B-NP, 48, 181
Sweet, W. H., B-NP, 85, 184
Swets, J. A., FP-HP, 44; WW-P, 78
Switzer, G., FP-HP, 106

Tabory, L., Z-SP, 67-70, 72
Taffel, C., Z-SP, 48
Taft, R., K-AHC, 67, 103
Tamura, M., Z-SP, 92
Tandler, B. F., W-CL, 41
Tannenbaum, P., M-CP, 61, 116
Tansley, K., ALW-SP, 64
Tatum, R., Z-SP, 25-27
Taylor, A. M., B-NP, 70, 183
Taylor, F. V., FP-HP, 118
Taylor, J. A., BV-MSA, 28, 47; K-AHC,
    89, 104
Taylor, W. L., M-CP, 69, 117
Teghtsoonian, M., FP-HP, 68-69
Teitelbaum, P., B-NP, 147, 188-189
Terfuolo, C. A., B-NP, 83, 126, 184, 186
Teuber, H. L., B-NP, 182
Thibaut, J. W., Z-SP, 58-60, 68-72
Thistlethwaite, D., M-CP, 102, 117
Thomas, D. R., W-CL, 49
Thompson, R., W-CL, 21
Thompson, R. F., W-CL, 83
Thompson, W. R., K-AHC, 4, 103;
    W-CL, 13-14, 16
Thomson, C. W., W-CL, 61
Thorndike, E. L., M-CP, 8, 10, 16, 81-82,
    117; WW-P, 83
Thruston, J. R., M-CP, 56, 113

Thurstone, L. L., H-QP, 30-31, 34, 43, 45, 69
Tinbergen, N., W-CL, 5-7; Z-SP, 54
Tolman, E. C., BV-MSA, 5, 15, 23; W-CL, 24, 27; WW-P, 8
Tombaugh, T. N., W-CL, 44-46
Tomita, T., B-NP, 48, 182
Topmiller, D. A., FP-HP, 98
Torgerson, W. S., H-QP, 23, 34
Torrey, R., Z-SP, 39
Towe, A. L., B-NP, 41, 83, 91, 101, 164, 183
Townsend, A., BV-MSA, 81
Trabasso, R., M-CP, 49, 113
Trapold, M., BV-MSA, 23; W-CL, 43, 44, 46, 80
Trautman, G. E., M-CP, 48, 116
Travis, L. E., Z-SP, 10-11
Triebel, W., WW-P, 64
Treisman, M., B-NP, 70, 183
Triesman, A., FP-HP, 58
Triplett, N., Z-SP, 2, 16
Trumbo, D., K-AHC, 75, 105
Tucker, A., FP-HP, 61
Turner, E.R.A., Z-SP, 30, 114
Tyler, L. E., H-QP, 68; K-AHC, 104-105

Ulrich, L., K-AHC, 75, 105
Underwood, B. J., FP-HP, 12, 69; M-CP, 30, 39, 117

Vandenberg, S. D., K-AHC, 4, 105
Verhave, T., W-CL, 100-101
Verney, E. B., B-NP, 146, 189
Vernon, P. E., K-AHC, 1-2, 29, 103, 105
Veroff, J., BV-MSA, 61, 78; WW-P, 84; Z-SP, 14
Verzeano, M., B-NP, 123, 186
Vinci, Leonardo da, M-CP, 105; WW-P, 25-30
Viney, W., W-CL, 76
Voeks, V., W-CL, 75
von Helmholtz, Hermann L. F., see Helmholtz
Von Kries, ALW-SP, 21
Von Senden, M., WW-P, 17, 96
Vroom, V., BV-MSA, 82

Wagner, A.R., W-CL, 84
Wagner, H. G., B-NP, 48, 182

Wald, G., ALW-SP, 28, 31, 34, 36, 49, 51, 63-64; B-NP, 44-45, 97, 181
Walker, E. L., B-NP, 5, 40, 191; BV-MSA, 4, 6, 14, 61, 67; FP-HP, 8, 19; M-CP, 26, 117; W-CL, 23, 26, 33-34, 75, 96; WW-P, 7, 74, 84-86, 88, 90, 92; Z-SP, 13, 88
Wallach, H., WW-P, 47
Waller, H. J., B-NP, 123, 186
Walls, G., B-NP, 41; WW-P, 65, 67
Walsh, J. W. T., ALW-SP, 63
Walter, A. A., M-CP, 25, 113
Walter, W. G., B-NP, 136; W-CL, 134-135
Walters, R. H., BV-MSA, 66, 76; W-CL, 115
Wapner, S., WW-P, 5, 70
Ward, C. D., M-CP, 76, 117
Ward, J. S., W-CL, 74
Warden, C. J., Z-SP, 34
Warren, J. M., Z-SP, 79-81, 93
Warren, R. P., B-NP, 91, 185
Warrick, M. J., FP-HP, 75, 98
Wasman, M., B-NP, 148, 189
Watson, J. B., M-CP, 85, 104; M-HD, 2-3; W-CL, 54
Weaver, W., FP-HP, 86, 90-92
Weber, E. H., H-QP, 24-25, 27
Weddell, G., B-NP, 73, 75, 183-184
Weiner, B., BV-MSA, 13-14
Weinstock, S., W-CL, 101-102
Weintraub, D. J., B-NP, 40, 190; WW-P, 70; Z-SP, 88
Weiskrantz, L., B-NP, 96, 156, 161, 185, 189
Weiss, P., M-HD, 6
Welford, A. T., FP-HP, 80
Wells, H. H., Z-SP, 39
Welty, J. C., Z-SP, 21-22, 29
Wendt, H. W., BV-MSA, 56
Wenger, M. A., K-AHC, 55, 105
Wenner, A. M., Z-SP, 55
Werner, G., B-NP, 77, 184
Werner, H., WW-P, 5, 70
Wertheimer, M., FP-HP, 75; WW-P, 13, 15
Werts, C. E., K-AHC, 84, 103
Westbrook, W. H., W-CL, 61
Westheimer, G., ALW-SP, 52, 63
Wever, E. G., ALW-SP, 73, 78-79, 92, 98, 101
Wheatstone, C. R., WW-P, 30, 37
White, B. W., FP-HP, 52-53
White, C. T., FP-HP, 77-78

White, S. D., ALW-SP, 78
Whiting, J. W. M., M-HD, 51
Whorf, B. L., M-CP, 86-91, 104
Wickelgren, W. O., B-NP, 155, 188
Wickens, D. D., W-CL, 83
Widen, L., B-NP, 56, 182
Wiener, N., B-NP, 116
Wiesel, T. N., B-NP, 48, 53, 55, 181-182;
    WW-P, 18-19
Williams, A., FP-HP, 11
Williams, C. D., Z-SP, 41-43
Williams, M. S., Z-SP, 39
Williams, R. G., B-NP, 74, 183
Willier, B. H., M-HD, 6
Wilska, A., ALW-SP, 73-74, 101
Wilson, K. V., Z-SP, 76-78
Wilson, M., B-NP, 161
Winnick, W. A., W-CL, 35
Witkin, H. A., WW-P, 71
Witthover, E. D., ALW-SP, 12
Wittmaack, ALW-SP, 93-94
Wolbarsht, M. L., B-NP, 48, 182
Wolf, I. S., W-CL, 85
Wollard, H. H., B-NP, 73
Wolpe, G., FP-HP, 100, 102-103
Wolsk, D., B-NP, 39; FP-HP, 5, 47;
    WW-P, 56, 63, 69, 79, 82
Wolstenholme, G., B-NP, 132-133
Woodbury, J. W., B-NP, 41, 91, 102, 164
Woodward, J. K., W-CL, 52
Woodworth, R. S., FP-HP, 12, 61-62, 71,
    74; M-CP, 20; WW-P, 25, 29, 32, 36, 57
Woolsey, C. L., B-NP, 97, 117, 179

Woolsey, C. N., ALW-SP, 11
Wright, W. D., ALW-SP, 64
Wulff, J. J., B-NP, 152, 189; W-CL, 79
Wulff, V., FP-HP, 108-109
Wundt, W., FP-HP, 94; M-CP, 6;
    W-PNSS, 2
Wurtman, R. J., B-NP, 155
Wyckoff, L. B., Z-SP, 67-70, 72
Wynne, L. C., BV-MSA, 22, 24
Wynne-Edwards, V. C., Z-SP, 8, 93
Wyrwicka, W., B-NP, 146, 188

Yamaguchi, H. G., BV-MSA, 37-39
Yarrow, Leon, M-HD, 60-61, 62
Yoshii, N., B-NP, 171
Young, Thomas, ALW-SP, 36, 43, 48

Zajonc, R. B., BV-MSA, 36; W-CL, 110,
    114-115; Z-SP, 14, 18, 60-61, 98,
    103, 108
Zanchetti, A., B-NP, 129, 186-187
Zander, A., Z-SP, 52
Zarriello, J. J., WW-P, 71
Zavadsky, W-CL, 70
Zeigarnik, B., M-CP, 32, 117
Zeller, A. F., M-CP, 31, 117
Zipf, G. K., M-CP, 70, 79, 87-88, 117
Zotterman, Y., ALW-SP, 123, B-NP, 77,
    183, 184
Zubek, J. P., M-HD, 15

CONCEPTUAL INDEX OF THE
BASIC CONCEPTS IN PSYCHOLOGY SERIES

This cross-index of the Basic Concepts in Psychology Series is composed of the entries in the indexes of the series volumes arranged in subject matter categories. The primary categories were chosen to reflect the traditional divisions within the field of psychology. Thus, each primary category has a heavy representation from one particular volume of the series, since each volume also represents a major traditional division of psychology.

Wherever possible, a secondary category represents a basic concept in psychology. Other categories were chosen as headings to make the index as convenient and as functional as possible.

The conceptual index can be used for many purposes, but it was devised primarily to aid the student in organizing a particular topic or problem across the different volumes of the series. To facilitate the use of the index, an outline of the primary categories and of the secondary categories that appear under them has been placed at the beginning of the index. The student should study this outline to become familiar with the general pattern. He will then find, in pursuing a particular topic, that the cross-references within the index will permit him to follow lines of conceptual association through different chapters within volumes as well as through different volumes in the series.

Each of the fourteen text volumes published as of July 1, 1969, is included in the conceptual index. Omitted from the index are A *Laboratory Manual for the Control and Analysis of Behavior* by Harlan L. Lane and Daryl J. Bem; *Teaching the Beginning Course in Psychology* by Edward L. Walker and Wilbert J. McKeachie, a book that is addressed to the instructor rather than the student; the *Perceptual Demonstration Kit* by Daniel J. Weintraub and Edward L. Walker; and two recent additions to the series, *Non-Freudian Personality Theories* by P. James Geiwitz and *Beliefs, Attitudes, and Human Affairs* by Daryl J. Bem. These last two volumes will be incorporated into a later revision of the index.

Each of the fourteen volumes included in the index is referred to by a set of code letters chosen because of their discriminability and mnemonic value. The code letters are:

ALW-SP   Alpern, Lawrence, and Wolsk,
                Sensory Processes

B-NP   Butter, *Neuropsychology*

B-PD   Blum, *Psychodynamics*

BV-MSA   Birch and Veroff, *Motivation: A Study of Action*

FP-HP   Fitts and Posner, *Human Performance*

H-BS   Hays, *Basic Statistics*

H-QP   Hays, *Quantification in Psychology*

K-AHC   Kelly, *Assessment of Human Characteristics*

M-CP   Manis, *Cognitive Processes*

M-HD   McNeil, *Human Development*

W-CL   Walker, *Conditioning and Instrumental Learning*

W-PNSS   Walker, *Psychology as a Natural and Social Science*

WW-P   Weintraub and Walker, *Perception*

Z-SP   Zajonc, *Social Psychology*

OUTLINE OF
THE CONCEPTUAL INDEX

§1 ASSESSMENT, 86

Assessment Psychologist, 86
General Characteristics and Problems, 86
Human Characteristics, 86
Human Judges, 88
Methods, 89
Reliability (of Tests), 90
Selection, 90
Tests, 90
Validity, 90

§2 COGNITION, 91

Biochemical Aspects of Memory, 91
Concept, 91
Creativity, 92
Language, 92
Memory, 93
Problem Solving, 93
Thinking and Thought, 94

§3 DEVELOPMENTAL, 94

Biological Factors, 94
Development, 95
Environment, 95
Life Themes, 95
Methods, 95
Personality, 95
Philosophical Issues, 96
Psychological Processes, 96
Social Factors, 96

§4 LEARNING, 97

Classes of, 97
Conditioning, 98
Discrimination, Generalization, Transfer, 98

Experimental Extinction, 99
Inhibition, 99
Instrumental, 99
Intervals, 99
Learning (General), 99
Mathematical Models, 100
Methods and Metatheory, 100
Motivation, Reward, Punishment, 100
Neurophysiology, 101
Operant Conditioning, 101
Theory, 102
Trace, 102

§5 METAPSYCHOLOGY,
PHILOSOPHY,
AND HISTORY, 102

Determinism vs. Indeterminism, 102
Experiment (Language of), 103
Free Will (Freedom), 103
Liberal Arts (Divisional Units), 103
Methods (in Psychology), 103
Philosophical Issues
    (including History), 103
Psychology, 104
Science (and Scientific), 105
Theory (Language of), 105

§6 MOTIVATION AND
EMOTION, 106

Achievement Incentive System, 106
Action, 106
Activity, 106
Affiliative Incentive System, 107
Aggressive Incentive System, 107
Arousal, 107
Availability, 108

Curiosity Incentive System, 108

Drive, 108

Emotions, 108

Goals, 108

Incentive (General), 109

Independence Incentive System, 109

Motivation, 109

Negative Incentives, 110

Power Incentive System, 110

Sensory Incentive System, 110

Sex, 110

Sleep, 110

Tendency, 111

§7 NEUROPSYCHOLOGY, 111

Anatomy (Non-neural), 111

Animals, 112

Behavior Relevant to Neuropsychology, 112

Cortices, 114

General Properties of Cells, 114

Lobes, 114

Mechanisms, 114

Methods of, 115

Nerve Cells (Fibers and Neurons), 115

Nerve Impulse, 116

Neurophysiology, 117

Nuclei, 118

Pathways (Tracts), 118

Peripheral Nervous System, 118

Physiology (Non-neural), 118

Reflex, 120

Structures, 120

Synapse, 121

Systems, 121

§8 PERCEPTUAL PROCESSES, 122

Afterimages, 122

Attention, 122

Color, 122

Complexity, 122

Constancy, 122

Depth Perception, 123

Figural Aftereffects, 123

Illusions, 123

Measurement (Threshold), 123

Organization, Principles of, 123

Perception (General), 124

Perceptual (Properties), 124

Rivalry, 124

Stimuli, 124

Theory, 124

§9 PERFORMANCE, 125

Feedback, 125

Group, 125

Information Processing, 125

Measurement, 125

Memory Processes, 125

Motivation, 125

Perceptual Processes, 125

Reaction Time, 125

Response to Stimuli, 125

Skill, 125

Stimulus, 126

Stress, 126

§10 PERSONALITY, 126

Anxiety, 126

Anxiety (Reactions to), 126

Cognition in Personality, 126

Consciousness, 127

Freudian Theory, 127

Measures (Tests), 128

Mechanisms of Defense, 128

Personality (General), 129

Psychoanalytic Viewpoints (Other), 129

Unconscious Influences upon, 130

§11 PSYCHOLOGICAL MEASUREMENT, 131

Differences, 131

Measurement, 131

Scaling, 131

Scores, 132
Stimulus, 132
Values, 132

§12   SENSORY, 133

General, 133
  Measurement, 133
  Psychological Properties, 133
  Receptors, 133
  Response Systems and Properties, 133
  Stimuli, 134
Bodily Orientation, 134
  Anatomy (Non-neural), 134
  Measurement, 134
  Psychological Properties, 134
  Receptors, 134
  Response Systems and Properties, 134
  Stimuli, 134
Hearing, 134
  Anatomy (Non-neural), 134
  Measurement, 134
  Psychological Properties, 135
  Receptors, 135
  Response Systems and Properties, 135
  Stimuli, 135
  Theories, 136
Smell, 136
  Anatomy (Non-neural), 136
  Measurement, 136
  Psychological Characteristics, 136
  Receptors (Nose), 136
  Response Systems and Properties, 137
  Stimuli, 137
Taste, 137
  Anatomy (Non-neural), 137
  Measurement, 137
  Psychological Characteristics, 137
  Receptors, 137
  Response Systems and Properties, 137
  Stimuli, 138
  Theory, 138

Touch and Kinesthesis, 138
  Anatomy (Non-neural), 138
  Measurement, 138
  Psychological Properties, 138
  Receptors, 139
  Response Systems and Properties, 139
  Stimuli, 139
Vision, 139
  Anatomy (Non-neural), 139
  Measurement, 140
  Psychological Properties, 140
  Receptors (Eye), 140
  Response Systems and Properties, 141
  Stimuli, 141
  Theories, 141

§13   SOCIAL, 142

Attitude, 142
Audience Effects, 142
Coaction Effects, 142
Communication, 142
Competition, 142
Conflict, 142
Conformity, 142
Cooperation, 142
Group, 142
Imitation, 142
Learning, 142
Moral, 142
Motivation, 142
Opinions, 143
Presence of Others, 143
Social (General), 143

§14   STATISTICS, 143

Association, 143
Central Tendency, 144
Characteristics and Properties, 144
Data and Variables, 144
Distributions, 144
Experimental Design, 145
Inference, 145
Variability, 145

CONCEPTUAL INDEX OF THE
BASIC CONCEPTS IN PSYCHOLOGY SERIES

§1 ASSESSMENT

Assessment Psychologist, K-AHC, 92-99
  role in applied science, K-AHC, 94-99
    cross-validation, K-AHC, 99
    defining task, K-AHC, 95
    determining value of experimental
      program, K-AHC, 98-99
    developing criterion measures,
      K-AHC, 96-98
    evaluating validity of current
      practice, K-AHC, 96
    specifying predictor traits, K-AHC,
      98
  role in basic science, K-AHC, 92-94
    experimenter, K-AHC, 93-94
    observer, K-AHC, 92
    personality theorist, K-AHC, 93
    systematist, K-AHC, 92-93
General Characteristics and Problems,
  K-AHC, 1-12, 49, 52, 78-94
  definition, K-AHC, 1
    meaning of, K-AHC, 49
    methods, K-AHC, 12, 67
    process, K-AHC, 73
    properties of, K-AHC, 52
  practical reasons for, K-AHC, 6-11
    choice of friends and associates,
      K-AHC, 7
      mutual assessment, K-AHC, 7
    choice of marital partners, K-AHC, 7
      premarital assessment, K-AHC, 7
    diagnosis of human malfunction,
      K-AHC, 10-11
      medical diagnosis, K-AHC, 10
      mental disease, K-AHC, 11
      psychodiagnosis, K-AHC, 11
      psychological breakdowns,
        K-AHC, 11
    educational counseling, K-AHC, 7-8
    key roles in society, K-AHC, 9-10
      astronauts, K-AHC, 10
      military personnel, K-AHC, 10
      military pilots, K-AHC, 10
      OSS, K-AHC, 10

General Characteristics and Problems
  (cont.)
      Peace Corps, K-AHC, 10
      selection, K-AHC, 9-10
      traditional methods, K-AHC, 10
    personnel, K-AHC, 8-9, 86, 94
      classification, K-AHC, 8
      decision, K-AHC, 86, 94
      occupations, K-AHC, 9
      promotions, K-AHC, 8
      selection, K-AHC, 8
    vocational counseling, K-AHC, 7-8
      educational achievement, K-AHC,
        8
      individual differences, K-AHC, 7
      personal adjustment, K-AHC, 8
      placement, K-AHC, 8
      vocational adjustment, K-AHC, 8
  problems of, K-AHC, 100
  status and outlook, K-AHC, 12, 78-79,
    85, 87-91
  fallibility of, K-AHC, 85
  popularity of personalized
    techniques, K-AHC, 78-79
  practice, K-AHC, 91
  present, K-AHC, 87
  toward better assessment, K-AHC, 91
  what shall be assessed, K-AHC,
    12, 23
Human Characteristics
  abilities, BV-MSA, 54-55, 62-63, 82;
    H-QP, 14, 58, 61-65, 67-68; K-AHC,
    1, 16
    intelligence, H-QP, 4, 8, 60-61;
      K-AHC, 4, 66, 100
      and achievement, BV-MSA, 62-63
      and curiosity, BV-MSA, 54-55
      and independence, BV-MSA, 82
      quotient, K-AHC, 100
      varieties of, K-AHC, 100
  characteristics (human), K-AHC, 1-5
    gullibility, K-AHC, 85
    honesty, K-AHC, 4
    morals, K-AHC, 4
    personal identity, K-AHC, 2
    range of, K-AHC, 2

Human Characteristics (cont.)

    self-concept, K-AHC, 16, 65
    talent, range of, K-AHC, 39
  individual differences (other), K-AHC,
    2-3, 7, 88-89
    acquiesence, K-AHC, 74
    anxiety, K-AHC, 20, 45, 48, 79, 83, 89
    arithmetic, H-QP, 17-18
    behavior, K-AHC, 50, 55-56, 86
      basis for judgment, K-AHC, 54-55
      expressive, K-AHC, 56
      gestures, K-AHC, 56
      mannerisms, K-AHC, 56
      posture, K-AHC, 56
      products, K-AHC, 54, 56, 86
      stylistic, K-AHC, 55
    cultural influences, K-AHC, 5
    ego development, K-AHC, 101
    emotional maturity, K-AHC, 100
    human values, H-QP, 2-3
    individual responsibility, K-AHC,
      100
    occupational choice, K-AHC, 4
    personal adjustment, K-AHC, 8
    personality, H-QP, 60-62, 68
      assessment, H-QP, 60
      dynamics, H-QP, 61
    reaction time, K-AHC, 40
    rigidity, K-AHC, 33
    sex, K-AHC, 45
      egalitarian ideal, K-AHC, 5
    social adjustment, K-AHC, 100
    social desirability, K-AHC, 74
    underprivileged groups, K-AHC, 5
    unifying schema, K-AHC, 3
  traits (modalities of), K-AHC, 15-23
    aptitudes, K-AHC, 16-17; H-QP,
      61-62
      athletic, K-AHC, 17
      clerical, K-AHC, 17
      defined, K-AHC, 16
      mechanical, K-AHC, 14, 17
      musical, K-AHC, 14, 17
      scholastic, K-AHC, 17
    attitudes, K-AHC, 4, 19; H-QP, 19,
      53, 58, 68-74
      tendencies, H-QP, 68
    drives, K-AHC, 18
      biological, K-AHC, 18
      motivational, K-AHC, 18, 88-89
      needs, K-AHC, 18, 46
      psychological, K-AHC, 18
    interests, K-AHC, 19

Human Characteristics (cont.)

    morphological, K-AHC, 16
      genetic determinants, K-AHC, 3,
      4, 15
      height, K-AHC, 3
      hermaphrodite, K-AHC, 4
      phrenology, K-AHC, 55, 86
      physiognomy, K-AHC, 55, 86
      physique, K-AHC, 14, 55
      race, K-AHC, 4-5
      sex, K-AHC, 66
      somatic, K-AHC, 16, 55
    physiological, K-AHC, 16
      age, K-AHC, 5, 66
      aging process, K-AHC, 5
      basal metabolic rate, K-AHC, 16
      blood, K-AHC, 15-16, 40-41, 55
      body temperature, K-AHC, 16
      brain waves, K-AHC, 16, 55
      heart rate, K-AHC, 16, 55
      life cycle, K-AHC, 5
      longevity, K-AHC, 4
      muscular tension, K-AHC, 55
      skin resistance, K-AHC, 55
    psychodiagnostic categories, K-AHC,
      20
      behavioral malfunction, K-AHC, 20
      diagnostic categories, K-AHC,
      91, 95
      pigeonholing, K-AHC, 13, 20
    skills and achievement, K-AHC,
      17-18
      achievement, K-AHC, 17-18, 45
      artistic, K-AHC, 18
      athletic, K-AHC, 18
      driver, K-AHC, 18
      educational achievement tests,
      K-AHC, 17
      learning, K-AHC, 89
      performance traits, K-AHC, 18
      reading, K-AHC, 18
    temperament, K-AHC, 19
    theories of personality, M-HD, 24
    values, K-AHC, 19
  traits (properties of), H-QP, 14, 58,
    61-65, 67-68; K-AHC, 16, 20-23
    bipolar, K-AHC, 20
    continuum, K-AHC, 20
    defined, K-AHC, 15
    interval scale of measurement,
      K-AHC, 21
    ratio scale, K-AHC, 21
    names, K-AHC, 25

Human Characteristics (cont.)
  number of, K-AHC, 16, 25
  objections to use of in assessment,
    K-AHC, 22
  unipolar, K-AHC, 20
  unique, K-AHC, 32
  value loadings, K-AHC, 21
  what traits shall be assessed,
    K-AHC, 23
  types, K-AHC, 3, 12-15
    blood, K-AHC, 15
    character, B-PD, 12-13, 16-18, 25-29
      aggressive, B-PD, 17
      anal, B-PD, 12-13
      average, B-PD, 16
      compliant, B-PD, 17
      creative, B-PD, 16
      detached, B-PD, 17
      exploitative, B-PD, 18
      genital, B-PD, 13
      hoarding, B-PD, 18
      marketing, B-PD, 18
      neurotic, B-PD, 16
      oral, B-PD, 12, 25-29
      phallic, B-PD, 13
      productive, B-PD, 18
      receptive, B-PD, 18
    constitutional (Kretschmer), K-AHC,
      13-14
      body build, K-AHC, 13
      personality, K-AHC, 13
    constitutional (Sheldon), K-AHC, 14
      somatotype, K-AHC, 14
      temperament, K-AHC, 14
    Hippocrates, K-AHC, 13
      humours, K-AHC, 13
      temperament, K-AHC, 13
    James, William, K-AHC, 14-15
      approach to life, K-AHC, 15
      voluntary actions, K-AHC, 14-15
    Jung, K-AHC, 14
      extrovert, K-AHC, 14
      introverts, K-AHC, 14
    Linnean (binomial) system,
      K-AHC, 13
      system of classification, K-AHC, 13
    popular, K-AHC, 15
      beatnik, K-AHC, 15
      bookworm, K-AHC, 15
      daredevil, K-AHC, 15
      dope, K-AHC, 15
      egghead, K-AHC, 15
      hippie, K-AHC, 15

Human Characteristics (cont.)
      jerk, K-AHC, 15
      killjoy, K-AHC, 15
      sad sack, K-AHC, 15
      teeniebopper, K-AHC, 15
    psychoanalytic theory, K-AHC, 14
      anal, B-PD, 12-13; K-AHC, 14
      genital, B-PD, 13; K-AHC, 14
      oral, B-PD, 12, 25-29; K-AHC, 14
    taste, K-AHC, 15
      tasters and non-tasters of PTC,
        K-AHC, 15
Human Judges, B-NP, 97; K-AHC, 52-68
  categories of judges, K-AHC, 60-65
    expert, K-AHC, 63
      expertise, K-AHC, 63, 76, 80, 87
    ideal, K-AHC, 59
    peer, K-AHC, 63
      ratings, K-AHC, 64
    self-ratings, K-AHC, 64-65
      ideal self, K-AHC, 65
      real self, K-AHC, 65
      social self, K-AHC, 65
    subordinates as judges, K-AHC, 64
  characteristics of good judges, K-AHC,
    65-67
    ability to judge, K-AHC, 65-66
    age, K-AHC, 66
    intelligence, K-AHC, 66-67
    sex, K-AHC, 66
    special training, K-AHC, 67
      clinician, K-AHC, 67, 72
  conditions essential for good ratings,
    K-AHC, 60-62
    increasing interjudge agreement,
      K-AHC, 61
    increasing the validity of ratings,
      K-AHC, 61
      conditions of, K-AHC, 61
    number of judges, K-AHC, 62
      errors of judgment, K-AHC, 62
      multiple interviewers, K-AHC, 62
      staff conferences, K-AHC, 62
  interjudge agreement, K-AHC, 61-72,
    77
  limitations of judges, K-AHC, 59-60
  anxiety of judges, K-AHC, 79, 81, 83
  biases of judges, K-AHC, 59
    contrast error, K-AHC, 60
    halo error, K-AHC, 59
    leniency error, K-AHC, 59
    rating error, K-AHC, 59-60
    similarity error, K-AHC, 60

Human Judges (cont.)
  role of judges in assessment, K-AHC,
    24, 41, 52-68, 91
  human assessors, K-AHC, 86

Methods
  behavior, K-AHC, 20, 24-25, 54, 56,
    61, 71; H-QP, 14, 16-19, 23, 59-61,
    65, 67, 71-75
  bases for assessment, K-AHC, 54
  criterion, H-QP, 73
  inferences from, K-AHC, 24
  invariant, H-QP, 72
  involuntary, H-QP, 59
  malfunction, K-AHC, 20
  measurement of, H-QP, 16-17
  observable, H-QP, 16-17
  products, K-AHC, 54, 56
  sample, K-AHC, 54, 61, 71
  voluntary, H-QP, 59
  what kinds shall be assessed,
    K-AHC, 25
  classification, K-AHC, 2, 8, 9, 52
  criterion, K-AHC, 31, 64, 96-99;
    H-QP, 66, 73
    behavior, H-QP, 73
    groups, K-AHC, 31
    independent, K-AHC, 98
    measures, K-AHC, 64, 96-97, 99
    performance, K-AHC, 98
    relation to items, H-QP, 66
    super-, K-AHC, 98
  data, K-AHC, 26, 74, 80
    collection, K-AHC, 74
    combination, K-AHC, 74
    life record, K-AHC, 26
    questionnaire, K-AHC, 26
    relevance of, K-AHC, 80
    test, K-AHC, 26
  important methodological issues,
    K-AHC, 35
  inferences from behavior, K-AHC, 24
  logic of, K-AHC, 25
  life record (L data), K-AHC, 26, 80
    history questionnaire, K-AHC, 86
  personal versus impersonal methods,
    K-AHC, 69-86
    combination of clinical and statistical
      methods, K-AHC, 74
    the evidence, K-AHC, 74-75
    format of report, K-AHC, 71
    impact on practice, K-AHC, 75-76
    the issue, K-AHC, 69-74

Methods (cont.)
    reasons for popularity of personal
      methods, K-AHC, 78
    synthesis of assessment methods,
      K-AHC, 74
  questionnaire (Q data), K-AHC, 26
  rating scales, K-AHC, 53-54, 64, 97
    adjective check list, K-AHC, 53
    forced choice, K-AHC, 54
    graphic, K-AHC, 53
    instructor, K-AHC, 64
    numerical, K-AHC, 53
    Q sort, K-AHC, 53
    sociometric, K-AHC, 54, 97
    types, K-AHC, 53
  strategies, K-AHC, 28-34
    empirical, K-AHC, 30-32
      criterion groups, K-AHC, 31
    factor analytic, K-AHC, 32-33, 91
      hypothetical construct, K-AHC, 32
    rational, K-AHC, 28-29, 33-34
      common sense, K-AHC, 28
      nontheoretical, K-AHC, 28
      theoretical, K-AHC, 29, 33-34
  techniques, K-AHC, 2, 10, 29-31, 56-58,
    60-61, 69-78, 80, 84-86, 89, 91,
    95, 100
    autobiography, K-AHC, 56, 61
    biography, K-AHC, 2
    clinical, K-AHC, 60-61, 69-72, 74
      assessment, K-AHC, 69-71
      inference, K-AHC, 74
      prediction, K-AHC, 71, 74
      ratings, K-AHC, 60-61, 72
    impersonal methods, K-AHC,
      69, 95
    information yield of, K-AHC, 80, 85
    interview, K-AHC, 57-58, 75, 84
      common elements of, K-AHC, 58
      diagnostic, K-AHC, 91
      selection, K-AHC, 29-30, 91
    inventory, K-AHC, 31, 80, 86, 91
      biographical, K-AHC, 31, 91
      personal, K-AHC, 80
      personality, K-AHC, 86
    observations of behavior, extensive,
      K-AHC, 58
    personal methods, K-AHC, 69, 76,
      78, 95
    role playing, K-AHC, 57
    situation tests, K-AHC, 57
      accomplice, K-AHC, 57

Methods (cont.)
  statistical methods, K-AHC, 69-70
  traditional methods, K-AHC, 10,
    89, 100
  test (T data), K-AHC, 26-28
    degree of structure, K-AHC, 27
    difficulty (of items), H-QP, 62-66
      equivalent, H-QP, 63
      graded (stepped), H-QP, 62-66
    discrimination (between groups),
      K-AHC, 47
    form, K-AHC, 27
    objective, K-AHC, 27
    power, H-QP, 61-64, 69; K-AHC, 27
    projective, B-PD, 22-23, K-AHC, 27
    speed, H-QP, 61-64; K-AHC, 27
    standardized, H-QP, 61-63; K-AHC,
      72
      evaluation, K-AHC, 44
      multiple keying, K-AHC, 74

Reliability (of Tests), H-QP, 67-68,
  75-76; K-AHC, 35-38, 40-43, 48, 50, 76
  alternate form (equivalence), K-AHC,
    36
    equivalent forms, K-AHC, 37
  assumptions, K-AHC, 36
  coefficient of, K-AHC, 36-38
    correlation, K-AHC, 36-37
    equivalence, K-AHC, 37
    reliability, K-AHC, 38
    stability, K-AHC, 37
  defined, K-AHC, 35ff
  estimates of, K-AHC, 36, 42
  heterogeneity, K-AHC, 38, 48
  homogeneity, H-QP, 38, 66, 73;
    K-AHC, 37-38, 43
  index of, K-AHC, 42, 50
  internal consistency, H-QP, 64, 70-71;
    K-AHC, 37, 43
    odd-even scores, K-AHC, 38
  kinds of, K-AHC, 36
  of measurement, H-QP, 75-76
  retest (stability), K-AHC, 36
  true score, K-AHC, 36, 40
  unreliability, H-QP, 66-67; K-AHC, 42,
    66-67, 76
    of personal assessment, K-AHC, 76
    sources of, K-AHC, 42
    of tests, H-QP, 66-67
Selection, K-AHC, 1, 8-10, 18, 45, 52,
  78-80
  of astronauts, K-AHC, 10

Selection (cont.)
  defined, K-AHC, 8-9
  drivers, K-AHC, 18
  Educational Testing Service, K-AHC,
    45
  for key roles, K-AHC, 9
  of medical students, K-AHC, 78, 96-97
  of military personnel, K-AHC, 10
  OSS, K-AHC, 1, 10, 52
  Peace Corps, K-AHC, 10
  of pilots, K-AHC, 10, 32, 80
    Naval Aviation, K-AHC, 80

Tests, K-AHC
  Bender-Gestalt, K-AHC, 57, 83
  Blacky Pictures, B-PD, 23-25, 44-47,
    51; K-AHC, 29
  Draw-a-Person, K-AHC, 75
  driver, K-AHC, 18
  essay, K-AHC, 75, 84
  HTP, K-AHC, 57
  inkblot, K-AHC, 27
  Minnesota Multiphasic Inventory,
    K-AHC, 30
  Mira Myokinetic, K-AHC, 57
  objective, K-AHC, 5, 27, 91
  Personal Preference Schedule, K-AHC,
    29, 46
  projective, K-AHC, 27, 29-30, 75, 91
  Rorschach, B-PD, 22-23; K-AHC, 27,
    75, 77, 83
  Scale of Values, K-AHC, 29
  Strong Vocational Interest Blank,
    K-AHC, 31
  Thematic Apperception Test, K-AHC,
    27, 75

Validity, H-QP, 19, 66-68, 72-76; K-AHC
  apparent, K-AHC, 91
  ceiling on, K-AHC, 50
  conditions reducing validity of human
    assessment, K-AHC, 77
  cross-validation, K-AHC, 99
  of current practice, K-AHC, 96
  defined, K-AHC, 43-44
  many different, K-AHC, 51
  of ratings, K-AHC, 61
  spurious criteria of, K-AHC, 81-84
    experienced validity, K-AHC, 82
    face validity, K-AHC, 81, 91
    faith validity, K-AHC, 83, 94
      fallibility, K-AHC, 85
      shared stereotypes, K-AHC, 84
    validity by fiat, K-AHC, 82

Validity (cont.)
  types, H-QP, 19, 66-68, 72-76; K-AHC, 45-48
    concurrent, H-QP, 68; K-AHC, 48
    consensual, K-AHC, 45
    construct, H-QP, 68; K-AHC, 33, 48, 89
    empirical, K-AHC, 46
    predictive, H-QP, 19, 66-68, 72-73; K-AHC, 47, 72, 99
    of relations, H-QP, 76

§2 COGNITION

Biochemical Aspects of Memory, B-NP, 174-179
  biochemical processes, B-NP, 174
  memory, B-NP, 174
    coding, B-NP, 174
    formation, B-NP, 174
    neuronal theory of, B-NP, 174
    storage, B-NP, 174
    trace, B-NP, 174
      theories of, B-NP, 174
  molecular genetics, B-NP, 174
  protein synthesis, B-NP, 174-175, 177
    amino acids, 174-175, 177
    bases, 175-177
    cell nucleus, B-NP, 175
    chromosomes, B-NP, 175
    cytoplasm, B-NP, 175
    daughter cells, B-NP, 175
    deoxyribonucleic acid (DNA), B-NP, 175
    deoxyribose, B-NP, 174, 176
    double helix, B-NP, 174-175
    genetic code, B-NP, 175
    messenger RNA, B-NP, 175, 177
    molecules, B-NP, 174
    nucleotide, B-NP, 174
    parent cell, B-NP, 175
    phosphoric acid, B-NP, 174-175
    proteins, B-NP, 174-176
    ribose, B-NP, 174
    sequence of bases, B-NP, 175

Biochemical Aspects of Memory (cont.)
    sugar, B-NP, 174
    synthesis, B-NP, 175, 179
    template, B-NP, 175
  ribonucleic acid (RNA), as a possible carrier of the memory code, B-NP, 174-179
    adenine, B-NP, 177
    biochemical analysis, B-NP, 177
    cytosine, B-NP, 177
    8-azaguanine, B-NP, 178-179
    enzyme formation, B-NP, 178
    guanine, B-NP, 177
    phosphate, B-NP, 176
    protein structure, B-NP, 175
    protein synthesis, B-NP, 174-175, 177
    puromycin, B-NP, 178
    ratio of bases, B-NP, 177
    ribosome, B-NP, 176-177
    rotation, B-NP, 177
    stimulation, B-NP, 177
    temporal area, B-NP, 178
    thyamine, B-NP, 177
    transfer RNA, B-NP, 177
    uricil, B-NP, 177
    vestibular neurones, B-NP, 177
    vestibular nucleus, B-NP, 177
    vestibular stimulation, B-NP, 177
  synaptic growth, B-NP, 174

Concept
  category, M-CP, 44-46, 54
    conjunctive, M-CP, 45, 54
    disjunctive, M-CP, 45, 54
    relational, M-C, 45-46, 54
  continuity vs. discontinuity, M-CP, 47-51, 53
  cues, relevant and irrelevant, M-CP, 46
  feedback, M-CP, 8-16, 37, 44
    (See PERFORMANCE)
    delay of, M-CP, 9-10, 16
      motivation, M-CP, 10
      programmed learning, M-CP, 13
    knowledge of results, M-CP, 8-10, 16
    proprioceptive, M-CP, 37, 44
  formation, M-CP, 44-46, 52-55
    awareness, M-CP, 46
    categories, M-CP, 44
    mediation, M-CP, 44
    strategies of, M-CP, 52-55
  generalization, M-CP, 35-43
    (See LEARNING)
    abstraction, M-CP, 41-42

Concept (cont.)
  cognition, M-CP, 40-41
  concreteness, M-CP, 41-42
  discrimination training, M-CP, 87
  mediation, M-CP, 36, 39
    proprioceptive feedback, M-CP, 37, 44, 59-60
    primary, M-CP, 39
    response, M-CP, 35, 39-40, 43, 110
      acquired, M-CP, 39
      originality, M-CP, 110
    response-produced stimuli, (s_m), M-CP, 37
    stimulus, M-CP, 35-40
  response, M-CP, 5
    generalization, M-CP, 35, 39-40, 43
      acquired, M-CP, 39
      originality, M-CP, 110
      primary, M-CP, 39
    light-weight, M-CP, 59
    observable, M-CP, 85
    -produced stimuli, (s_m), M-CP, 37
    specific vs. response clusters, M-CP, 39-40
    symbolic process, M-CP, 91
  semantic differential, M-CP, 61
  stimulus, M-CP, 5, 35
    generalization, M-CP, 35-40
      mediated, M-CP, 36-39
      primary, M-CP, 35
    observable, M-CP, 85
    similarity and retroactive inhibition, M-CP, 27-29
    symbolic process, M-CP, 91

Creativity, M-CP, 105, 112
  age, M-CP, 107-109
  associations, M-CP, 61, 78, 111-112
    controlled, B-PD, 55
    free, B-PD, 2, 21, 55-56
    ideas, B-PD, 55-56
    principles, B-PD, 57
    remote, M-CP, 111-112
      test (RAT), M-CP, 111-112
    semantic differential, M-CP, 61, 78
  brainstorming, M-CP, 109-110, 112
  intelligence, M-CP, 105
  originality, M-CP, 105, 111
    stimulation of, M-CP, 109-110
  personal characteristics, M-CP, 106-109, 111-112
  psychological health, M-CP, 106

Language, FP-HP, 4, 123-145; M-CP, 56-79
  development, M-HD, 34-36
  emotion, M-HD, 48-49
  general semantics, M-CP, 65-67, 78
    extensional meaning, M-CP, 65-67, 78
      agreement, M-CP, 66-67
      attitude, M-CP, 66
      meaning, M-CP, 65
  interpreting persuasive messages, M-CP, 71-76, 79
    assimilation effect, M-CP, 72-75, 79
    contrast effect, M-CP, 72-76, 79
    consensual validation, M-CP, 71, 76, 79
    involvement, M-CP, 76-77
    perspective effect, M-CP, 77
  labeling, B-PD, 9

Osgood's approach, M-CP, 59-65
  "extremity effect," M-CP, 62
  compound stimuli, M-CP, 62-63
  learning, M-CP, 59-60
    assign, M-CP, 60
    sign, M-CP, 59
  meaning, M-CP, 59, 78
    connotative, M-CP, 60-62, 78
    denotative, M-CP, 60-61, 78
    learning, M-CP, 59-60
    response (r_m), M-CP, 59-60
  mediating response, M-CP, 60, 65
  semantic differential, M-CP, 60-65
  semantic satiation, M-CP, 64

semantic (See General Semantics, Osgood, Skinner)
  differential, M-CP, 60-65
  satiation, M-CP, 64
  set relations, FP-HP, 143
    disjunctive, FP-HP, 143
    exclusion, FP-HP, 143
    identity, FP-HP, 143
    inclusion, FP-HP, 143
    nested, FP-HP, 143
    overgeneralization, FP-HP, 143
    pseudodiscrimination, FP-HP, 143

Skinner's approach, M-CP, 56-59
  conditioning, M-CP, 59
  intraverbal behavior, M-CP, 59
  mand, M-CP, 58
  tact, M-CP, 58
  textual behavior, M-CP, 59

Language (cont.)
    reading, M-CP, 6, 59
    verbal behavior, M-CP, 56-57
    control of, M-CP, 57-58
    discriminative stimulus, M-CP, 56-57
    reinforcement, M-CP, 10-12, 16, 56-57
    vocal behavior, M-CP, 57
  speech, role of, B-PD, 3, 9
  statistical approach, M-CP, 70-71
    law of least effort (Zipf), M-CP, 70-71, 87
    word
      familiarity, M-CP, 69, 79
      frequency, M-CP, 70, 79
      length, M-CP, 70, 79
      order, M-CP, 67-70, 79
  syntactics, M-CP, 67-70, 79
    cloze technique, M-CP, 69
    comprehensible writing, M-CP, 69
    lexical, M-CP, 67
    linguistic, M-CP, 67
    readability, M-CP, 69
    redundancy, M-CP, 68
    structural, M-CP, 67
  words
    autistic, B-PD, 19
    denial, B-PD, 35
    ego planning, B-PD, 9
    US pictures, B-PD, 3
Memory, FP-HP, 61-72; M-CP, 18-34; M-HD, 34; WW-P, 83-84
  amnesia, B-PD, 54
  attention span, FP-HP, 61-63
  autonomous changes, WW-P, 84
  biochemical aspects (See Biochemical Aspects of Memory), B-NP, 174-179
  chain association, coaction effects, Z-SP, 20
  codability, M-CP, 88-89
  coding, M-CP, 22-24
    RNA, B-NP, 175
  distortion and organization, M-CP, 24-26; WW-P, 83
  experimental extinction, M-CP, 19
  forgetting, M-CP, 2, 19-22, 26, 33; B-PD, 54-55
    closure, M-CP, 26
    disuse, M-CP, 19-20, 33
    ease of and learning, M-CP, 2
    organization, M-CP, 21-22, 33

Memory (cont.)
  inhibition of, B-NP, 179
  long-term memory, FP-HP, 68-70
  methods, M-CP, 14, 17-19
    nonsense syllables, M-CP, 18-19
    savings, M-CP, 18-19
    socratic, M-CP, 14
    successive approximations (shaping), M-CP, 14, 17
  motivation, M-CP, 30
  nonsense syllable learning, audience effects, Z-SP, 12
  normalization, WW-P, 84
  organization, M-CP, 21-25
  pointing, WW-P, 84
  proactive inhibition, M-CP, 29-30, 34
  punishment, M-CP, 19-20
  repression, M-CP, 30-32, 34; B-PD, 35-37, 42, 51, 55, 60, 63-64
  retention, B-NP, 178-179; M-CP, 19-20
  retroactive inhibition, M-CP, 27-29, 34
    stimulus similarity, M-CP, 27-29, 34
  screen, B-PD, 55
  sensory storage, FP-HP, 63-65
  serial tasks, FP-HP, 70-72
  sharpening, WW-P, 84
  short term memory, FP-HP, 65-70
  span, FP-HP, 66
  trace, FP-HP, 26
  transfer, B-NP, 177
  word association, audience effects, Z-SP, 12
  Zeigarnik effect, M-CP, 32-34
    self (ego) orientation, M-CP, 33
    task orientation, M-CP, 33
Problem Solving, B-NP, 135; B-PD, 60-61; M-CP, 80-102
  coaction effects, Z-SP, 20
  diversity of group members, M-CP, 110
  fixation of incorrect response, M-CP, 96-100, 104
    drive level, M-CP, 97-98, 100, 104
    past experience, M-CP, 98-99
  habit-family hierarchy, M-CP, 96-97
  insight, M-CP, 80-85, 103-104
  motivation, M-CP, 97-98, 100
    cognitive dissonance, M-CP, 102-104; Z-SP, 6
  representation as aid, M-CP, 94-96
  restructuring, M-CP, 100
    attitude and
      logic, M-CP, 102

Problem Solving (cont.)
    memory, M-CP, 32
    message interpretation, M-CP,
      72-79
    hints, M-CP, 101
    rewording, M-CP, 100
    through varied sequence, M-CP, 101

Thinking and Thought, B-NP, 127; B-PD,
    3, 8-9, 15, 54; M-CP, 80-104
    central neural mechanism, M-CP, 86
    cognition and generalization, M-CP,
      40-41
    cognitive activity, B-NP, 118
    cognitive controls, B-PD, 59-60
      style, B-PD, 59
    cognitive dissonance and motivation,
      M-CP, 102-103; Z-SP, 6
    disorganization, B-PD, 54
    ego development, B-PD, 9
    ideas
      association, B-PD, 55-56
      condensation, B-PD, 3, 56-57, 59
      displacement, B-PD, 3, 57, 59
      energy, B-PD, 3
      id as container, B-PD, 5
      repression, B-PD, 35, 42
      separation from emotion, B-PD, 36
      strength, B-PD, 1
      warded off, B-PD, 36
    implicit speech, M-CP, 85-86
    information processing, B-NP, 135
    insight, M-CP, 81-85
    language, M-CP, 85-95, 104
    learning, M-CP, 81
    learning set, M-CP, 83-84
    learning to learn, M-CP, 84
    magical, B-PD, 8-9
    motivation, M-CP, 102-103
    peripheral motor activity, M-CP, 86
    primitive, B-PD, 3
    productive, M-CP, 80-81
    representation, M-CP, 91-96
      in animals, M-CP, 92-93
        delayed reaction experiment,
          M-CP, 92
        double alternation problem,
          M-CP, 92
      of future, M-CP, 93-94
    reproductive, M-CP, 80
    subvocal speech, M-CP, 85-86
    symbolic process, M-CP, 91
      stimulus, M-CP, 91

Thinking and Thought (cont.)
    response, M-CP, 91
    symbolization, M-HD, 7
    type, B-PD, 15
    Whorfian hypothesis, M-CP, 86-91
      codability and memory, M-CP, 88-89
      vocabulary, M-CP, 87-91

§3 DEVELOPMENTAL

Biological Factors, M-HD, 10-20, 41,
    43-44, 47-48, 50-51, 59
    embryological
      amnion, M-HD, 16
      ectoderm, M-HD, 16
      embryo, M-HD, 5-6, 16
      encephalization, M-HD, 5
      endoderm, M-HD, 16
      fetus, M-HD, 16-17
      mesoderm, M-HD, 16
      neonate, M-HD, 17-18
      placenta, M-HD, 16
      prenatal development, M-HD, 16-17
      retrolental fibroplasia, M-HD, 14
    general
      heredity, K-AHC, 3-4; M-HD,
        10-16 passim
      homeostasis, M-HD, 44, 46
      nature-nurture, K-AHC, 3-5
      organism, B-NP, 135
      physiological factors, M-HD, 43-44,
        47-48
    genetics, M-HD, vii, 12
      chromosomes, M-HD, 11-13
      damage, M-HD, 13-14
      DNA, M-HD, 11-12
      dominance, M-HD, 12
      eugenics movement, M-HD, vii-viii
      family studies
        Jukes, M-HD, vii
        Kallikak, M-HD, vii-viii
        Nam, M-HD, vii
        Piney, M-HD, vii
        Sixty, M-HD, vii

Biological Factors (cont.)
  gametes, M-HD, 11
  genes, M-HD, 11
  genotype, M-HD, 12
  homunculus, M-HD, 1
  mongolism, M-HD, 11, 17
  mutation, M-HD, 13-14
  phenotypes, M-HD, 12
  preformationism, M-HD, 1-2
  radiation effects, M-HD, 13-14
  recessiveness, M-HD, 12
  zygote, M-HD, 11
  maturation, B-NP, 19-20; M-HD, 16-17
  adult, B-NP, 134
  age, M-HD, 65-66
  fetal stage, B-NP, 135
  growth, B-NP, 135; M-HD, 18-19
  neuronal, B-NP, 135
  newborn, B-NP, 135
  teething, M-HD, 29
  structure
    cells, M-HD, 5-6
      organizer, M-HD, 56
    central nervous system, M-HD, 4-5, 13
    organs
      adjustment, M-HD, 13-14
      connector, M-HD, 13
      effector, M-HD, 13
      maintenance, M-HD, 12-13
      receptor, M-HD, 13

Development, M-HD, 4-7; B-NP, 135
  adolescence, M-HD, 39-40, 65-66; B-PD, 11-12, 20
  ages and stages, M-HD, 65-67
  animal, M-HD, 7, 50
  childhood, B-PD, 8-11
    early, B-PD, 8-10
    late, B-PD, 10-11
  definition of, M-HD, 1
  human, M-HD, 7, 50
  infancy, B-PD, 7-8
  interferences
    abnormal environment, M-HD, 13-15
    separation from mother, M-HD, 59-63
  judgment, B-PD, 9
  maturation and, M-HD, 17-20, 39-40, 46-47
    emotion, M-HD, 56-57
    time factors, M-HP, 39-40
  neonate, M-HD, 17-18

Development (cont.)
  passive-dependent period, M-HD, 26-28
  prenatal, M-HD, 16-17
  stages of, M-HD, 65-66

Environment, M-HD, 2-4, 10, K-AHC, 3-5
  family factors, M-HD, 41-42, 70-73
  genetic damage, M-HD, 13-14
  maturation, M-HD, 40
  organs of adjustment to, M-HD, 13
  peer influences, M-HD, 36-37, 51-52, 53, 64
  prenatal influences, M-HD, 17
  school, M-HD, 36-42 passim, 63-64
  twins, K-AHC, 2

Life Themes, M-HD, 21-42 passim
  generalization of, M-HD, 35-36
  language and, M-HD, 34-36
  passive-dependence, M-HD, 26-28
  self-assertiveness, M-HD, 28-31
  sexual identity and, M-HD, 33

Methods, M-HD, 8-9
  diary studies, M-HD, 8-9
  longitudinal studies, M-HD, 8-9
  idiographic studies, M-HD, 9
  naturalist child studies, M-HD, 8-9
  nomothetic studies, M-HD, 9

Personality (See also §10)
  defense mechanisms, M-HD, 55-56
  deprivation and, M-HD, 44-45, 59-62 passim
  developmental theories of, M-HD, 23-24
  dynamic theories of, M-HD, 24
  fantasy, M-HD, 68
  food relationships and, M-HD, 44-45
  frustration tolerance, M-HD, 27-28
  life space, M-HD, 24
  life themes, M-HD, 21-28 passim (See Life Themes)
  mother relationships and, M-HD, 26-28, 59-62 passim
  motivation, M-HD, 43-46
  neo-Freudian views, M-HD, 21
  oral character, M-HD, 27
  passive-dependent period, M-HD, 26-28
  psychological development, M-HD, 21-42, 58-73 passim
  psychological disorders, M-HD, 44-46, 59-62 passim

Personality (cont.)

self, M-HD, 45-46, 64-73 passim
-assertion, M-HD, 28-31
sexual identity, M-HD, 31-33, 51-52, 72
trait theories of, M-HD, 23
types, M-HD, 22-23

Philosophical Issues (See also §5)
behaviorism, M-HD, 2-3
cultural determinism and relativity,
M-HD, 3-4, 41, 47, 51-52, 63-64
environmentalism, M-HD, 3
epigenesis, M-HD, 4
humanism, M-HD, 2-4
innate ideas, M-HD, 1-2
instinct, M-HD, 2, 59
human, M-HD, 2
prediction, M-HD, 8
racial unconscious, M-HD, 1-2
scientific method, M-HD, 7-9
teleology, M-HD, 4

Psychological Processes (See also §§3, 4,
6, 8, and 9)
perceptual processes
deprivation, sensory, M-HD, 46-47
functions, sensory, M-HD, 13-15
perception, M-HD, 14-15, 21-22, 42,
55-56
infantile, B-PD, 7
of self, M-HD, 64-73 passim
and stimulus-response, M-HD, 22
white noise, M-HD, 15
learning, M-HD, 18-19
aggression, M-HD, 49-57 passim
conditioning, M-HD, 28, 47
emotion, M-HD, 46-49
play, M-HD, 67
socialization, M-HD, 58-73
stimulus-response, M-HD, 28
motivation and emotion
aggression, M-HD, 49-57
instrumental, M-HD, 50-51
curiosity, M-HD, 31
deprivation, biological, M-HD, 44-45
drives, M-HD, 43
emotion
development of, M-HD, 46-49,
61-62
language development, M-HD,
48-49
learning, M-HD, 46-49
stimulus-response, M-HD, 47-48

Psychological Processes (cont.)
frustration-aggression hypothesis,
M-HD, 51
hunger drive, M-HD, 44
motivation, M-HD, 43-46
stimulus-response, M-HD, 43-46
passim
performance
body expression, M-HD, 30-31
galvanic skin response, M-HD, 48
games, M-HD, 66-69
mechanization of response, M-HD, 7
pilomotor response, M-HD, 48
play, M-HD, 66-69
walking, M-HD, 30
cognition
communication, M-HD, 34-36, 66-67
language development, M-HD, 34-36
memory, M-HD, 34
symbolization, M-HD, 7

Social Factors
education
development theory and, M-HD, 2-3
readiness, M-HD, 19
school, M-HD, 36-42, 63-64
teacher's values, M-HD, 64
family
courtship, K-AHC, 4
food experiences, M-HD, 26-27,
44-45
maternal deprivation, M-HD, 59-63
separation from mother, M-HD,
59-63
mixed marriages, M-HD, 70-71
parental values and roles, M-HD,
29-31, 37-39, 58-59, 70-71
values and functions, M-HD, 32,
41-42, 70-73
mother's role, M-HD, 26-28, 59-63
social class factors, M-HD, 29-31,
37-39, 59, 63-64, 70-71
lower class values, M-HD, 31, 38-39,
63
middle class values, M-HD, 29-31,
38, 64
status, M-HD, 29-31, 37-39, 58-59,
70-71
society and socialization, M-HD,
58-73 passim; Z-SP, 5
agents of socialization, M-HD, 36-42,
63-64
aggression, M-HD, 54-57

Social Factors (cont.)

attitudes, M-HD, 23

complexity of interdependence, M-HD, 40-41

cooperation, development of, M-HD, 53

deprivation (social), M-HD, 59-63 passim

ethnic factors, M-HD, 59

institutional child rearing, M-HD, 61-62

Judeo-Christian ethic, M-HD, 41

norms, M-HD, 58-59, 66-67

peer group functions, M-HD, 36-37, 51-53, 63-64

play functions, M-HD, 66-69

role behavior, M-HD, 37-38, 58-59, 68

school as microcosm, M-HD, 37-38, 63-64

sociocultural behavior, M-HD, 5

Sparta, treatment of youth, M-HD, 66

values and value conflicts, M-HD, 29-33, 58

aggression, M-HD, 50-51, 54-57

biological needs, M-HD, 41

cultural norms, M-HD, 58-59

emotional expression, M-HD, 47

family functions, M-HD, 41-42

Judeo-Christian ethic, M-HD, 41

moral development, Z-SP, 49

school's role, M-HD, 36-39, 63-64

social structure, M-HD, 40-41

§4 LEARNING

Classes of

classical conditioning, B-NP, 156, 169-170; W-CL, 4 (See also *Conditioning*)

conditioned reflex method, ALW-SP, 143-144

contiguity learning, W-CL, 86

Classes of (cont.)

delayed alternation, B-NP, 160, 162; M-CP, 92

discrimination, B-NP, 156, 162

reversal, B-NP, 162

sensory, B-NP, 162

imitation, W-CL, 4, 110ff; Z-SP, 29-40

instinct, Z-SP, 29-30

low probability response, Z-SP, 40

social reinforcement, Z-SP, 48-50

imprinting, W-CL, 4, 7-12, 16

critical period, W-CL, 9-11

learning, W-CL, 12

information processing, W-CL, 4

instrumental (See Instrumental), W-CL, 4

latent, BV-MSA, 15-17; M-CP, 7-8; W-CL, 84

learning to learn, M-CP, 84; W-CL, 86ff, 93

learning sets, M-CP, 83-84; W-CL, 91ff

repeated learning and extinction, W-CL, 87ff

avoidance conditioning, W-CL, 88

selective learning, W-CL, 87ff

repeated reversal learning, W-CL, 88ff, 92

modeling, W-CL, 110ff

imitation, W-CL, 4, 110ff

copying behavior, W-CL, 110

matched dependent behavior, W-CL, 110ff

paradigm, W-CL, 115

social learning, W-CL, 110

successive approximation, W-CL, 108, 115-116

vicarious

conditioning, Z-SP, 35-37

learning, Z-SP, 29-40

punishment, W-CL, 117-118

reinforcement, W-CL, 116-118

operant conditioning (See Operant Conditioning), W-CL, 4

paradigms of

conditioning, W-CL, 17-18

instrumental learning, W-CL, 17-18

modeling, W-CL, 115

perceptual learning, B-NP; WW-P, 81ff

programmed learning, M-CP, 12-15

Classes of (cont.)
skill (See also §9), FP-HP, 8-15; W-CL, 4
  early phase, FP-HP, 11-12
  final phase, FP-HP, 14-15
  habit transfer, FP-HP, 19-20
  intermediate phase, FP-HP, 12-14
  motor, B-NP, 156; W-CL, 4; FP-HP,
    8-15
  perceptual-motor, FP-HP, 8-15;
    W-CL, 4
  plateaus, FP-HP, 8-9
  practice conditions, FP-HP, 13-14
  verbal learning (See also §2), W-CL, 4

Conditioning, B-NP, 156-157, 169-171;
  M-CP, 59; M-HD, 28, 47; W-CL, 17-19,
  21, 24, 30, 38ff, 52
  amount of training, W-CL, 30
  avoidance, B-NP, 167-168, 178; W-CL,
    19
  classical, W-CL, 17
    as association, W-CL, 21
    as paradigm, W-CL, 17, 18
    autonomic, W-CL, 24
    backward, W-CL, 52
    CR, definition, B-NP, 156, 168,
      172-173; W-CL, 17
    CS, definition, B-NP, 156, 166,
      168-170, 172-173; W-CL, 17
      intensity and learning, W-CL, 38ff
      omission of, W-CL, 84
    CS-US interaction, W-CL, 21
      interval, W-CL, 51
      pairings, W-CL, 30ff
    definition, W-CL, 17
    delayed, W-CL, 51
    generality of, W-CL, 20
    neutral stimulus, W-CL, 17
    pseudoconditioning, W-CL, 21ff
    sensitization, W-CL, 21ff
    sensory preconditioning, W-CL, 82
      CS-CS interval, W-CL, 83
      definition, W-CL, 82
      generalization, W-CL, 83
      number of pairings, W-CL, 83
    stimulus adaptation, W-CL, 21
    temporal, W-CL, 20
    trace, W-CL, 51
    UR definition, B-NP, 156; W-CL, 17
    US definition, B-NP, 156; W-CL, 17
      intensity, W-CL, 39ff
    volition, W-CL, 24
  contiguity, W-CL, 25, 76, 86

Conditioning (cont.)
  association principle, W-CL, 76
  learning principle, W-CL, 25
  ease of, W-CL, 29
  electrical responses in CNS, B-NP,
    168-171
    arousal, B-NP, 170
    association, B-NP, 170
    behavioral conditioning, B-NP, 169
    conditioned desynchronization,
      B-NP, 169
    desynchronization (EEG), B-NP,
      169-173
    discrimination, B-NP, 169-170
    electrical activity of the brain, B-NP,
      168
    electrical response, B-NP, 169
    emotional responses, B-NP, 170
    flickering light, B-NP, 166-169, 171
    instrumental conditioning, B-NP, 169
    sensory messages, B-NP, 170
    tone, B-NP, 169-170
    reconditioning, B-NP, 168
    suppression, W-CL, 22

Discrimination, Generalization, Transfer
  discrimination, W-CL, 66ff
    definition, W-CL, 62
    operant, W-CL, 163ff
    relevant and irrelevant cues, M-CP,
      46
    training, M-CP, 40, 87
    transposition, W-CL, 66
  generalization, W-CL, 61-66
    cognition, M-CP, 40-41
    gradient, W-CL, 62
    mediation
      concept formation, M-CP, 44
      generalization, M-CP, 36-37
    response, M-CP, 35, 39-40, 48, 110;
      W-CL, 65ff
      acquired, M-CP, 39
      definition, W-CL, 61
      habit-family-hierarchy, M-CP, 5,
        15, 96-97; W-CL, 65
      meaning (r_m), M-CP, 37
      originality, M-CP, 110
      primary, M-CP, 39
      -produced stimulus (s_m), M-CP, 37
    stimulus, M-CP, 35-39; W-CL, 61ff
      explanations, M-CP, 35-39; W-CL,
        62-66
      octave, W-CL, 64

Discrimination, Generalization, Transfer (cont.)

  similarity definition, M-CP, 27-29; W-CL, 63ff
  transposition, W-CL, 66
transfer of training, W-CL, 61ff
Experimental Extinction, B-NP, 168-169; M-CP, 6; W-CL, 67ff
amount of, W-CL
  effort, W-CL, 72
  training, W-CL, 67ff
    overtraining, W-CL, 67
below zero, W-CL, 72
defined as, W-CL
  procedure, W-CL, 67
  process, W-CL, 67
disinhibition, W-CL, 69ff
  inhibition of inhibition, W-CL, 70
elimination of learned responses, W-CL, 67
explanations of, W-CL, 73
  decrease in, W-CL, 73
  changes in, W-CL, 73, 75
  conditioned inhibition, W-CL, 75
  counter conditioning, W-CL, 75
  learning a different response, W-CL, 74
  orienting response, W-CL, 75
  reactive inhibition, W-CL, 75
forgetting, W-CL, 69
frustration, BV-MSA, 25
high resistance to, W-CL, 72, 73, 101ff
latent, W-CL, 85
memory, M-CP, 6
punishment for responding, W-CL, 72
spontaneous recovery, W-CL, 71ff
Inhibition, W-CL, 23, 34-36, 70
disinhibition, W-CL, 69ff
external, W-CL, 35, 36
of, W-CL, 23, 34, 70
  delay, W-CL, 23
  inhibition, W-CL, 70
  reinforcement, W-CL, 34
Instrumental, B-NP, 156; W-CL, 4, 17, 18ff
acquisition of responses, W-CL, 29
  without responding, W-CL, 85-86
alternation phenomena, W-CL, 19
amount of training, W-CL, 30
as paradigm, W-CL, 17, 18
available response, W-CL, 18
avoidance conditioning, W-CL, 19
definition, M-CP, 4; W-CL, 18

Instrumental (cont.)
ease of, M-CP, 2; W-CL, 29
  forgetting, M-CP, 2
escape learning, W-CL, 19
generality of, W-CL, 20
law of effect, M-CP, 10, 16
number of trials, W-CL, 32
SS (stimulus situation), W-CL, 18
Intervals, W-CL
CS-US, W-CL, 51ff
intertrial, W-CL, 55-57ff
massed practice, W-CL, 57
reinforcement, W-CL
  delay of, W-CL, 54ff
  fixed, W-CL, 100
  variable, W-CL, 100
spaced practice, W-CL, 57
temporal rhythms, W-CL, 38
Learning (General)
apparatus
  water maze, B-NP, 178
  Y-maze, B-NP, 178
association, B-NP, 157, 171
behavior, B-NP, 147
continuity-discontinuity, M-CP, 47, 51, 55
cues, B-NP, 161
  electric shock, B-NP, 156, 166-167
  olfactory, B-NP, 161
  tactile, B-NP, 161
  verbal command, B-NP, 156
  visual, B-NP, 161
delayed feedback
  programmed learning, M-CP, 13
  Socratic method, M-CP, 14
habit, BV-MSA, 4; W-CL, 27, 36, 60-61, 65
  antecedent conditions, BV-MSA, 4
  availability, BV-MSA, 6
  D-H, drive-habit distinction, W-CL, 36, 60-61
  family hierarchy, W-CL, 65
  H, W-CL, 27
  maze, B-NP, 159, 161
habituation, B-NP, 167, 172
overlearning, W-CL, 33
  new problem, W-CL, 89-90
  resistance to extinction, W-CL, 92
  reversal learning, W-CL, 88-89, 92
response, B-NP, 161
  alternation, B-NP, 161
  clusters, M-CP, 39-40

Learning (General) (cont.)
  learning, B-NP, 159
  maze running, B-NP, 152, 159
  observable, M-CP, 85
  orienting, B-NP, 172-174
    conditioned reflex, B-NP, 173
    facilitation, B-NP, 172
    inhibition, B-NP, 173
    instrumental, B-NP, 172-173
    investigatory, B-NP, 172
    release, B-NP, 173
    synchronization (EEG), B-NP, 173
  preferred modes of, B-NP, 162-163
  sequence, B-NP, 161
  shifting, B-NP, 162-163
  specific, M-CP, 39-40
  symbolic process, M-CP, 91
  suppression, B-NP, 157
  stimulus, M-CP, 5, 35
  symbolic process, M-CP, 91
Mathematical Models, W-CL, 119
  as a continuous process, W-CL, 123ff
  as a discrete process, W-CL, 123ff
  computer simulation, W-CL, 134
  deterministic, W-CL, 124ff, 128, 134
  mathematical concepts, W-CL
    asymptote, W-CL, 121
    constant, W-CL, 127
    exponential equation, W-CL, 121, 123
      learning-performance, W-CL, 122
      negative exponential curve, W-CL, 31
    growth equation, W-CL, 121
    parameters, W-CL, 127
    set theory, W-CL, 128
    variables, mathematical, W-CL, 127
  predictive, W-CL, 124
  probabilistic, W-CL, 128
  process, W-CL, 135
  stimulus sampling, W-CL, 128
    theory, W-CL, 133
  stochastic, W-CL, 128, 132
Methods and Metatheory, W-CL
  constructs, W-CL
    empirical, W-CL, 133
    theoretical, W-CL, 126, 133
  curves
    negative exponential, W-CL, 31
    S-shaped, W-CL, 31
    inverted-U, W-CL, 36
    definitions of, W-CL, 1ff
      fatigue, W-CL, 2

Methods and Metatheory (cont.)
    maturation, W-CL, 2
    motivation, W-CL, 3
    stimulus change, W-CL, 3
    variability concept, W-CL, 2
  definition types
    coordinating, W-CL, 126
    implicit, W-CL, 126
  measures of, W-CL
    amplitude, W-CL, 23
    correlations between, W-CL, 23
    frequency, W-CL, 23
    latency, W-CL, 3
    operant level, W-CL, 95
    rate of responding, W-CL, 95
    resistance to extinction, W-CL, 23
    trials to extinguish, W-CL, 23
    trials to learn, W-CL, 23
  variable types
    dependent, W-CL, 126
    independent, W-CL, 126
    intervening, W-CL, 26, 126
    mathematical, W-CL, 127
    performance, W-CL, 126
    situational, W-CL, 36
  scales, W-CL
    physical, W-CL, 64
    psychological, W-CL, 64

Motivation, Reward, Punishment (See also §6)
  audience effects, Z-SP
    in nonsense syllable learning, Z-SP, 12
    in relearning, Z-SP, 13
    in word association, Z-SP, 12
  coaction effects, Z-SP
    in avoidance learning, Z-SP, 24-28
    in discrimination learning, Z-SP, 18
    in maze learning, Z-SP, 18-19, 21-24
  drive, W-CL, 36-73, 41, 47, 60-61
    acquired, W-CL, 47ff
    D-H, drive-habit distinction, W-CL, 36, 60-61
    level and performance, W-CL, 36ff
      Yerkes-Dodson Law, W-CL, 37
    strength and learning, W-CL, 41
  incentive function, W-CL, 41
  law of least effort, M-CP, 70-71, 87
  punishment, M-CP, 19-20; W-CL, 80
    aversive stimulus, B-NP, 156
    fixated behavior, W-CL, 81-82
    frustration, W-CL, 74, 81

Motivation, Reward, Punishment (cont.)
  masochistic-like behavior, W-CL, 81
  memory, M-CP, 19-20
  paradox, W-CL, 80
  vicarious, W-CL, 117, 118

  reinforcement, M-CP, 5-8, 15; W-CL, 76-80
  awareness, M-CP, 11-12
  blood sugar level, W-CL, 78
  brain stimulation, W-CL
  consumption, W-CL, 78
  explanations of, W-CL, 79
    increased probability of response, W-CL, 80
    need reduction, W-CL, 79-80
    primitive axiom, W-CL, 80
    stimulus reduction, W-CL, 80
  exploration, W-CL, 79
  feedback, FP-HP, 28
  incentive function, W-CL, 76
  inhibition of, W-CL, 34
  language, M-CP, 56
  learning principle, W-CL, 25
  manipulation, W-CL, 79
  nature of, W-CL, 76
  need reduction, W-CL, 77ff
  negative, W-CL, 76
    definition, W-CL, 76
    punishment, W-CL, 77
    Skinner's definition, W-CL, 95
  positive, W-CL, 76
    definition, W-CL, 76
    reward, W-CL, 77
    Skinner's definition, W-CL, 95
  principle of association, W-CL, 76
  punishment, W-CL, 80
  reciprocity, Z-SP, 53
  reduction of biological need, W-CL, 77
  secondary, stimulus roles, W-CL, 50
  social reinforcement, Z-SP, 9, 41-50
    behavior control, Z-SP, 42-43
    differentiation, Z-SP, 83, 92-98
    facilitation, Z-SP, 16
    imitation, Z-SP, 48-50
    instincts, Z-SP, 7-8
    interaction, Z-SP, 5, 51-82
    of tantrum, Z-SP, 41-43
    situation, minimal, Z-SP, 67-72
  stimulus change, W-CL, 79
  stimulus increase, W-CL, 79
  stomach loading, W-CL, 78

Motivation, Reward, Punishment (cont.)
  verbal, Z-SP, 43-48
    opinions, Z-SP, 44-46
    self-acceptance, Z-SP, 48
  vicarious, W-CL, 116, 117, 118
  reward, B-NP, 156; W-CL
    acquired, W-CL, 48ff
    amount of, W-CL, 43
    delay of, W-CL, 54ff
    gradient of, W-CL, 55
    secondary, W-CL, 48, 50

Neurophysiology, B-NP, 162-174
  electrical correlates of learning, B-NP, 166-168
    discharge, B-NP, 166
    familiarization stage, B-NP, 166-167
    frequency-specific response, B-NP, 166, 167, 171
    response, B-NP, 166
  electrophysiological investigations of learning and memory, B-NP, 166-174
    learning situation, B-NP, 166
  interhemispheric transfer of the memory trace, B-NP, 163-165
    deficits in learned behavior, B-NP, 165
    difficulty of discrimination, B-NP, 165
    learning curve, B-NP, 164
    split brain preparation, B-NP, 163
      animal, B-NP, 163-165
      interocular transfer, B-NP, 163-165
  localization of cortical functions and learning, B-NP, 160-163
    patterns, B-NP, 162
    trial and error, B-NP, 162
  structural representation of the memory trace, B-NP, 168

Operant Conditioning, W-CL, 94ff
  cumulative curves, W-CL, 96
    grain of record, W-CL, 98
    recorder, W-CL, 96
  discrimination, W-CL, 103
    operant, W-CL, 103ff
  discriminative stimulus, M-CP, 56-57
  elicited behavior, W-CL, 94ff
  emitted behavior, W-CL, 94ff
  experimental analysis of behavior, W-CL, 95
    experimental style, W-CL, 96
    theory, W-CL, 96
  experimenter-controlled, W-CL, 94

Operant Conditioning (cont.)
  learning and performance, W-CL, 96
  punishment, W-CL, 95
  reinforcement, W-CL, 95
    negative, W-CL, 95
  resistance to extinction, W-CL, 101ff
  respondent conditioning, W-CL, 94
  schedules of reinforcement, W-CL, 98ff
    intermittent, W-CL, 99
    interval, W-CL, 100ff
      fixed, W-CL, 99-100
      variable, W-CL, 100
    other schedules, W-CL, 101
    ratio reinforcement, W-CL, 99ff
      continuous, W-CL, 99
      fixed, W-CL, 99
      variable, W-CL, 100
  shaping, W-CL, 106, 115
    external, W-CL, 106
    internal, W-CL, 107
    successive approximation, M-CP,
      14, 17; W-CL, 108, 115-116
  "superstition," W-CL, 108ff
  subject-controlled, W-CL, 94

Theory, W-CL, 25ff
  behaviorism, W-CL, 26ff
    strict, W-CL, 26, 27
    theoretical, W-CL, 26
  cognitive, W-CL, 26ff
    expectancy, W-CL, 26, 27
  contiguity, W-CL, 86
  empty organism, W-CL, 26
  intervening variables, W-CL, 26
  issues, W-CL, 25, 29
  necessary conditions for, W-CL, 82
  principles of, W-CL
    contiguity, W-CL, 25
    reinforcement, W-CL, 25
  radical empiricism, W-CL, 26
  S-R, W-CL, 26ff, 86
    excitatory potential, W-CL, 25
  S-S, W-CL, 86
  unitary process, W-CL, 23

Trace
  active, W-CL, 51
  consolidation, B-NP, 158, 178; W-CL,
    59, 61
    ECS, W-CL, 59-61
    hypothesis, W-CL, 57ff
    intertrial interval, W-CL, 57
  inactive, W-CL, 51
  long term, B-NP, 158, 178

Trace (cont.)
  memory, B-NP, 157-159, 163, 165,
    167-169; W-CL, 51, 59
    biochemical aspects, B-NP, 174-179
    retrieval, B-NP, 168
  permanent storage, B-NP, 158
  perseveration, W-CL, 51
    memory, B-NP, 174, FP-HP, 26;
      W-CL, 59
    stimulus, W-CL, 59
  response, W-CL, 51
  short term, B-NP, 158, 178
  stimulus, W-CL, 51
  structural, W-CL, 51
  temporary, B-NP, 158
  time factors, W-CL, 50

§5 METAPSYCHOLOGY, PHILOSOPHY, AND HISTORY

Determinism vs. Indeterminism
  causal determinism, W-PNSS, 14
  determinism, B-NP, 2; W-PNSS, 12,
    15, 18, 20, 23-24, 27-28, 30
    cultural, M-HD, 3-4, 41, 47, 51-52,
      63-64
    in contemporary physics, W-PNSS,
      10
    mechanistic, B-NP, 2; W-PNSS, 18
    uncertainty, W-PNSS, 11, 18
      Heisenberg principle, W-PNSS,
        11, 60
  determinist, W-PNSS, 14
  physical, W-PNSS, 17
  physics, W-PNSS, 10
    deterministic model, W-PNSS, 11
    indeterministic model, W-PNSS, 11
    Newtonian physics, W-PNSS, 11
      certain, W-PNSS, 11
      deterministic, W-PNSS, 11
    quantum mechanics, W-PNSS, 11
      probabilistic, W-PNSS, 11
      statistical, W-PNSS, 11
      uncertainty (fundamental),
        W-PNSS, 11

Determinism vs. Indeterminism (cont.)
political implications, W-PNSS, 24-30
democracy, W-PNSS, 24, 26-28, 30
compatibility, W-PNSS, 29
determinism, W-PNSS, 26
democratic tradition, W-PNSS, 27
law (jurisprudence), W-PNSS, 27-28
totalitarianism, W-PNSS, 29
relativity (cultural), M-HD, 3-4, 41,
47, 51-52, 63-64

Experiment (Language of), W-PNSS, 35,
40, 45
conceiving, W-PNSS, 35
control, W-PNSS, 41
experimental, W-PNSS, 40, 54
manipulative, W-PNSS, 40
operation, W-PNSS, 40
statistical, W-PNSS, 40, 54
variable, W-PNSS, 40
deduction, W-PNSS, 36, 53
experiment, W-PNSS, 36, 39
classical, K-AHC, 90
control, W-PNSS, 41
essence of, W-PNSS, 36
field, W-PNSS, 39
laboratory, W-PNSS, 39
as multiplicity of experiments,
W-PNSS, 39
pilot, W-PNSS, 54
psychological, W-PNSS, 52ff
executing, W-PNSS, 35
experimental design, W-PNSS, 41
experimental proof, W-PNSS, 35
gigabucks, W-PNSS, 35
hypothesis, W-PNSS, 36
immediate experience, W-PNSS, 36
induction, H-BS, 2; W-PNSS, 36, 53
observing, W-PNSS, 35-36
naturalistic, W-PNSS, 38
scientific, W-PNSS, 36
objective, W-PNSS, 36
purposeful, W-PNSS, 36
systematic, W-PNSS, 36
problems of measurement, W-PNSS, 41
responses, W-PNSS, 40
stimulus, W-PNSS, 40
situation, W-PNSS, 40
statistical analysis, W-PNSS, 41
control, W-PNSS, 41
significance, W-PNSS, 55
variables
assessment, W-PNSS, 40, 54

Experiment (Language of) (cont.)
behavioral, W-PNSS, 40
control, W-PNSS, 40-41
dependent, H-BS, 88, 92; W-PNSS,
39-40, 45-46, 54
independent, H-BS, 88, 92;
W-PNSS, 39-40, 45-46, 54
manipulative, W-PNSS, 39-40, 54
nuisance, H-BS, 89-91
random, H-BS, 50-61
response, W-PNSS, 40
situational, W-PNSS, 40
stimulus, W-PNSS, 40
Free Will (Freedom), W-PNSS, 13, 22-24,
27
action (human choice), W-PNSS, 21
epiphenomenon, W-PNSS, 21
ignorance, W-PNSS, 21
illusory, W-PNSS, 21
perceptual distortion, W-PNSS, 21
phenomenological error, W-PNSS, 21
reality, W-PNSS, 20
voluntarist, W-PNSS, 14
Liberal Arts (Divisional Units),
W-PNSS, 5
behavioral sciences, K-AHC, 68;
W-PNSS, 6
biological sciences, W-PNSS, 17
humanities, W-PNSS, 5, 10, 17
natural sciences, W-PNSS, 5, 10, 17
physical sciences, W-PNSS, 17
social sciences, W-PNSS, 5-6, 10, 17
"two cultures," W-PNSS, 30
Methods (in Psychology) (See also the
relevant categories in other sections.)
case history, W-PNSS, 37
clinical methods, W-PNSS, 4, 37-38
limitations of, W-PNSS, 38
clinical psychologist, W-PNSS, 37
experimental, W-PNSS, 2, 39ff
free-association, B-PD, 2; W-PNSS, 4
idiographic, M-HD, 9
intelligence tests, W-PNSS, 3
interpretation of
dreams, B-PD, 2
wishes, B-PD, 2
naturalistic observation, W-PNSS, 38
nomothetic, M-HD, 9
psychological test, W-PNSS, 3
scientific, M-HD, 7-9
Philosophical Issues (including History)
(See also *Determinism vs.
Indeterminism, Free Will,* and *Science*)

Philosophical Issues (including History) (cont.)
apperception, B-PD, 1
becoming, W-PNSS, 15
behaviorism, M-HD, 2-3; W-CL, 26ff
behavioristic view, B-NP, 1-2
conflict of ideas, B-NP, 1
depth perception, history of, WW-P, 21-23, 33
  artist's approach, WW-P, 22-23
  experimental approach, WW-P, 33
  philosophical approach, WW-P, 21-22
doctor, original meaning, W-PNSS, 5
dualism, W-PNSS, 2, 16
empiricism, WW-P, 7, 22
English philosophers, W-PNSS, 3
ethics, W-PNSS, 24
existentialism, W-PNSS, 12-13, 15-16
fact, W-PNSS, 24
French philosophers, W-PNSS, 3
Freudian thought, W-PNSS, 3
fulfillment, W-PNSS, 13ff
German philosophers, B-PD, 1; W-PNSS, 2
Gestalt, M-CP, 26, 81
Greek philosophy, W-PNSS, 2
  Aristotle, W-PNSS, 2
  rationalism, W-PNSS, 2
humanism, M-HD, 2-4
innate ideas, M-HD, 1-2
irrational behavior, explanations of, W-PNSS, 2-3
  evil forces, W-PNSS, 2
  rational, W-PNSS, 2-3
  science, W-PNSS, 2
  theology, W-PNSS, 2
mathematics, original meaning, W-PNSS, 5
monads, B-PD, 1
monism, W-PNSS, 15-16
naive realism, WW-P, 1
nativism, WW-P, 4, 17
negative sensations, B-PD, 1
philosophy, original meaning of, W-PNSS, 5
positivism, W-PNSS, 12, 15-16, 33, 46
  logical positivism, W-PNSS, 12, 33, 46
  positivistic philosophy, W-PNSS, 12-13, 15-16
pragmatism, K-AHC, 48
psychoneural isomorphism, WW-P, 5
stimulus-response, M-HD, 6-7, 13
subjective, W-PNSS, 15
  experience, W-PNSS, 15, 20

Philosophical Issues (including History) (cont.)
  idealism, W-PNSS, 16
  world, W-PNSS, 14
tabula rasa, M-HD, 2
threshold of consciousness, B-PD, 1
unconscious determinants, of behavior, W-PNSS, 3
  degrees of consciousness, B-PD, 1
  dynamic theory of, B-PD, 1
unconscious inference, B-PD, 1
understanding, K-AHC, 2, 80, 82, 88
value, W-PNSS, 24

Psychology
academic disciplines (among), W-PNSS, 4ff
contemporary perspective (in), W-PNSS, 4ff
definition of, W-PNSS, 1; Z-SP, 1
determinism in, W-PNSS, 12
development of, Z-SP, 2-5
languages of W-PNSS, 33ff
metapsychology, W-PNSS, 7
modern characteristics of, W-PNSS, 4ff
  empiricism, W-PNSS, 2-4
  experimentalism, W-PNSS, 2-4, 33
  human variability, W-PNSS, 4
   individual differences, W-PNSS, 2-3
  natural origins of behavior, W-PNSS, 3-4
modern university (in the), W-PNSS, 4ff
neuropsychology, B-NP, 1-6
  definition, B-NP, 3
perspective, W-PNSS, 1ff
  contemporary, W-PNSS, 4ff
  of time, W-PNSS, 2
  within, W-PNSS, 6ff
philosophical issues in (See also *Philosophical Issues*), W-PNSS, 10ff
professional schools, W-PNSS, 9
and science, W-PNSS, 33
separation from philosophy, W-PNSS, 33
subdivisions of, W-PNSS, 7-9, 17
  applied, W-PNSS, 9
  experimental, W-PNSS, 7
  general, W-PNSS, 6-7
  interdisciplinary, W-PNSS, 6-8
  natural science, W-PNSS, 6-7, 17
  social science, W-PNSS, 6, 8, 17
systematic body of knowledge, W-PNSS, 33

Science (and Scientific)
  aims of, W-PNSS, 36
    control, W-PNSS, 36
      deliberate, W-PNSS, 37
      intellectual, W-PNSS, 36
      statistical, W-PNSS, 36
    describe, W-PNSS, 36
    predict, W-PNSS, 36
  approach to psychological problems,
    W-PNSS, 1-2
  as humanistic and subjective product,
    W-PNSS, 15
  curiosity, W-PNSS, 2
  definition, W-PNSS, 33
  general commitment to, W-PNSS, 30
  measurement in, H-QP, 1
    human values, H-QP, 2
    theoretical and empirical base,
      H-QP, 12, 14-15, 18-20, 22-25, 58,
      64-68, 75-76
  method, M-HD, 7-9
  models of the universe, W-PNSS, 12,
    14, 24
    deterministic, W-PNSS, 12, 20, 24
    indeterministic, W-PNSS, 12
    probabilistic, W-PNSS, 12
    statistical, W-PNSS, 12
    status of, W-PNSS, 26

  observation, W-PNSS, 36
    objective, W-PNSS, 36
    purposive, W-PNSS, 36
    systematic, W-PNSS, 36

  of human behavior, W-PNSS, 12

  study, H-QP, 4-6
    human component, H-QP, 4-6
    principles, H-QP, 4-6
    procedures, H-QP, 4-6

Theory (Language of), W-PNSS, 35, 42,
  45

  abstraction (loss of information), H-BS,
    8-10

  concepts (constructs), W-PNSS, 43
    empirical, W-PNSS, 43-45, 48-50, 53
    entities, W-PNSS, 47
    higher level, W-PNSS, 43
    hypothetical, K-AHC, 32, 44, 93,
      100; W-PNSS, 48, 55
    theoretical, W-PNSS, 43-45, 48-50, 53

  data, W-PNSS, 42, 55
    datum, W-PNSS, 42

Theory (Language of) (cont.)
    events, H-BS, 45; W-PNSS, 42
      actual, W-PNSS, 44
    collection, K-AHC, 74
    combination, K-AHC, 74
    life record, K-AHC, 26
    numerical, H-BS, 1, 17, 23, 28
    qualitative, H-BS, 17, 28
    questionnaire, K-AHC, 26
    relevance of, K-AHC, 80
    symbolic record, W-PNSS, 42
    symbolic representation, W-PNSS, 43
    test, K-AHC, 26
    weights, K-AHC, 76, 78, 98
      empirical, K-AHC, 91

  definitions (types)
    coordinating, W-PNSS, 43-44, 53
    implicit, W-PNSS, 44, 53
    operation, W-PNSS, 43
    operational, W-PNSS, 43-44, 54
      arrangements, W-PNSS, 43
    ostensive, W-PNSS, 42, 54
      pointing, W-PNSS, 42
      symbolic representation, W-PNSS,
        43

  epistemology, W-PNSS, 2
  evaluation of, W-PNSS, 58-60
    comprehensiveness, W-PNSS, 58
    control of behavior, W-PNSS, 59
    elegance, W-PNSS, 58
    good and bad theories, W-PNSS, 58
    heuristic, W-PNSS, 59
    humanistic importance, W-PNSS, 59
    internal consistency, W-PNSS, 58
    prediction (of behavior), W-PNSS, 59
    Pretzel Bell, W-PNSS, 60
    simplicity, W-PNSS, 58

  hypothesis, K-AHC, 92, 94; W-PNSS,
    36
    null form, W-PNSS, 53
    positive form, W-PNSS, 53
    source of, W-PNSS, 47

  inference from behavior (strategies),
    K-AHC, 25, 28
    common sense, K-AHC, 20, 93
    empirical, K-AHC, 30-31; W-PNSS,
      46
    factor analytic, K-AHC, 32
    inferential leap, K-AHC, 76, 80
    logic of, K-AHC, 24, 77
    rational, K-AHC, 28, 33, 46, 77
      hazards of, K-AHC, 33
    theoretical, K-AHC, 29

Theory (Language of) (cont.)
  meaning
    connotative, W-PNSS, 47
    denotative, W-PNSS, 47
    surplus, W-PNSS, 46-47
  ostensively defined events, W-PNSS, 44
  perception, as illustration, W-PNSS, 48-50
    awareness and behavior, WW-P, 78ff
    empirical construct, W-PNSS, 48ff
    logical status of, WW-P, 3
    nonperceptual behavior, W-PNSS, 48
    perceptual behavior, W-PNSS, 48-50
    theory, W-PNSS, 49; WW-P, 91
    relation to other concepts in psychology, WW-P, 21-22
    subjective experience, W-PNSS, 48-49ff
    theoretical construct, W-PNSS, 49ff; WW-P, 2, 76ff
  positivism, W-PNSS, 12, 15-16, 33, 46
    logical, W-PNSS, 12, 33, 46
  postulate, H-QP, 18
    psychological and physical, H-QP, 18
  prediction, M-HD, 8; K-AHC, 48
  real world, W-PNSS, 43; WW-P, 1
  scores, H-BS, 41-43, 62
    raw, H-BS, 41-42
    standardized, H-BS, 41-43, 62
    values, H-BS, 41
  stimulus, W-PNSS, 48
  variable types, W-PNSS, 45
    assessment, W-PNSS, 40, 54
    dependent, W-PNSS, 45
    hypothetical, K-AHC, 32, 44, 93, 100; W-PNSS, 48, 55
    independent, W-PNSS, 45
    intervening, BV-MSA, 4; W-PNSS, 45-46, 55
      defined, BV-MSA, 4
      Hull, BV-MSA, 4
      Tolman, BV-MSA, 5
    manipulable, W-PNSS, 39-40
    predictor, K-AHC, 97, 99
    theoretical, W-PNSS, 46

§6 MOTIVATION AND EMOTION

Achievement Incentive System,
  BV-MSA, 56-64
  aspiration, level of, BV-MSA, 57-58
    defined, BV-MSA, 57
    goal discrepancy, BV-MSA, 57
    social influence on, BV-MSA, 57-58
    Zeigarnik phenomenon, BV-MSA, 62
  available responses, BV-MSA, 62-64
    among Jews and Italian Catholics, BV-MSA, 63-64
    cautiousness, BV-MSA, 63
    competence, BV-MSA, 62-63
    sense of effectiveness, BV-MSA, 63-64
    sexual identity, BV-MSA, 64
  consummatory value, BV-MSA, 61-62
    feeling of completion, BV-MSA
    psychological difficulty, BV-MSA, 61
    Zeigarnik phenomenon, BV-MSA; M-CP, 23-34
  incentives, BV-MSA, 20-22, 31, 56-60
    absolute standards, BV-MSA, 56-57
    vs. cooperation, BV-MSA, 59-60
    defined, BV-MSA, 56
    independence, BV-MSA, 58, 82
    internal goals, BV-MSA, 56
    level of aspiration, BV-MSA, 57-58
    negative type, BV-MSA, 59-60
    public recognition, BV-MSA, 56-57
    vocational success, BV-MSA, 58-59
  motive, BV-MSA, 29-31, 60-61
    in different groups, BV-MSA, 61
    in predicting behavior, BV-MSA, 60
    stability of, BV-MSA, 61
    and vocational activity, BV-MSA, 60

Action
  determinants of
    conscious, BV-MSA, 3
    unconscious, BV-MSA, 3
  hedonism, BV-MSA, 3
  Hull, BV-MSA, 3-4
  Lewin, BV-MSA, 3
  pain (minimizing), BV-MSA, 3
  pleasure (maximizing), BV-MSA, 3
  principles of, BV-MSA, 2-4

Activity
  alternative, BV-MSA, 12-14

Activity (cont.)
assumptions about, BV-MSA, 1
consummatory, BV-MSA, 1-2, 9-11
availability, BV-MSA, 9
expectancy, BV-MSA, 9
incentive, BV-MSA, 9, 22-23
instinct, BV-MSA, 9-10
motive, BV-MSA, 9-10
response, B-NP, 138, 152
value, BV-MSA, 9, 33-35
achievement, BV-MSA, 61-62
affiliation, BV-MSA, 67-68
aggression, BV-MSA, 74-75
curiosity, BV-MSA, 54
defined, BV-MSA, 9
incentive, BV-MSA, 33-35
independence, BV-MSA, 82
power, BV-MSA, 79
resting, BV-MSA, 48
sensory, BV-MSA, 48-49
copulation, B-NP, 152
drinking, B-NP, 138
eating, B-NP, 138
ejaculation, B-NP, 152
escape from pain, B-NP, 138
hex maze, BV-MSA, 12-13
instrumental, BV-MSA, 1-2, 4-9, 11
intensity of, BV-MSA, 1, 20-21, 33-36
maternal care, B-NP, 152
motivational response, B-NP, 152
ongoing, BV-MSA, 12-14, 23
persistence, BV-MSA, 1, 10, 13-14, 26, 36
selection of, BV-MSA, 1, 18-19, 23-24, 36
sexual behavior, B-NP, 139
shifts in, BV-MSA, 11-14
social behavior, B-NP, 139, 154
Affiliative Incentive System, BV-MSA, 64-70; Z-SP, 6
available responses, BV-MSA, 69-70
empathy, BV-MSA, 69
maturity, BV-MSA, 70
sympathy, BV-MSA, 69-70
conformity, BV-MSA
and affiliation, BV-MSA, 67
pressures for, BV-MSA, 82
consummatory value, BV-MSA, 67-68
self-perception and, BV-MSA, 68
stability of friendship and, BV-MSA, 68
friendship, stability of, BV-MSA, 68
marriage and, BV-MSA, 68

Affiliative Incentive System (cont.)
functional autonomy, BV-MSA, 65
incentive, BV-MSA, 64-66
attraction to similarity, BV-MSA, 66
cognitive ambiguity and, BV-MSA, 65
defined, BV-MSA, 65
fear of rejection, BV-MSA, 66
independence, BV-MSA, 81
physical contact, BV-MSA, 64-65
sensory, BV-MSA, 65
social isolation and, BV-MSA, 66
to love, BV-MSA, 66
motive, BV-MSA, 66-67
conformity, BV-MSA, 67
measured, BV-MSA, 66
related to behavior, BV-MSA, 67
self, BV-MSA, 65, 68
sympathy, BV-MSA, 69-70

Aggressive Incentive System, B-PD, 3-6, 8-9, 11-13, 17, 24, 34-36, 40-41, 61; BV-MSA, 70-76; M-HD, 49-57; Z-SP, 6
conflict
of aggressive incentives, BV-MSA, 71-72
displacement, BV-MSA, 72-73
consummatory value, BV-MSA, 74-75
catharsis and, BV-MSA, 74-75
depression
and aggression, BV-MSA, 73
dominance, Z-SP, 79-80
imitation of physical aggression, BV-MSA, 76
incentive, BV-MSA, 70-73
defined, BV-MSA, 70
displacement of, BV-MSA, 72
frustration of, BV-MSA, 71
negative type of, BV-MSA, 71
instrumental, M-HD, 50-51
motive, BV-MSA, 73-74
as resentment, BV-MSA, 74
constitutional differences and, BV-MSA, 74
physical vs. verbal responses, BV-MSA, 75-76
resentment, BV-MSA, 74
self and displaced aggression, BV-MSA, 73

Arousal, WW-P, 92; Z-SP, 13-15, 52
curiosity, WW-P, 92
novelty, WW-P, 92
optimal, WW-P, 92
presence of others, Z-SP, 13-15

Arousal (cont.)
surprisingness, WW-P, 92
Availability, BV-MSA, 5-7
achievement responses, BV-MSA, 62-64
affiliative response, BV-MSA, 69-70
aggressive responses, BV-MSA, 75-76
curiosity responses, BV-MSA, 54-55
defined, BV-MSA, 6
goals, BV-MSA
habit, BV-MSA
incentive system, BV-MSA, 42
independent responses, BV-MSA, 82-83
power responses, BV-MSA, 79-80
sensory responses, BV-MSA, 49
Curiosity Incentive System, B-NP, 139; BV-MSA, 50-55; M-HD, 31
available responses, BV-MSA, 54
consummatory value and the, BV-MSA, 35, 54
exploratory behavior, B-NP, 139
independence and the, BV-MSA, 82
motive, BV-MSA, 53-54
and basic disposition, BV-MSA, 53
and individual differences, BV-MSA, 53-54
and intelligence, BV-MSA, 54
Drive, B-NP, 138-139, 149, 151-152; B-PD, 3-4; BV-MSA, 4-5, 35-40; M-HD, 43; W-CL, 36-37, 41, 47, 60-61
acquired, W-CL, 47ff
aim, B-PD, 3-4
antecedent conditions, BV-MSA, 4, 36-40
anxiety, BV-MSA, 28, 47
biological, B-NP, 134
constitutional differences, BV-MSA, 47
deprivation, BV-MSA, 4-5, 37-40
demand, BV-MSA, 5
food, B-NP, 152
sensory goals, BV-MSA, 43
drive-habit (D-H) distinction, W-CL, 36, 60-61
fear, BV-MSA, 36
hunger, B-NP, 118, 134, 138-139, 147; M-HD, 44
individual differences, BV-MSA, 47
intensity, B-PD, 3-4
level, BV-MAS, 47
performance, W-CL, 36ff
Yerkes-Dodson Law, W-CL, 37

Drive (cont.)
noxious stimuli, B-NP, 138
electric shock, B-NP, 155
pain (escape from), B-NP, 138
reduction, B-NP, 152
source, B-PD, 3-4
state, B-NP, 139
strength and learning, W-CL, 41
stress, B-NP, 154
thirst, B-PD, 134, 138, 146
use of term, B-PD, 4

Emotions
adaptive value, B-NP, 139
aggression, B-NP, 139-140, 148, 150, 153-155
anxiety, B-PD, 30-34, 42-44
attack, B-NP, 139-140, 147, 155
autonomic reactions, B-NP, 140
behavior, B-NP, 139, 155
blood flow, B-NP, 139-140
development of, M-HD, 46-49, 61-62
disturbances, B-NP, 153
emotional states, B-NP, 140
evaluative aspects, B-NP, 140, 155
experience of, B-NP, 139
exuberance, B-NP, 139
fear, B-NP, 139, 153-154; B-PD, 8-9, 30, 63-64; BV-MSA, 24-25, 36; WW-P, 84ff
fleeing, B-NP, 139-140
hate, B-NP, 139
heart rate, B-NP, 139-140, 142
integration, B-NP, 140
joy, B-NP, 139
language development, M-HD, 48-49
learning, M-HD, 46-49
playfulness, B-NP, 139
predator, B-NP, 140
reactions, B-NP, 139-140
respiration, B-NP, 139-140, 142
response, B-NP, 140, 154
sadness, B-NP, 140
snarling, B-NP, 139
S-R, M-HD, 47-48
submission, B-NP, 139
sweating, B-NP, 139, 143
threat, B-NP, 139-140, 154
withdrawal, B-NP, 139

Goals, BV-MSA, 2
availability, BV-MSA, 6
-directed activities, B-NP, 139; BV-MSA, 2

Goals (cont.)
Tolman, BV-MSA, 5
elation effect, BV-MSA, 18, 23
gradients, BV-MSA, 72-73
incentive, BV-MSA, 14, 17-22

Incentive (General) (See also *Achievement, Affiliative, Aggressive, Curiosity, Independence, Negative, Power, Sensory,* and *Sex*), BV-MSA, 5, 7-8, 14-28
achievement, BV-MSA, 56-60
affiliative, BV-MSA, 64-66
aggressive, BV-MSA, 70-71
consummatory value of, BV-MSA, 33-35
curiosity, BV-MSA, 50-53
defined, BV-MSA, 7
expectancy, BV-MSA, 5, 7, 20-21
defined, BV-MSA, 7
and incentive, BV-MSA, 20-21
goals and, BV-MSA, 14
goal magnitude and, BV-MSA, 17-22
independence, BV-MSA, 58, 80-81
latent learning and, BV-MSA, 15-17
measurement of, BV-MSA, 8
motive and, BV-MSA, 8, 31
negative, BV-MSA, 7-8, 22-28, 31, 44-46
positive, BV-MSA, 7-8, 15-22, 31
power, BV-MSA, 76-78
regression and, BV-MSA, 26-28
sensory, BV-MSA, 42-46
system, BV-MSA
availability, BV-MSA, 42
conflict of, BV-MSA, 55
defined, BV-MSA, 41
developmental tasks and, BV-MSA, 42
instincts and, BV-MSA, 41

Independence Incentive System, BV-MSA, 80-83
availability, BV-MSA, 82
available responses, BV-MSA, 82-83
sex role and, BV-MSA, 83
test anxiety and, BV-MSA, 83
confidence in one's effectiveness, BV-MSA, 83
consummatory value, BV-MSA, 82
dependence, BV-MSA, 81
goal attainment, BV-MSA, 80
incentive, BV-MSA, 80-81
achievement, BV-MSA, 58, 80

Independence Incentive System (cont.)
affiliative, BV-MSA, 80
power, BV-MSA
motive, BV-MSA, 81-82
measured, BV-MSA, 81-82
to participate in decisions, BV-MSA, 82
negative affiliation, BV-MSA, 81
pressures for conformity, BV-MSA, 82

Motivation (See also §4), B-NP, 34, 138-139, 146, 152, 155, 157; BV-MSA, 1, 5, 8-10, 28-32; FP-HP, 18-19, 26-41, 147; M-HD, 43-46 passim; WW-P, 84ff; Z-SP, 14-15, 51
achievement, BV-MSA, 60-61
affiliation, BV-MSA, 66-67
aggression, BV-MSA, 73-74
alertness loss, FP-HP, 37-41
anxiety, BV-MSA, 28, 30; FP-HP, 37
cognitive dissonance, M-CP, 102-103; Z-SP, 6
conflict, Z-SP, 53
conventionalized, Z-SP, 81
dominance, Z-SP, 79-80
frustration tolerance, M-HD, 27-28
incentive systems, BV-MSA, 55
curiosity, BV-MSA, 53-54
defined, BV-MSA, 8
delayed feedback, M-CP, 10
domain of, BV-MSA, 1, 10
fatigue, FP-HP, 37-41
feedback, FP-HP, 28
hex maze, BV-MSA, 31-32
hypothesis, of par, FP-HP, 26-27
improvement, FP, HP, 33
incentive, BV-MSA, 8, 31
independence, BV-MSA, 81-82
memory, M-CP, 30
needs, B-PD, 3, 50
perceptual selection, WW-P, 84ff
achievement, WW-P, 87, 90
affiliation, WW-P, 86-90
appetitive, WW-P, 84
conflict, WW-P, 88, 90
performance, FP-HP, 18-19, 26-27
physiological factors, M-HD, 43-44, 47-48
autonomic responses, B-NP, 138-140
body heat, B-NP, 138, 143
loss of, B-NP, 143
constriction of blood vessels, B-NP, 138

Motivation (cont.)
food regulation, B-NP, 138
homeostasis, B-NP, 138
homeostatic imbalance, B-NP, 139
hypothalamic control of, B-NP,
142-152
hypothalamic mechanisms, B-NP,
139
hypothalamic stimulation, B-NP,
152
nutritional needs, B-NP, 138
self stimulation, B-NP, 151-152
temperature regulation, B-NP, 138
tissue need, B-NP, 139
water regulation, B-NP, 138, 147
power, BV-MSA, 78-79
problem solving, M-CP, 97-98, 100
process, B-NP, 142-152
repression, M-CP, 30-32, 34
sensory, BV-MSA, 42-46
social
coaction effects, Z-SP, 16, 24-25, 48
drinking, Z-SP, 25
eating, Z-SP, 25
stress tolerance, Z-SP, 16, 24, 48
interdependence, Z-SP, 52
system, B-NP, 155
TAT, as measure, BV-MSA, 28-30
theory, BV-MSA, 2
tracking tasks, FP-HP, 38, 117-119
vigilance tasks, FP-HP, 37-39, 147
Negative Incentives, BV-MSA, 22-25
anxiety, B-PD, 30-34, 42-44; BV-MSA,
28, 30, 47
test of, BV-MSA, 60, 63, 83
depression, effect of, BV-MSA, 17, 23
fear, B-NP, 139, 153-154; B-PD, 8-9,
30, 63-64; BV-MSA, 24-25, 36;
WW-P, 81ff
drive, BV-MSA, 36
frustration, BV-MSA
aggression, BV-MSA, 71; M-HD, 51
extinction, BV-MSA, 25
tolerance, B-PD, 4, 8-9
pain
escape from, B-NP, 138
minimizing, BV-MSA, 3
noxious stimuli, B-NP, 138, 155
threat, B-NP, 139-140, 154
Power Incentive System, B-PD, 14, 18,
BV-MSA, 76-80
available responses, BV-MSA, 79-80
types of influence, BV-MSA, 79-80

Power Incentive System (cont.)
consummatory value, BV-MSA, 79
dominance, Z-SP, 93
conflict, Z-SP, 79-80
incentive, BV-MSA, 76-78
affiliative, BV-MSA, 81
defined, BV-MSA, 77
negative, BV-MSA, 77-78
inferiority, BV-MSA, 76
motive, BV-MSA, 78-79
measured, BV-MSA, 78
origins of, BV-MSA, 78-79
related to behavior, BV-MSA, 78
Sensory Incentive System, BV-MSA,
42-50
available responses, BV-MSA, 49
consummatory value, BV-MSA, 48-49
incentive, BV-MSA, 42-46
affiliative, BV-MSA, 65
bodily responses, BV-MSA, 43-44
negative, BV-MSA, 44-46
sexual behavior, BV-MSA, 43-44
motive, BV-MSA, 44, 47-48
and drive level, BV-MSA, 47
and libido, BV-MSA, 47
and sex, BV-MSA, 47
and survival, BV-MSA, 49-50
stimulation
aesthetics, BV-MSA, 53
change, BV-MSA, 52-53
and curiosity, BV-MSA, 51-53
optimal level of, BV-MSA, 48, 53
spontaneous alternation, BV-MSA,
51-53
stimulus hunger, B-PD, 7
Sex
achievement, BV-MSA, 59
copulation, B-NP, 152
drive (impulse), B-PD, 3-6, 10-13,
34-35, 37, 40, 49
ejaculation, B-NP, 152
female, B-NP, 153
identity, BV-MSA, 64
independence, BV-MSA, 83
mate, B-NP, 153
motivation, BV-MSA, 43-44, 47-48
motive, BV-MSA, 47-48
sexual behavior, B-NP, 139, 149-150,
152, 155
Sleep, B-NP, 118-136
activity, B-NP, 119
cognitive, B-NP, 118

Sleep (cont.)
adult, B-NP, 135
alertness, B-NP, 118-119, 123, 126
arousal, B-NP, 119, 122-123, 127, 131, 135
attention, B-NP, 118
awakening, B-NP, 122, 131
threshold of, B-NP, 131
body functions, B-NP, 118
circling, B-NP, 127
comatose, B-NP, 133
common mechanism of, B-NP, 130
consciousness, B-NP, 118-119
curling up, B-NP, 127
cycles, B-NP, 134
activity, B-NP, 118
biological, B-NP, 118
celestial, B-NP, 118
day-night, B-NP, 118
wakefulness, B-NP, 118-120, 127,
129-134
daydreaming, B-NP, 119
depth of, B-NP, 119
digestion, B-NP, 118
dreaming, B-NP, 127-135; B-PD, 2, 19,
36, 40, 56-59, 63
content, B-NP, 134
deprivation, B-NP, 134-135
irritability, B-NP, 134
psychotic-like behavior, B-NP, 134
restlessness, B-NP, 134
energy conservation, B-NP, 118, 135
exhaustion, B-NP, 135
fatigue, B-NP, 118
inhibitory mechanism of, B-NP,
127-130
deafferentiation of the cortex, B-NP,
127
diminution of stimulation, B-NP, 127
excitation, B-NP, 127
medulla, B-NP, 127-130
thalamic reticular system, B-NP, 127
metabolic activity, B-NP, 118
motor integration, B-NP, 118
nocturnal animals, B-NP, 118
paradoxical sleep, B-NP, 130-135
neurochemical mechanism, B-NP,
133
relaxation, B-NP, 135
rest, B-NP, 119
sensory stimulation, B-NP, 119-121
sleepwalking, B-PD, 63
theories of, B-NP, 134-135

Sleep (cont.)
wakefulness, B-NP, 118-120, 127,
129-131, 134
yawning, B-NP, 127
Tendency, BV-MSA, 1
defined, BV-MSA, 1
determinants of, BV-MSA, 4-10, 14-40
Hull, BV-MSA, 4-5
Tolman, BV-MSA, 5
negative, BV-MSA, 7, 24
positive, BV-MSA, 7, 24
principle of action, BV-MSA, 2-3

§7   NEUROPSYCHOLOGY

Anatomy (Non-neural)
ankle, B-NP, 104
anterior pituitary, B-NP, 149-150
anterior pituitary-gonadal system,
B-NP, 150
arm, B-NP, 98, 113
arteries, B-NP, 129, 142
back, B-NP, 100
bladder, B-NP, 141, 144
blood, B-NP, 144
blood vessels, B-NP, 2, 10, 15
body, B-NP, 98, 102, 104, 107-108, 113,
137-138
body organs, B-NP, 142
bones, B-NP, 10
bronchioles, B-NP, 140, 142
cells, glandular, B-NP, 149
effector, B-NP, 10, 15, 25, 27-30,
137-138, 140-142
organs, M-HD, 13
esophagus, B-NP, 146
esophageal fistula, B-NP, 146, 149
eye, B-NP, 110
face, B-NP, 113
feet, B-NP, 166
finger, B-NP, 114
glands, B-NP, 10, 29, 138
adrenal, B-NP, 138-140
endocrine, B-NP, 141
gonads, B-NP, 149

Anatomy (Non-neural) (cont.)
  mammary, B-NP, 151
  pancreas, B-NP, 141
  pituitary, B-NP, 138
  salivary, B-NP, 141
  secretion, B-NP, 10
 hand, B-NP, 113-114
 head, B-NP, 107-108
 heart, B-NP, 10, 137, 141-142
 hips, B-NP, 98-99, 104
 inner ear, B-NP, 99
 kidney, B-NP, 137, 144, 146
 kidney tubules, B-NP, 144
 knee, B-NP, 104
 large intestines, B-NP, 141
 leg, B-NP, 104, 113
 limbs, B-NP, 102-105, 112, 117
  hind, B-NP, 104
 lungs, B-NP, 140, 142, 144
 mouth, B-NP, 114, 146, 153, 156; B-PD,
  4, 12, 25, 63
 muscles, B-NP, 2-3, 10, 14, 30, 98-99,
  101, 103-104, 110, 113-114, 135, 140
  ankle flexor, B-NP, 105
  antagonist, B-NP, 100, 102-103, 105
  cardiac, B-NP, 10-11
  extensor, B-NP, 100, 102, 104-105
  eye, B-NP, 30
  facial, B-NP, 169
  fibers, B-NP, 10-11, 103-104
  flexor, B-NP, 7, 101-102
  quadriceps, B-NP, 101
  receptors, B-NP, 99
  skeletal, B-NP, 10, 131, 142
  smooth, B-NP, 10-11, 29
  spindle, B-NP, 101-103
  striped, B-NP, 10-11, 29
  synergist, B-NP, 100, 114
 neck, B-NP, 108
 paw, B-NP, 100, 165
 posterior pituitary, B-NP, 144-145
 saddle region, B-NP, 100
 scalp, B-NP, 119, 126
 sexual organs, B-NP, 149-150
 shoulders, B-NP, 98
 skin, B-NP, 10, 27, 29, 104-105, 114
 small intestine, B-NP, 141
 stomach, B-NP, 110, 141, 148
 tendon, B-NP, 101, 103
 throat, B-NP, 146
 trunk, B-NP, 98, 113-114
 uterus, B-NP, 149-150
 vascular portal system, B-NP, 150

Anatomy (Non-neural) (cont.)
 vein, B-NP, 145
 vertebra, B-NP, 27
 visceral organ, B-NP, 28-29
Animals
 bats, B-NP, 58
 bird, African village weaverbird
  (textor cucullatus), B-NP, 59
 bird song, B-NP, 58
 bug, B-NP, 51
 carnivores, B-NP, 86, 148
 cat, B-NP, 38, 47, 50, 52, 84-85, 87-88,
  94, 96, 107, 118, 121, 124-125, 127,
  129, 131, 133, 143, 147, 150,
  163-165, 168, 172-173
  female, B-NP, 150
  kitten, B-NP, 38
  retina, B-NP, 50
  tongue, B-NP, 87-88, 94, 96
 dog, B-NP, 6, 107, 146, 156
  footpad, 100, 104
 fish, B-NP, 38, 47
  goldfish, B-NP, 178
 frog, B-NP, 47, 49, 51, 88-89
 goat, B-NP, 146
 guinea pigs, B-NP, 91
 hamsters, B-NP, 93
 human, B-NP, 107, 111-112, 116,
  118-119, 126, 131, 133
  patients, B-NP, 111-112, 117, 162
 insect, B-NP, 51
 interspecies comparisons, B-NP, 86-87
 mammals, B-NP, 35, 92, 134, 151-152
 monkey, B-NP, 35, 55, 64, 77, 81-82,
  110, 114, 126, 152, 154-155,
  160-162, 170
 mouse, B-NP, 178
 patients, B-NP, 111-112, 117, 162
 porpoises, B-NP, 58, 86
 primates, B-NP, 86
 rabbits, B-NP, 39, 90
 rats, B-NP, 93, 139, 144, 151, 155,
  161-162, 177-178
 rodents, B-NP, 86
 snakes, B-NP, 153
 vertebrates, B-NP, 152
 whales, B-NP, 86
Behavior Relevant to Neuropsychology
 abduction, B-NP, 100
 adaptation, B-NP, 137, 139-140
 adduction, B-NP, 100
 adjustment, B-NP, 100
 alertness, B-NP, 157

Behavior Relevant to
  Neuropsychology (cont.)
anticipation of movement, B-NP, 114
approach reaction, B-NP, 112
arousal, B-NP, 112
athetosis, B-NP, 112
avoidance, B-NP, 155
avoidance movements, B-NP, 114
avoidance reaction, B-NP, 112
awake, B-NP, 166, 169
balance, B-NP, 98-99
beg for food, B-NP, 156
behavioral abnormalities, B-NP, 122
body movements, B-NP, 108
body posture, B-NP, 110
body support, B-NP, 107
chewing, B-NP, 2-3
chorea, B-NP, 112
circling, B-NP, 127
cognitive functions, B-NP, 37
conditioned avoidance response,
  B-NP, 114
contraction, B-NP, 101-103, 105
coordination, B-NP, 98, 103, 109, 117
copulatory behavior, B-NP, 151
curling up, B-NP, 127
deactivation, B-NP, 173
discrimination learning, B-NP, 111
dominance, B-NP, 154-155
dominance hierarchy, B-NP, 154
  boss, B-NP, 154
  lowest man on totem pole,
    B-NP, 154
dreaming, B-NP, 1
eating, B-NP, 147, 149
emotional behavior, B-NP, 35, 139,
  155
excitation, B-NP, 172
exertion of effort, B-NP, 140
extension, B-NP, 98, 104
eye movements, B-NP, 114
facilitation, B-NP, 110-112
feeding, B-NP, 147-148
  efferent control of, B-NP, 148
feeding, hypothalamic regulation of,
  B-NP, 147-149
ferocity, B-NP, 154
flex, B-NP, 98
flexion, B-NP, 98, 104
food-directed response, B-NP, 155
food intake, B-NP, 3
food preferences, B-NP, 2
gesture, B-NP, 154

Behavior Relevant to
  Neuropsychology (cont.)
goal-directed movements, B-NP, 114
gymnastics, B-NP, 98-99
hunger, B-NP, 1
hyperkinesis, B-NP, 112
inactivation, B-NP, 172
ingestion of water, B-NP, 146
inhibition, B-NP, 110
initiating movement, B-NP, 57
integration, B-NP, 98
  spatial, B-NP, 98, 103-104
  temporal, B-NP, 98
intellectual functions, B-NP, 37
intention, B-NP, 112
leap, B-NP, 107
learned response, B-NP, 146
learning, B-NP, 5
lengthening reaction, B-NP, 103
limb withdrawal, B-NP, 6-7
memory, B-NP, 5
motivational, B-NP, 5
motor activity, B-NP, 110
motor response, B-NP, 116
motor skills, B-NP, 5
movement, B-NP, 35, 118, 146
  skilled, B-NP, 135
movement, hierarchial organization of,
  B-NP, 98
movement patterns, B-NP, 100
movements, B-NP, 31, 98-101, 104,
  108-113, 116-117
muscle tension, B-NP, 99, 172
muscular inhibition, B-NP, 133
obstinate progression, B-NP, 111
oral behavior, B-NP, 153-155
orienting, B-NP, 111
panting, B-NP, 143
parallel bars, B-NP, 98
Parkinson's disease, B-NP, 112
past experience, B-NP, 151
pedaling a bicycle, B-NP, 98
performance, B-NP, 98-99, 101,
  110-111
performance of skilled movements,
  B-NP, 117
pilomotor response, M-HD, 45
postural adjustment, B-NP, 98, 101,
  103-104, 108, 110, 112
postural reaction, B-NP, 108
posture, B-NP, 35
postures, B-NP, 98-99, 102, 104, 107,
  110-112

Behavior Relevant to
  Neuropsychology (cont.)
  preferences, B-NP, 147
  problem solving, B-NP, 2-3
  reaching out, B-NP, 99
  release, B-NP, 112
  release phenomena, B-NP, 155
  respiration, B-NP, 172
  response, B-NP, 156
  riding a bicycle, B-NP, 156
  right, B-NP, 107
  rotation of joints, B-NP, 99
  salivation, B-NP, 156
  sexual activity, B-NP, 151, 153, 154
  sexual behavior, B-NP, 151
    female, B-NP, 151
    male, B-NP, 151
  sexual receptivity, B-NP, 150
    to males, B-NP, 150
  sham feeding, B-NP, 149
  shivering, B-NP, 143-144
  shortening, B-NP, 103
  skilled movements, B-NP, 114
  sleep, B-NP, 1, 4, 31, 34, 111-112
  social position, B-NP, 155
  social response, B-NP, 154
  somersault, B-NP, 98-99
  somnolence, B-NP, 111
  spontaneous movements, B-NP, 116
    loss of, B-NP, 111
  stalk(ing behavior), B-NP, 147
  stand, B-NP, 104, 107, 110
  startle response, B-NP, 155
  submission, B-NP, 154
  suppression, B-NP, 111, 172
  swallowing, B-NP, 2, 3
  sympathetic activation, B-NP, 172
  tameness, B-NP, 154
  thinking, B-NP, 2
  thoughts, B-NP, 2, 126
  timing, B-NP, 98, 117
  tremor, B-NP, 112, 117
  vicious, B-NP, 155
  vocalization, B-NP, 154
  voluntary movement, B-NP, 111
  wakefulness, B-NP, 157, 112
  waking, B-NP, 4, 34
  walking, B-NP, 3, 99, 107-108
  withdrawal movements, B-NP, 104, 112
  yawning, B-NP, 127
Cortices
  anterior, B-NP, 162
  association, B-NP, 158, 161
    posterior, B-NP, 161

Cortices (cont.)
  auditory, B-NP, 63, 66-67, 70, 132, 167
  cerebral, B-NP, 31, 35-37, 81, 94,
    111-113, 115-116, 119-123, 125-127,
    129-131, 143, 151-152, 159-160,
    163, 165, 169-171, 173
  cingulate, B-NP, 153
  frontal, B-NP, 111-112, 161-162
  motor, B-NP, 6-7, 83, 113-117, 158-159,
    165, 173
  parietal, B-NP, 112
  posterior, B-NP, 161
  prepyriform (prepiriform), B-NP, 87,
    90, 153
  prestriate, B-NP, 55-56
  receptor area, B-NP, 81-85,
    158-159
  somatosensory, B-NP, 80, 82-83, 165
    overlap, B-NP, 81
    second somatosensory, B-NP, 84
  striate, B-NP, 53-54, 56
  tactile projection, B-NP, 94
  taste area, B-NP, 95
  temporal, B-NP, 56, 112
  visual, B-NP, 38, 52, 159, 169

General Properties of Cells, B-NP, 7-8
  cell irritability, B-NP, 8
  cell membrane, B-NP, 8
  chromosomes, B-NP, 8
  heredity, B-NP, 8
  metabolism, B-NP, 8
  nucleus, B-NP, 8
  protoplasm, B-NP, 8
  reproduction, B-NP, 8

Lobes
  frontal, B-NP, 35, 86, 112, 114, 157,
    162
  lobe, B-NP, 31, 35, 115
    lobule, B-NP, 115
  occipital, B-NP, 35, 53, 169
  parietal, B-NP, 35, 83, 85
  temporal, B-NP, 35, 55, 69, 152

Mechanisms
  central, B-NP, 94-96
  cerebral motor, B-NP, 116
  common of sleep and waking, B-NP,
    130
  comparator, B-NP, 168
  emotion, B-NP, 139-155
  encephalization, M-HD, 5
  homeostatic, B-NP, 137, 138, 140, 142,
    144-145, 148; ALW-SP, 124,
    130-133, 142-144

Mechanisms (cont.)
hypothalamic, B-NP, 139
inhibitory, B-NP, 127
inhibitory of slow-wave sleep, B-NP, 127
thalamic reticular system, B-NP, 127
the medulla, B-NP, 127-130
internal regulation, B-NP, 137-155
motivation, B-NP, 137-155
motor, B-NP, 158
neural mechanisms of sleep and dreaming, B-NP, 127-135
neurochemical, B-NP, 133
neurophysiological of paradoxical sleep, 130-135
reflex of the brain stem, B-NP, 107-110
reflex of the higher brain stem, B-NP, 107-109
reflex of the medulla, B-NP, 107
respiratory, B-NP, 137
reticular, B-NP, 174
sleep and wakefulness, B-NP, 118-136
spinal motor, B-NP, 109
wakefulness and arousal, B-NP, 119-127

Methods of
ablation, B-NP, 4, 90, 158, 165
brain damage, M-CP, 42-43
cortical damage, B-NP, 151
decortication, B-NP, 132-133
electrical recording, B-NP, 4, 47, 158, 166, 172
electrical stimulation, B-NP, 5, 111, 113-114, 116, 121-124, 127, 129-130, 133, 146-147, 149, 151-152
reticular, B-NP, 131
electrodes, B-NP, 122
recording, B-NP, 61
electroencephalogram (EEG), B-NP, 119-127, 130-133
activation, B-NP, 119-123, 126-127, 133-135
cortical excitability, B-NP, 119
cortical rhythm, B-NP, 119
deep sleep, B-NP, 119
desynchronization, B-NP, 119-120, 122, 132-133
electrical activity, B-NP, 131
electrical discharge, B-NP, 123
electrical recording, B-NP, 134
electrical stimulation, B-NP, 121-124, 127, 129-130, 133

Methods of (cont.)
fast, low amplitude waves, B-NP, 119
fast waves, B-NP, 131
high voltage waves, B-NP, 119
light sleep, B-NP, 119
slow waves, B-NP, 120, 127, 130, 133-135
spindle, B-NP, 119, 131, 133
spindle burst, B-NP, 129
spontaneous discharge, B-NP, 130
electrographic recording, B-NP, 167
EMG, B-NP, 132
recording electrode, B-NP, 131
eye muscle, B-NP, 131
evoked potentials, B-NP, 124, 126
amplitude, B-NP, 124, 126
general anesthesia, B-NP, 111
lesion, B-NP, 96, 111-112, 129, 133
medullar transection, B-NP, 107
microelectrodes, B-NP, 47, 53, 61, 93-94
microscope, B-NP, 157
neurosurgery, B-NP, 83
lesions, B-NP, 82-83, 85
prefrontal lobotomy, B-NP, 86
other methods, B-NP, 5
reflex stimulation, B-NP, 116
self-stimulation, B-NP, 151-152
spinal transection, B-NP, 101
split-brain technique, B-NP, 163-165
surgery, B-NP, 122, 153
transection, B-NP, 120, 129, 131

Nerve Cells (Fibers and Neurons)
afferent, B-NP, 92, 100, 101, 106, 103-106, 123, 130, 165
afferent to ARAS, B-NP, 123, 130
ascending reticular, B-NP, 123
autonomic afferent, B-NP, 142
bipolar, B-NP, 87
cells, B-NP, 53-54, 125-126; M-HD, 5-6
complex, B-NP, 53-54
ganglion, B-NP, 125, 126
hypercomplex, B-NP, 54
organizer, M-HD, 5-6
simple, B-NP, 53-54
corticospinal, B-NP, 113
cutaneous afferents, B-NP, 115
dorsal root, B-NP, 30
efferent, B-NP, 38, 61, 69, 103, 144, 165
efferent signals, B-NP, 117

Nerve Cells (Fibers and Neurons) (cont.)
electrophysiology of, B-NP, 93
exteroceptive, B-NP, 117
fiber, B-NP
afferent, B-NP, 79
axon, B-NP, 76-77
cold, B-NP, 77-79
mechanicoreceptor, B-NP, 77
mylinated, B-NP, 74, 77
pain, B-NP, 79
physiological response of afferent,
B-NP, 76-79, 84
somatic, B-NP, 76, 83
tactile, B-NP, 79
unmyelinated, B-NP, 77, 79
warm, B-NP, 77-79
gamma efferent, B-NP, 102, 110, 116
interneuron, B-NP, 106-107
internuncial, B-NP, 30, 100, 102, 103
lemniscal, B-NP, 79-80
motoneurons, B-NP, 101, 103-105,
108, 110, 116, 128
gamma, B-NP, 103, 110

motor, B-NP, 30, 106

muscle spindle afferents, B-NP, 101, 110

nerve, B-NP, 25, 64, 75, 101, 108, 144,
olfactory, B-NP, 88-89
optic, B-NP, 163
parasympathetic, B-NP, 142
peripheral, B-NP, 87
proprioceptive, B-NP, 115, 116, 117
neuroglia, B-NP, 15
neuron, B-NP, 10-14
axon, B-NP, 12-14, 17, 20-21, 45, 89
axon hillock, B-NP, 12
cell body, B-NP, 10, 12, 25
cell membrane, B-NP, 12-13
classes of, B-NP
afferent, B-NP, 14
bipolar, B-NP, 11
cortical, B-NP, 14
definition of, B-NP, 10-14
internuncial, B-NP, 14
monopolar, B-NP, 11
motor, B-NP, 12-14
multipolar, B-NP, 12
sensory, B-NP, 14
dendrites, B-NP, 12-14
general characteristics, B-NP, 10-14
myelin, B-NP, 12-13
neurilemma, B-NP, 13
neuro-effector junction, B-NP, 11

Nerve Cells (Fibers and Neurons) (cont.)
node of Ranvier, B-NP, 12-13, 19
nucleus, B-NP, 10, 13, 25, 31, 35
protoplasm, B-NP, 10
soma, B-NP, 10-11, 13-14
telodendria, B-NP, 12-13
proprioceptive afferents, B-NP, 115
reafference, B-NP, 117
reafferent, B-NP, 99-100
reafferent signals, B-NP, 117
sensory, B-NP, 130
somatic, B-NP, 142
somatosensory to ARAS, B-NP, 123
taste, B-NP, 93-96
tracts, B-NP, 30, 34
transverse (of pons), B-NP, 31, 32
(undesignated), B-NP, 113-114,
115, 121
ventral root, B-NP, 30-32
vestibular, B-NP, 177
vestibular afferents, B-NP, 115
vestibulospinal, B-NP, 108

Nerve Impulse, B-NP, 15-21, 23, 38, 48,
53, 59, 61, 64, 77, 81, 88, 94, 96,
101-102, 143, 148, 157-158, 174, 177
absolute refractory period, B-NP, 17
afterpotential, B-NP, 17-18
all-or-none principle, B-NP, 15
amplitude of response, B-NP, 76
conduction speed, B-NP, 15
electrical potential, B-NP, 16
excitability, B-NP, 17
fiber diameter, B-NP, 17
membrane, B-NP, 15, 19
refractory period, B-NP, 64
relative refractory period, B-NP, 17
spike potential, B-NP, 17-19
subnormal period, B-NP, 17
supernormal period, B-NP, 17
transmission of, B-NP, 17-20
action potential, B-NP, 17, 43, 47
chloride, B-NP, 18
ions, B-NP, 17-18
membrane permeability, B-NP, 18-19
metabolism, B-NP, 18
molecules, B-NP, 17
neuron membrane, B-NP, 17-18, 23
potassium, B-NP, 18
resting potential, B-NP, 18-19
saltatory, B-NP, 19
sink, B-NP, 18-19
sodium, B-NP, 18

Nerve Impulse (cont.)
  sodium ion, B-NP, 18-19
  source, B-NP, 18

Neurophysiology
  action potential, B-NP, 63, 75-77, 89
  activation, B-NP, 111, 119, 123, 127,
    134-135
  adaptiveness, B-NP, 100
  adjustment, B-NP, 100
  adrenocortical activity, Z-SP, 14
    and presence of others, Z-SP, 14
  afferent messages, B-NP, 158
  afterdischarge, B-NP, 107
  arousal, B-NP, 84, 90, 95, 151
  associative linkage, B-NP,
  auditory information transmission,
    B-NP, 70
  barbiturate, B-NP, 129
  basic neural processes, B-NP, 6-24
  bilateral representation, B-NP, 114
  brain waves, B-NP, 70, 168
  characteristic frequency, B-NP, 64, 66
  coding, B-NP
    frequency, B-NP, 58, 61, 64-66
    hierarchical, B-NP, 69
    intensity, B-NP, 58-64
    tonal patterns, B-NP, 58
  conduction, B-NP, 110
  convergence, B-NP, 79, 81, 171
  cortical modulation of reticular
    activity, B-NP, 126-127
  divergence, B-NP, 79
  efferent, B-NP
    discharge, B-NP, 57
    processes, B-NP, 56
  efferent control (auditory information),
    B-NP, 69-70
    processes, B-NP, 69
  electrical, B-NP
    activity, B-NP, 83
    recording, B-NP, 84
    stimulation, B-NP, 83-85
  electrical activity, B-NP, 89, 168
  electrical activity of the brain, B-NP, 4
  electrical discharge, B-NP, 123
  excitability, B-NP, 126-127
  excitation, B-NP, 148-149
  facilitation, B-NP, 128, 135
  feedback, B-NP, 7, 39, 151
    negative, B-NP, 126-127, 151
  feedback mechanisms, B-NP, 69-70, 83
  filtering, B-NP, 39

Neurophysiology (cont.)
  frequency, B-NP
    analysis, B-NP, 66
    following, B-NP, 64
    tuning, B-NP, 64, 66
  frequency code, B-NP, 46
  frequency following, B-NP, 79
  hierarchical coding, B-NP, 55
  hierarchical organization, B-NP, 109
  hydrocortisone, Z-SP, 14
    and presence of others, Z-SP, 14
  generator potential, B-NP, 38
  inhibition, B-NP, 68-70, 102, 110
    inhibitory surrounds, B-NP, 81-82
  integration, B-NP, 144
  intensity (reflex), B-NP, 104
  internuncial process, B-NP, 6
  load, B-NP, 103
  membrane depolarization, B-NP, 61
  modulation, B-NP, 116, 155
  molar responses, B-NP, 6
  molecular responses, B-NP, 6
  negative sign, B-NP, 114
  off-response, B-NP, 49
  on-response, B-NP, 49
  paradoxical discharge, B-NP, 77-78
  priming, B-NP, 110
  priming, function, B-NP, 99
  positive symptoms, B-NP, 112
  reafference, B-NP, 51
  receptive field, B-NP, 49-50, 53, 55
    complex, B-NP, 53, 55
  reticular control of attention, B-NP, 126
  reticular control of sensory
    transmission, B-NP, 126
  self-regulation, B-NP, 101
  sensitivity, B-NP, 103
  sensory information, B-NP, 123, 138,
    151, 158
  sensory transmission and attention,
    B-NP, 126
    reticular control of, B-NP, 126
  slow waves, B-NP, 173
  spatial code, B-NP, 81
  spatial coding, B-NP, 48-51
  spatial integration, B-NP, 3
  spatial patterning, B-NP, 104
  spatial representation, B-NP, 113-114
  spontaneous discharge, B-NP, 51, 130
  stages of neural control, B-NP, 6-7
  suppression, B-NP, 148, 150, 155
  synaptic growth, B-NP, 158
  temporal integration, B-NP, 3, 116

Neurophysiology (cont.)
  temporal lobe syndrome, B-NP, 153
  temporal patterning, B-NP, 104
  theta rhythms, B-NP, 172-173
  transmission of visual information,
    B-NP, 56
Nuclei
  brainstem, B-NP, 142
  caudate, B-NP, 33, 36, 109, 111-112,
    127
  centrum medianum (thalamus), B-NP,
    171
  cerebellar, B-NP, 115
  cranial nerve, B-NP, 34, 113
  eye muscle, B-NP, 108
  lateral geniculate, B-NP, 48, 52-56,
    124, 167
  mammillary, B-NP, 150
  medial geniculate, B-NP, 63, 66-67
  midline, B-NP, 33
  motor, B-NP, 113
  nucleus, B-NP, 115
  paraventricular, B-NP, 145
  pontile, B-NP, 31-32
  of pons, B-NP, 115
  posterolateral ventral, B-NP, 80, 95
  preoptic, B-NP, 129
  red, B-NP, 109-110, 33-34
  sensory, B-NP, 38
  septal, B-NP, 87
  sixth (VI) nerve, B-NP, 32
  solitarious, B-NP, 94-95
  subcortical, B-NP, 83
  supraoptic, B-NP, 145
  thalamic, B-NP, 37, 115, 121
    specific, B-NP, 123
    unspecific, B-NP, 123
  third (III) nerve, B-NP, 33
  ventralis anterior (thalamus), B-NP, 171
  vestibular, B-NP, 108, 115, 177
Pathways (Tracts)
  afferent, B-NP, 31-32, 34, 37, 109
  auditory, B-NP, 123
  auditory to ARAS, B-NP, 123
  central somatic, B-NP, 79-86
  centrifugal, B-NP, 39
  cerebro-cerebellar, B-NP, 116
  circuits, B-NP, 99-102, 104-105, 117
  corticopontile, B-NP, 32-33
  corticospinal, B-NP, 32-33
  cortifugal, B-NP, 70
  efferent, B-NP, 31, 37, 56, 83, 94, 111,
    115, 125-126, 146

Pathways (Tracts) (cont.)
  extrapyramidal, B-NP, 116
  fiber, B-NP, 152
  hypothalamico-hypophysial, B-NP, 145
  mammillothalamic, B-NP, 153
  neural, B-NP, 133
  nucleus, B-NP, 34
  olfactory, B-NP, 87, 90
  optic, B-NP, 33, 41, 48, 51-53
  sensory, 126, 158
  solitary, B-NP, 130
  somatosensory, B-NP, 123
  specific sensory, B-NP, 122
  spinocerebellar, B-NP, 116
  spinothalamic, B-NP, 84
  visual, B-NP, 166-167
    central visual, B-NP, 51-56, 166-167
Peripheral Nervous System, B-NP, 27-30
  afferent fibers, B-NP, 6, 25, 27-29, 34
  autonomic nervous system, B-NP, 29
  central canal, B-NP, 29
  cranial nerves (and spinal), B-NP, 27,
    30-31, 121, 141
    abducens (VI), B-NP, 30
    accessory (XI), B-NP, 30
    facial (VII), B-NP, 30, 32, 95, 141
    glossopharyngeal (IX), B-NP, 30, 95,
      141
    hypoglossal (XII), B-NP, 30, 32
    oculomotor (III), B-NP, 30, 141
    olfactory (I), B-NP, 30
    optic (II), B-NP, 30, 125
    stato-acoustic (vestibular) (VIII),
      B-NP, 30, 60-61, 65, 108
    trigeminal (V), B-NP, 30, 125
    trochlear (IV), B-NP, 30
    vagus (X), B-NP, 30, 32, 95, 141
  dorsal root, B-NP, 27-29, 79
    ganglion, B-NP, 25, 27, 29
  efferent fibers, B-NP, 7, 11, 25, 27-30,
    34, 39
  nerves, B-NP, 2, 10-12, 15-18, 20, 25, 27
  sense organs, B-NP, 29
  somatic fibers, B-NP, 29
  visceral fibers, B-NP, 29
Physiology (Non-neural)
  activation, B-NP, 142
  adrenocorticotropic hormone (ACTH),
    B-NP, 151
  antidiuretic hormone (ADH), B-NP,
    144-146
  autonomic reactions, B-NP, 140
  blood flow, B-NP, 139, 140

Physiology (Non-neural) (cont.)
blood plasma, B-NP, 27
blood pressure, B-NP, 31
blood stream, B-NP, 137, 140-144, 148
blood supply, B-NP, 146
bodily reactions, B-NP, 141
body activity, B-NP, 144
body needs, B-NP, 138
body state, B-NP, 137
body temperature, B-NP, 137, 142-144
breakdown of foodstuffs, B-NP, 137
carbon dioxide, B-NP, 142
castration, B-NP, 149, 151
cell membrane, B-NP, 145
cellular metabolism, B-NP, 137
CNS biochemistry, B-NP, 5
    DNA, M-HD, 11-12
conservation of energy, B-NP, 142
constriction of peripheral vessels,
    B-NP, 144
contraction (muscular), B-NP, 10
dehydration, B-NP, 137-138, 145-146
development, B-NP, 149
diabetes insipidus, B-NP, 145
diet, B-NP, 147
digestion, B-NP, 140, 142
drinking, B-NP, 146, 152
ejection of milk, B-NP, 151
elimination, B-NP, 142
emotional response, B-NP, 140
endocrines, B-NP, 138
endocrines and internal regulation,
    B-NP, 138
energy, B-NP, 140
epinephrine, B-NP, 141
estrogen, B-NP, 150-151
evaporàtion, B-NP, 137
exertion of effort, B-NP, 140
feedback (neuro-hormonal), B-NP,
137, 142, 150
    negative, B-NP, 150
fluid intake, B-NP, 145
fluid reabsorption, B-NP, 145
food, B-NP, 137, 139, 148, 151, 153
food intake, B-NP, 147-148
food regulation, B-NP, 138
fuel, B-NP, 137
galvanic skin response (GSR), B-PD,
43-44, 51-52, 55; M-HD, 48
general circulation, B-NP, 145
glucose (blood stream), B-NP, 148
gonadal hormones, B-NP, 149-151

Physiology (Non-neural) (cont.)
gonadotrophic hormones, B-NP,
    149-150
gonadotrophins, B-NP, 149-150
growth, B-NP, 149
    biological factors in, M-HD, 10-20,
    41, 43-44, 50-51, 59
heart rate, B-NP, 139-140, 142
heat, B-NP, 143
heating, B-NP, 143
heat loss, B-NP, 143
heat production, B-NP, 144
homeostasis, B-NP, 137; B-PD, 4;
    M-HD, 44, 46
homeostasis and motivation, B-NP,
    138
homeostatic balance, B-NP, 138, 142
homeostatic imbalance, B-NP, 139
homeostatic reaction, B-NP, 142
homeostatic regulation, B-NP, 138
hormones, B-NP, 138, 141, 144-145, 151
hunger, B-NP, 138, 139, 147
hypertonic saline, B-NP, 146
ingestion, B-NP, 137
internal regulation, B-NP, 138
lactation, B-NP, 151
male sex hormone, B-NP, 149
meal, B-NP, 147
metabolic needs, B-NP, 147
metabolic processes, B-NP, 5, 137
non-food, B-NP, 153
nutritional needs, B-NP, 138
osmotic pressure, B-NP, 145-146
ovulation, B-NP, 149-150
oxygen, B-NP, 137, 140, 142
oxytoxin, B-NP, 151
pituitary hormones, B-NP, 151
    hypothalamic control of, B-NP, 151
progesterone, B-NP, 149-150
reflex, B-NP, 29
regulation of water loss, B-NP, 146
respiration, B-NP, 31, 131, 139-140, 142
respiratory mechanisms, B-NP, 137
saccharine, B-NP, 152
satiation, B-NP, 147
self-regulation, B-NP, 137, 142, 151
sexual functions, B-NP, 138, 149-151
stress, B-NP, 138, 151
sweating, B-NP, 139, 143
sympathetic reactions, B-NP, 142
temperature regulation, B-NP, 138,
    142-144, 146-147

Physiology (Non-neural) (cont.)
thermal probe, B-NP, 143
thermostat, B-NP, 142
thirst, B-NP, 138, 146
tissue need, B-NP, 139
vegetative functions, B-NP, 137
wakefulness, B-NP, 31
water, B-NP, 137
water balance, B-NP, 138, 144-146
water concentration, B-NP, 145-146
water intake, B-NP, 144, 146
water loss, B-NP, 144-146
water regulation, B-NP, 138, 147
Reflex
afterdischarge, B-NP, 107
arc, concept of, B-NP, 158-160
autonomic, B-NP, 142
response, B-NP, 143-144
center, B-NP, 146
circuit, B-NP, 101, 158, 163
cortical, B-NP, 161
feeding, B-NP, 148
flexion, B-NP, 1, 100-105
general features of, B-NP, 99-101
knee jerk, B-NP, 101
locomotion, B-NP, 101, 104, 107, 110-111
mechanisms of, B-NP, 107-110
brain stem, B-NP, 107-110
medulla, B-NP, 107
higher brain stem, B-NP, 107-109
monosynaptic, B-NP, 101
neural control of, B-NP, 99-107
righting, B-NP, 107, 110
scratch, B-NP, 100, 101, 105
spinal, B-NP, 101, 104, 109
dynamic properties of, B-NP, 104-107
stepping, B-NP, 104, 107
stretch, B-NP, 101-103, 110
withdrawal, B-NP, 100, 101, 103
Structures
amygdala, B-NP, 36, 87, 90, 154-155
anterior commissure, B-NP, 87, 89
autonomic nervous system (ANS),
B-NP, 138-141
internal regulation, B-NP, 140-142
parasympathetic, B-NP, 142
sympathetic, B-NP, 142
basal ganglia, B-NP, 35-36, 111-114
brain, B-NP, 3-6, 25-30, 34, 38-39, 45,
51, 55, 58, 69, 71, 84, 101, 108,
112, 132, 135, 138, 140, 143, 145-156,
163, 168, 177-178

Structures (cont.)
brain stem, B-NP, 25, 27, 29, 31, 34-35,
56, 67, 70, 84, 86, 94, 99, 107, 109,
111, 113, 115, 117, 120-123, 125-126,
129, 138, 140, 142, 144, 165, 172
central fissure, B-NP, 35, 113
central nervous system (CNS), B-NP,
2-7, 14, 27, 30-39, 64, 79, 98-99,
137-138, 140, 145, 147, 159, 169;
M-HD, 4, 5, 13
development of, B-NP, 25-27
cerebellar vermis, B-NP, 67
cerebellum, B-NP, 14, 31-32, 35, 108,
115-117, 153
cerebral aqueduct, B-NP, 33
cerebral hemisphere, B-NP, 27, 31-32,
34-36, 52-53, 86, 111, 115, 163, 165
cerebral peduncle, B-NP, 33, 113
cerebrospinal fluid, B-NP, 27
cerebrum, B-NP, 14, 115
claustrum, B-NP, 36
corpus callosum, B-NP, 32-33, 37, 153,
163-165
diencephalon, B-NP, 33-34, 86, 111,
131, 152
dorsal column, B-NP, 79
epithalamus, B-NP, 34
extrapyramidal (structures), B-NP, 113
fissures, B-NP, 31, 35
forebrain, B-NP, 25, 31, 34-35, 86,
89-90, 123, 151-152
fornix, B-NP, 32-33, 36, 153
ganglion, B-NP, 140, 142
globus pallidus, B-NP, 36, 109, 111
hindbrain, B-NP, 25, 31
hippocampus, B-NP, 87, 132, 153, 155,
167, 172-174
hypothalamus, B-NP, 32-35, 87, 122,
138-141, 143-144, 147-149, 151,
153, 155
anterior, B-NP, 142-152
lateral, B-NP, 147-152
medial, B-NP, 147-149
posterior, B-NP, 144, 149-150
inferior colliculus, B-NP, 32, 34, 64,
66-67
inferior olive, B-NP, 32
insula, B-NP, 36, 94-96
internal capsule, B-NP, 33, 36
lateral lemniscus, B-NP, 32, 67
limbic, B-NP, 154-155
mammillary body, B-NP, 33

Structures (cont.)
  medial lemniscus, B-NP, 32-33, 80,
    94-95
  medulla, B-NP, 27, 31-32, 80, 84, 86,
    95, 120, 122, 131
  mesencephalon, B-NP, 31-32, 34, 121
  midbrain, B-NP, 25, 31, 52, 80, 84, 86,
    95, 120, 122, 131
  neural tube, B-NP, 25-27, 31
  neuroglia, B-NP, 15
  olfactory bulb, B-NP, 87, 89-90
  olfactory tubercle, B-NP, 87, 90
  optic chiasm, B-NP, 36, 163-165
  pineal body, B-NP, 1, 32, 34
  pituitary, B-NP, 32, 34
  pons, B-NP, 31-32, 80, 129, 131, 133
  precentral gyrus, B-NP, 113-114
  putamen, B-NP, 36, 109, 112
  pyramid, B-NP, 113
  reticular formation, B-NP, 31-34, 56,
    67, 84, 109-112, 121, 125-126, 157,
    166-167, 171-173
    ascending, B-NP, 110, 112
      projections, B-NP, 123-126
    descending, B-NP, 109-110
    mesencephalic, B-NP, 132
    pontile, B-NP, 131-133
    thalamic, B-NP, 123-124
  rhinencephelon, B-NP, 90
  septum, B-NP, 153, 155, 167
  smell brain, B-NP, 90
  spatial representation of body parts,
    B-NP, 81
    bilateral representation, B-NP, 84
    topographical projections, B-NP,
      89-90
  spinal cord, B-NP, 6, 25, 27, 29-31,
    34-35, 79, 84, 98-99, 101, 103-104,
    107-108, 113, 120, 140-142, 144, 158
    cervical, B-NP, 80
    lumbar, B-NP, 80
    sacral, B-NP, 80
    thoracic, B-NP, 80
  spinal gray matter, B-NP, 29-30, 84
  subarachnoid space, B-NP, 27
  subcortical, B-NP, 165-166, 170-171
  substantia nigra, 33-34, 109, 112
  subthalamus, B-NP, 33-34
  sulcus, B-NP, 35
  superior colliculus, B-NP, 32-34, 52, 56
  superior olive, B-NP, 67-68
  sylvian fissure, B-NP, 35

Structures (cont.)
  tectum, B-NP, 34, 52
  tegmentum, B-NP, 34, 153
  telencephalon, B-NP, 34
  thalamus, B-NP, 32-35, 52, 80, 84, 86,
    95, 109, 111, 122, 125, 143, 153,
    159, 165, 172
  trapezoidal body, B-NP, 63, 67
  ventricular system, B-NP, 27
    fourth ventricle, B-NP, 27, 32
    lateral ventricle, B-NP, 33, 36
    third ventricle, B-NP, 33-34, 36
  white matter, B-NP, 29-30, 115
Synapse
  acetylcholine, B-NP, 142
  afferent, B-NP, 23
  afferent fibers, B-NP, 21, 38
  axosomatic, B-NP, 13
  chemical transmitters, 20, 22-23,
    141-142
  efferent, B-NP, 23
  excitability, B-NP, 23
  excitatory postsynaptic potentials,
    B-NP, 20, 23
  hyperpolarization, B-NP, 22-23
  inhibition, B-NP, 23, 48, 56
  inhibitory postsynaptic potential,
    B-NP, 22-23
  internuncial, B-NP, 23
  membrane depolarization, B-NP,
    20-22, 43
  membrane potential, B-NP, 22
  multisynaptic networks, B-NP, 123
  neuron membrane, B-NP, 21
  postsynaptic potential, B-NP, 21-22,
    104
  refractory period, B-NP, 21
  summation, B-NP, 21, 23
  synaptic potential, B-NP, 20-23
Systems
  ascending reticular activating system
    (ARAS), B-NP, 109, 121-130
    activation, B-NP, 121-123
    arousal, B-NP, 121-123
    awakening, B-NP, 122
    comatose state, B-NP, 122
    cortical modulation of, B-NP, 126-127
    desynchronization, B-NP, 122
    electrical stimulation, B-NP, 121-124,
      127, 129-131, 133, 135
      frequency code, B-NP, 130
      frequency modulation, B-NP, 130

Systems (cont.)
    high frequency, B-NP, 127, 130
    low frequency, B-NP, 127, 130
    inputs, B-NP, 123
    projections, B-NP, 123-126
    reticular control of attention, B-NP, 126
    reticular control of sensory transmission, B-NP, 126
    reticular formation, B-NP, 121, 125-126
  auditory, B-NP, 34, 81, 115
  autonomic, B-NP, 138-141
    parasympathetic, B-NP, 140-141
    sympathetic, B-NP, 140-141
  component (color code), B-NP, 47
  descending reticular, B-NP, 109-110
  extrapyramidal, B-NP, 109, 114-115
    motor, B-NP, 110-113
  lemniscal, B-NP, 79-86, 165
  limbic, ALW-SP, 10-11; B-NP, 35-36, 95-96, 140, 152-155, 157, 170-172
  medial lemniscal, ALW-SP, 138
  motivational B-NP, 155
  motor, B-NP, 98-117
  nervous, structure of, B-NP, 25-37
  olfactory, B-NP, 152
  opponent (color code), B-NP, 48
  pyramidal, B-NP, 111, 113-115
  reticular, B-NP, 130
  sensory, 38-97, 157
  spinothalamic, B-NP, 84-86
  taste, B-NP, 96
  thalamic reticular, B-NP, 127, 129-130
  visual, B-NP, 34, 69, 81, 115, 168

Attention (cont.)
  selective, B-NP, 126; FP-HP, 55-58
    doctrine of prior entry, FP-HP, 56
  sensory transmission, B-NP, 126
  span, FP-HP, 61-63
Color, WW-P, 52-69
  binocular, WW-P, 67
  brightness, WW-P, 52ff
  circle, WW-P, 53
  complementary, WW-P, 53ff
  constancy, WW-P, 58ff
  contrast, ALW-SP, 44; WW-P, 64-65
    simultaneous, ALW-SP, 44; WW-P, 65
    successive, ALW-SP, 44; WW-P, 64
    adaptation level theory, WW-P, 64
  depth cue, WW-P, 28, 32
  flicker frequency (critical) (cff), ALW-SP, 53; WW-P, 61
  Ganzfeld, WW-P, 64
  hue, ALW-SP, 18-19, 23, WW-P, 52ff
  Land demonstration, WW-P, 66
  mixture
    additive, WW-P, 55ff
    metameric pairs, WW-P, 55
    subtractive, WW-P, 55ff
  Munsell, WW-P, 54
  nonvisual sensory influences, WW-P, 69
  saturation, ALW-SP, 18-19; WW-P, 52ff
    supersaturation, WW-P, 65
  solid, WW-P, 53-54
  stimulus for, WW-P, 52
  subjective, WW-P, 60ff
    Benham's top, WW-P, 61
    colorimetry, WW-P, 60
Complexity, WW-P, 92
  arousal, WW-P, 92
    curiosity, WW-P, 92
    ideal, WW-P, 91
    novelty, WW-P, 92
    optimal, WW-P, 92
    preferred, WW-P, 91
    psychological, WW-P, 92
    stimulus, WW-P, 92
  surprisingness, WW-P, 92
Constancy, WW-P, 38-58
  brightness, ALW-SP, 18-57; WW-P, 56ff
    albedo, WW-P, 57
    penumbra, WW-P, 57
    umbra, WW-P, 57

§8   PERCEPTUAL PROCESSES

Afterimages, WW-P, 39ff, 63-64
  negative, WW-P, 64
  positive, WW-P, 63
  size constancy, WW-P, 39ff
Attention, ALW-SP, 76; B-NP, 52, 70, 96, 118, 126, 157, 172; FP-HP, 55-58, 61-63

Constancy (cont.)
chromatic, WW-P, 58
color, WW-P, 58
object, WW-P, 38
shape, WW-P, 38ff
size, B-PD, 51; WW-P, 38ff
stimulus
distal, WW-P, 38, 56
objective, WW-P, 38
perceived, WW-P, 38
physical, WW-P, 38
proximal, WW-P, 38, 39, 56
afterimage, WW-P, 43
equation for, WW-P, 40
Emmert's law, WW-P, 43

Depth Perception

approach to
artist's, WW-P, 22-23
experimental, WW-P, 33
philosophical, WW-P, 21-22
cues of
binocular, WW-P, 29, 33
color filters, WW-P, 31
crossed and uncrossed images,
WW-P, 31-33
disparity, WW-P, 30, 33-36
head movement parallax, WW-P,
31, 33, 38
movement perspective, WW-P,
32-33
parallax, WW-P, 31, 33, 38
polarized light, WW-P, 31
seeing behind near object, WW-P,
32-33
stereoscope, WW-P, 30
muscular, WW-P, 38
kinesthesia, WW-P, 21
sensations of accommodation,
WW-P, 21, 33
sensations of convergence, WW-P,
21, 33
two-dimensional, WW-P, 23ff
attached shadow, WW-P, 25, 32
blurring, WW-P, 29, 32
cast shadow, WW-P, 25, 32
color, WW-P, 28, 32
filled and unfilled space, WW-P,
28, 32
partial overlap, WW-P, 23, 32
perspective, WW-P, 26-27, 32-33, 38
size, WW-P, 23, 32
texture gradient, WW-P, 23, 32

Figural Aftereffects, WW-P, 46ff
augmenters, WW-P, 49ff
distance paradox, WW-P, 49
FAE, WW-P, 48ff
I-figure, WW-P, 47-48
KAE, WW-P, 48ff
kinesthetic aftereffects, WW-P, 48
reducers, WW-P, 49ff
satiation theory, WW-P, 50
T-figure, WW-P, 47-48

Illusions, WW-P, 45ff
autokinetic effect, WW-P, 91; Z-SP, 88
Delboeuf, WW-P, 49
distorted room, WW-P, 50
Kopfermann cubes, WW-P, 44
moon, WW-P, 42
Müller-Lyer, WW-P, 45-46
oculogravic, WW-P, 72
real world, WW-P, 1
reversible perspective, coaction effects,
Z-SP, 20
Schröder staircase, WW-P, 16
three dimensional, WW-P, 50ff
trapezoidal window, WW-P, 51

Measurement (Threshold)
absolute, WW-P, 77ff
forced choice, WW-P, 77ff
limen, WW-P, 78; H-QP, 26, 71-72
subception, WW-P, 76
subliminal, WW-P, 78
advertising, WW-P, 80
stimuli, WW-P, 92
tachistoscope, WW-P, 47
unconscious, WW-P, 78

Organization, Principles of
acquired vs. innate, WW-P, 17
congenital cataracts, WW-P, 17
optical prism experiments, WW-P, 18
role of experience, WW-P, 17ff
apparent motion, WW-P, 15
figure-ground
distinctions between, WW-P, 11
nonsensory, WW-P, 75
opposition, WW-P, 15
phi phenomenon, WW-P, 15
Prägnanz, law of, WW-P, 12-13
grouping, laws of, WW-P, 13
closure, WW-P, 13, 84
common fate, WW-P, 14
configuration, WW-P, 12
continuation, WW-P, 14-15
familiarity, WW-P, 13

Organization, Principles of (cont.)
    figure, WW-P, 12, 15
    proximity, WW-P, 13, 15-16
    similarity, WW-P, 14, 16
Perception (General), B-NP, 5, 39, 118, 127; H-QP, 22, 29-35, 38, 43, 49-51, 58; M-HD, 14-15, 21-22, 42, 55-56
    awareness and behavior, WW-P, 76ff
    classical, WW-P, 74
    defense (perceptual), B-PD, 51-53
      inhibition, B-PD, 53
      vigilance, B-PD, 51-52
    definition of perception, WW-P, 1
      logical status of, WW-P, 2
      as a construct, WW-P, 69
      meanings of, WW-P, 3
    horizontal-vertical, WW-P, 69
    infantile, B-PD, 7-8
    learning, WW-P, 81
    memory, WW-P, 83
    motivation, WW-P, 84ff
      appetitive, WW-P, 84
      fear, WW-P, 84ff
    penumbra of, WW-P, 75
    personal characteristics, WW-P, 75
    practical problems of, WW-P, 2-3
    real world, WW-P, 1
    relation to other psychological constructs, WW-P, 80
    social behavior, WW-P, 86
    social characteristics, WW-P, 75
Perceptual (Properties)
    categorization, WW-P, 9
    coding, B-NP, 126
    distortion of present stimulus, WW-P, 85
    learning, WW-P, 81ff
    memory, WW-P, 83
      autonomous changes, WW-P, 84
      distortions, WW-P, 83
      normalization, WW-P, 84
      pointing, WW-P, 84
      sharpening, WW-P, 84
    motivation, WW-P, 84ff
      appetitive, WW-P, 84
      conflict situation, WW-P, 88, 90
      fear, WW-P, 84ff
      need for achievement, WW-P, 87, 90
      need for affiliation, WW-P, 86, 90
      need for selection, WW-P, 86
    -motor, FP-HP, 5, 93-122, 147-148
    organization and experience, WW-P, 17ff

Perceptual (Properties) (cont.)
    pattern recognition, FP-HP, 51-55, 59-61
      effects of distortion, FP-HP, 51-55
      rate of search, FP-HP, 59-61
    plasticity, WW-P, 74ff
    processes, FP-HP, 50
    psychophysics, WW-P, 8
    readiness, WW-P, 9
    response, WW-P, 78
    selection and motivation, WW-P, 86
    social behavior, WW-P, 86
Rivalry, WW-P, 23, 33-34
    binocular, WW-P, 23
    contour, WW-P, 33-34
Stimuli, WW-P, 38-39, 56, 79-80, 92
    change detection, FP-HP, 46, 50
    complexity, WW-P, 92
    distal, WW-P, 38, 56
    objective, WW-P, 38
    pacer, WW-P, 92
    perceived, WW-P, 38
    physical, WW-P, 38
    proximal, WW-P, 38-39, 56
    subliminal, WW-P, 80
    unavailability to awareness, WW-P, 79
Theory
    adaptation level, WW-P, 7, 64
    apperception, B-PD, 1
    behavior theory, WW-P, 74
    Gestalt, WW-P, 5, 11-12; M-CP, 26, 81
      psychologists, WW-P, 45, 47, 50, 84
      theory, WW-P, 4, 70
    nativism, WW-P, 4, 17
    neurophysiological, WW-P, 6
      cell assembly, WW-P, 6
      identity, WW-P, 6
      phase sequence, WW-P, 7
      primitive unity, WW-P, 6, 12
    perceptual psychophysics, WW-P, 8
    probabilistic functionalism, WW-P, 8
      functional tradition, WW-P, 8
      representative design, WW-P, 8
    readiness, WW-P, 9
      categorization, WW-P, 9

§9 PERFORMANCE

Feedback, FP-HP, 2-3, 27-33, 73, 116
  augmented, FP-HP, 31-33
  delayed, FP-HP, 3, 31; M-CP, 9-10, 16
    programmed learning, M-CP, 13
  distorted, FP-HP, 28-30
  elimination of, FP-HP, 30-31
  intrinsic, FP-HP, 28-31
  knowledge of results, M-CP, 8-10, 16
  proprioceptive, M-CP, 37, 44, 59-60
  reinforcement effect, FP-HP, 28
Group, Z-SP, 2, 10-28, 99-103, 108
  coordination, Z-SP, 103
  presence of others, Z-SP, 2, 10-29
  vs. individual, Z-SP, 99-103
Information Processing, B-NP, 135;
  FP-HP, 5-6, 124-131
  conservation tasks, FP-HP, 5-6,
    124-136, 132
  creation tasks, FP-HP, 5-6, 130-131
  memory, FP-HP, 133-135
  reading and listening, FP-HP, 136-145
  reduction tasks, FP-HP, 5-6, 126, 130
  single-channel hypothesis, FP-HP,
    131-136
  theory, FP-HP, 85-92, 113
Measurement
  computer languages, FP-HP, 4-5
    programs, FP-HP, 10-11
  input-output relations, FP-HP, 84-85
  judgment
    absolute, FP-HP, 47-50
    comparative, FP-HP, 46-48
  sensory capacities, FP-HP, 43-50
    stimulus comparison, FP-HP, 46-47
    stimulus recognition, FP-HP, 47-50
  signal detection theory, FP-HP, 44-46
    signal to noise ratio, FP-HP, 52
  skills, FP-HP, 83-92
  thresholds, FP-HP, 43, 46
  Weber's law, FP-HP, 46, 113
Memory Processes, FP-HP, 61-72
  attention span, FP-HP, 61-63
  long term memory, FP-HP, 68-70
  sensory storage, FP-HP, 63-65
  serial tasks, FP-HP, 70-72
  short term memory, FP-HP, 65-70
  span, FP-HP, 66
Motivation, FP-HP, 26-41, 147
  alertness, FP-HP, 37-41

Motivation (cont.)
  anxious subjects, FP-HP, 37
  audience effects in, Z-SP, 10-12
    monitoring task, Z-SP, 11-12
    multiplication, Z-SP, 12
    pursuit rotor, Z-SP, 10-11
  coaction effects, Z-SP, 20
    judgment, Z-SP, 20
    multiplication, Z-SP, 20
    vowel cancellation, Z-SP, 20
  fatigue, FP-HP, 37-41
  feedback, FP-HP, 28
  hypothesis of par, FP-HP, 26-27
  improvement, FP-HP, 33
  individual differences, FP-HP, 40-41
  performance, FP-HP, 26-27
  tracking tasks, FP-HP, 38, 117-119
  vigilance tasks, FP-HP, 37-39, 147
Perceptual Processes, FP-HP, 50
  pattern recognition
    effects of distortion, FP-HP, 51-55
    rate of search, FP-HP, 59-61
  perceptual-motor, FP-HP, 4, 93-122,
    147-148
  selective attention, FP-HP, 55-58
    doctrine of prior entry, FP-HP, 56
Reaction Time, FP-HP, 73-75, 93-122
  accuracy of performance, FP-HP,
    109-112
  choice, FP-HP, 97, 104
  continuous tasks, FP-HP, 117-121
  discrete movement tasks, FP-HP,
    113-115
  index of difficulty, FP-HP, 114-115
  movement amplitude, FP-HP, 112-113
  serial tasks, FP-HP, 115-117
  simple, FP-HP, 95-96
  stimulus intensity, FP-HP, 40-41
  stimulus response code compatibility,
    FP-HP, 104-109
  stimulus-response codes, FP-HP, 22-24
  temporal uncertainty, FP-HP, 97-98
Response to Stimuli, FP-HP, 72-82
  precision, FP-HP, 73
  psychological refractory period,
    FP-HP, 80-82
  quantization, FP-HP, 79
  rate of response, FP-HP, 78-79
  reaction time, FP-HP, 73-75
  stimulus repetition, FP-HP, 75-78
  variety, FP-HP, 73
Skill, FP-HP
  association norms, FP-HP, 21

Skill (cont.)
categories of, FP-HP, 3-5
language, FP-HP, 4, 123-145
semantic level, FP-HP, 141ff
set relations, FP-HP, 143
learning, FP-HP, 8-15
early phase, FP-HP, 11-12
final phase, FP-HP, 14-15
habit transfer, FP-HP, 19-20
intermediate phase, FP-HP, 12-14
plateaus, FP-HP, 8-9
practice conditions, FP-HP, 13-14
nature of, FP-HP, 1-3
organization, FP-HP, 9-10
perceptual-motor, FP-HP, 4, 93-122, 147-148
performance
characteristics, FP-HP, 2
effects of practice, FP-HP, 16
improvement, FP-HP, 15-19
limits, FP-HP, 15-19
role of feedback, FP-HP, 2-3
role of motivation, FP-HP, 18-19
population stereotypes, FP-HP, 21
transfer, FP-HP, 19-25
Stimulus
change, detection of, FP-HP, 46-50
events, FP-HP, 83-84
-response codes
compatibility, FP-HP, 21, 25
high performance levels, FP-HP, 106-107
information rate, FP-HP, 107-109
learning, FP-HP, 104-106, 121
-response matrix, FP-HP, 47-48, 89
Stress, FP-HP, 33-37, 146
environmental, FP-HP, 35-36
input overload, FP-HP, 34-35
nature of, FP-HP, 33-34
optimal, FP-HP, 36-37
Yerkes-Dodson law, FP-HP, 36
performance, FP-HP, 27
sensory deprivation, FP-HP, 33, 37

§10   PERSONALITY

Anxiety
fear, B-PD, 8-9, 30, 63-64
free-floating, B-PD, 30
functions, B-PD, 33-34
identification of, B-PD, 32-33, 43
nature of, B-PD, 30
neurotic, B-PD, 30
objective, B-PD, 30
origins, B-PD, 31
physical manifestations, B-PD, 33
predispositions to, B-PD, 31
primary, B-PD, 34
taming of, B-PD, 34
unconscious, B-PD, 32, 42-44
warning signal, B-PD, 34, 36-37
Anxiety (Reactions to), B-PD, 41-42
accidents, B-PD, 42
acts of reparation, B-PD, 42
belated mastery, B-PD, 41
blindness, B-NP, 43-44
hypnotic, B-NP, 43-44
catatonia, B-NP, 40, 62
compartmentalization, B-PD, 37
confession, B-PD, 42
criminal acts, B-PD, 42
daydreaming, B-PD, 36, 56
delusions, B-NP, 40, 54, 60
derivatives, B-PD, 36
encouraging others, B-PD, 42
hallucinations, B-PD, 40, 48-49, 54
humor, B-PD, 42
intimidation of others, B-PD, 42
making light of ominous, B-PD, 42
masochism, B-PD, 42
repetition compulsion, B-PD, 39, 41-42
paranoia, B-PD, 40, 49, 51, 54, 60
seeking atonement, B-PD, 42
seeking reassurance, B-PD, 42
self-destructive behavior, B-PD, 42
slips of speech, B-PD, 36, 64
Cognition in Personality
ideas
association of, B-PD, 55-56
condensation of, B-PD, 3, 56-57, 59
displacement of, B-PD, 3, 57, 59
energy of, B-PD, 3
id as container, B-PD, 5
repression of, B-PD, 35, 42
separation from emotion, B-PD, 36

Cognition in Personality (cont.)
    strength of, B-PD, 1
    warded-off, B-PD, 36
   judgment, B-PD, 9, 50-51
   labeling, B-PD, 9
   symbols
    as equivalents, B-PD, 12
    dream, B-PD, 14, 57-59
    in incorporation, B-PD, 39, 63
    role in thinking, B-PD, 3, 9
   thinking
    disorganization of, B-PD, 54
    in ego development, B-PD, 9
    magical, B-PD, 8-9
    primitive, B-PD, 3
    type, B-PD, 15
   words
    autistic, B-PD, 19
    ego planning, B-PD, 9
    in denial, B-PD, 35
    vs. pictures, B-PD, 3
Consciousness
   hypnosis, B-PD, ix, 6, 43, 49, 58, 62, 65-66, 68, 71
   levels of, B-PD, ix, 1, 4-5
   negative sensations, B-PD, 1
   preconscious, B-PD, ix, 3, 35, 43, 61
   threshold of, B-PD, 1
   unconscious
    anxiety, B-PD, 32, 42-44
    contents of, B-PD, 42
    defenses in, B-PD, 30-47
    inference, B-PD, 2
    influences of, B-PD, 48-71
    mental forces in, B-PD, 1-29
    personal vs. collective, B-PD, 14-15
    vs. preconscious, B-PD, ix, 43-44
    subception, WW-P, 76
    subliminal, WW-P, 78
     advertising, WW-P, 80
     stimuli, WW-P, 92
    "unconscious", WW-P, 78
Freudian Theory, B-PD, 2-13; BV-MSA, 44-46
   aggression, B-PD, 3-6, 8-9, 11-13, 17, 24, 34-36, 40-41, 49, 61
   cathexis, B-PD, 5
   counter cathexis, B-PD, 5, 35-37, 52, 63
   divisions of personality, B-PD, 4-7
    ego, B-PD, 4-5
     alliances, B-PD, 6
     anxiety disruption of, B-PD, 33

Freudian Theory (cont.)
    autonomy, B-PD, 19, 61
    conflict-free sphere, B-PD, 19
    defenses, B-PD, 34-41
    development, B-PD, 7-13
    energy of, B-PD, 5, 37
    functions, B-PD, 5, 19, 48
    ideal, B-PD, 6, 24
    identity, B-PD, 20
    psychology, B-PD, 19-20, 59
    undifferentiated phase, B-PD, 19
   id, B-PD, 4
    container of unconscious ideas, B-PD, 5
    in adolescence, B-PD, 11
    in daydreaming, B-PD, 56
    source of energy, B-PD, 4
    undifferentiated phase, B-PD, 19
   superego, B-PD, 4, 6
    conscience, B-PD, 6, 17-18, 42
    divisions of personality, B-PD, 6
    early formation, B-PD, 9
    guilt, B-PD, 6, 16, 18, 28, 30, 42-43, 49
    heir of Oedipus complex, B-PD, 10
    later development, B-PD, 11, 24-25, 39
   dreams, B-PD, 2, 19, 36, 40, 56-69, 63
   interpretation of, B-PD, 2, 56
   drives, B-PD, 3-4
    aim, B-PD, 3-4
    intensity, B-PD, 3-4
    object, B-PD, 3-4
    source, B-PD, 3-4
    use of term, B-PD, 4
   economic interpretation of unconscious forces, B-PD, 6
   energy (psychic)
    bound, B-PD, 3
    discharge, B-PD, 4
    displacement, B-PD, 6
    economy, B-PD, 6
    of ego, B-PD, 5, 37
    fatigue, B-PD, 6, 63
    fixed quantity, B-PD, 6, 36
    free floating, B-PD, 3
    homeostasis, B-PD, 4
    id as source, B-PD, 4
    of ideas, B-PD, 3
    indirect measurement, B-PD, 4
    investment, B-PD, 5
    neutralized, B-PD, 19, 41, 61

Freudian Theory (cont.)
vs. physical energy, B-PD, 6-7
free association, B-PD, 2, 21, 55-56
frustration tolerance, B-PD, 4, 8-9
gratification
delay, B-PD, 3, 9
development of self, B-PD, 7
homeostasis, B-PD, 4
impulses, B-PD, 4-5, 35-37, 41, 49
libido, B-PD, 5-6, 17, 61; BV-MSA, 47
love, B-PD, 4, 8, 10-13, 18
love choice
anaclitic, B-PD, 24
homosexual, B-PD, 4, 12, 40, 54
needs, B-PD, 3, 50
pleasure, B-PD, 4-5, 7
pleasure principle, B-PD, 2-3, 5, 8, 61
pain (minimizing), B-PD, 5, 7
preconscious, B-PD, ix, 3, 35, 43, 61
primary process, B-PD, 2-3, 5, 9, 40,
54, 57, 59, 61
psychoanalysis, B-PD, 2, 21
psychodynamics, B-PD, ix, 2
psychosexual development, B-PD,
7-13, 23-25
infancy, B-PD, 7-8
ambivalence, B-PD, 8, 10, 13, 24, 37
biting, B-PD, 8
dependency, B-PD, 8, 26
mouth, B-PD, 4, 12, 25, 63
omnipotence, B-PD, 7-8, 11, 39
oral sadistic, B-PD, 8
oral stage, B-PD, 8
passive-receptive mastery, B-PD, 8
perception, B-PD, 7
self-esteem, B-PD, 7, 12
stimulus hunger, B-PD, 7
sucking, B-PD, 8, 20, 40
early childhood, B-PD, 8-10
anal stage, B-PD, 9, 18, 20, 24, 38,
41
beginning of superego formation,
B-PD, 9
mastery, B-PD, 8-9, 41-42
oral stage, B-PD, 10, 11, 13, 14,
17-18, 20, 22, 24-25, 36-39, 59
speech acquisition, B-PD, 9
later childhood and adolescence,
B-PD, 10-12
cultural influences, B-PD, 11
latency period, B-PD, 11, 36
adult character structure, B-PD,
12-13

Freudian Theory (cont.)
adult character, B-PD, 12
fixations, B-PD, 12-13, 25-29, 40-41
reality
principle, B-PD, 3, 5, 8
testing, B-PD, 5-6, 35, 49
secondary process, B-PD, 2-3, 5, 9, 40,
57, 61
sex, B-PD, 3-6, 10-13, 34-35, 37,
40, 49
sexual and aggressive forces, B-PD, 3
sexual regulation, BV-MSA, 46
sleep, B-NP, 135
discharge of drive, B-NP, 134
discharge of impulse, B-NP, 134
safety valve, B-NP, 134
speech, role of, B-PD, 3, 6
tension, B-PD, 4, 7, 9, 31, 63
Trieb, B-PD, 4
wishes
fulfillment, B-PD, 2-3, 7, 9, 34, 49
54, 56
role of, B-PD, 2, 35, 63
Measures (Tests)
abilities and traits, H-QP, 14, 58,
61-65, 67-68
Blacky pictures, B-PD, 23-25, 44-47, 51
E-scale, Z-SP, 46-48
F-scale, Z-SP, 46-48
galvanic skin response (GSR), B-PD,
43-44, 51-52, 55
personality, H-QP, 60-61
assessment, H-QP, 60
dynamics, H-QP, 61
speed and power tests, H-QP, 61
standardized tests, H-QP, 61
tests, H-QP, 61-62, 68
projective techniques, B-PD, 22-23
Rorschach, B-PD, 22-23
Mechanisms of Defense, B-PD, 34-41,
44-47; M-HD, 55-56
avoidance, B-PD, 45
denial, B-PD, 34-36
displacement, B-PD, 38, 57-59
defensive, B-PD, 38
dream, B-PD, 57-58
intellectualization, B-PD, 45
introjection, B-PD, 10, 39
incorporation, B-PD, 8, 20, 39
internalization, B-PD, 9
isolation, B-PD, 36-37, 51
projection, B-PD, 39, 45-46, 49, 54
reaction formation, B-PD, 37-38, 45-46

Mechanisms of Defense (cont.)
  regression, B-PD, 40-41, 45-46, 61
  repression, B-PD, 35-37, 42, 51, 55,
    60, 63-64; BV-MSA, 45-46; M-CP,
    30-32, 34
  suppression, B-PD, 35
  sublimation, B-PD, 41
  undoing, B-PD, 38-39
Personality (General)
  mechanisms
    boredom, BV-MSA, 50
    conversion reaction, B-PD, 62-63
    deprivation, B-PD, 7, 31, 41; M-HD,
      44-45, 59-62 passim
      sleep, B-NP, 134
    fantasy, B-PD, 11, 35-36, 39, 56, 61
    food relationships, M-HD, 44-45
    indulgence, B-PD, 7, 11, 41
    life themes, M-HD, 24-28, 59-62
      passim
    motivation, M-HD, 43-46
    multiple function principle, B-PD,
      64
    overdetermination, B-PD, 64
    perception of personal
      characteristics, WW-P, 75
    sexual identity, M-HD, 31-33, 51-52,
      72
  moral
    development, Z-SP, 49
    judgment, Z-SP, 49-50
  pathological characteristics
    authoritarianism, Z-SP, 45-46
    compulsion, B-PD, 6, 37-39, 42,
      63-64
    depression, BV-MSA, 73
    homosexual object choice, B-PD,
      4, 12, 40, 54
    maladjustment, K-AHC, 65
    mental disorder, K-AHC, 1, 11, 13
    obsession, B-PD, 6, 11, 53-54, 63-64
    phobias, B-PD, 6, 64
      counterphobic attitudes, B-PD, 64
    psychological disorders, M-HD,
      44-46, 59-62
    psychopathology, K-AHC, 30
    psychotic-like behavior, B-NP, 134
    schizophrenia, B-PD, 49, 51, 54,
      60, 62
    psychotherapy, K-AHC, 65
    psychoanalysis, K-AHC, 88, 90
  self, B-PD, 19, 34, 37-38; M-HD,
    45-46, 64-73 passim; Z-SP, 5, 48

Personality (General) (cont.)
  -actualization, B-PD, 34
  -destructive behavior, B-PD, 42
  -esteem, B-PD, 6-8
  -orientation, M-CP, 33
  theories of, K-AHC, 25, 29-30, 48, 67,
    90, 93
    developmental, M-HD, 23-24
    dynamic, M-HD, 24
    organization of personality, K-AHC,
      6, 11
    psychoanalytic, K-AHC, 12, 29
      of sleep, B-NP, 135
    structural analysis of, K-AHC, 90
    types, M-HD, 22-23
Psychoanalytic Viewpoints (Other),
  B-PD, 13-21
  Adler, B-PD, 13-14
    compensation, B-PD, 14
    inferiority, B-PD, 13-14
    life style, B-PD, 14
    masculine protest, B-PD, 14
    overprotection (maternal), B-PD, 13
    power, B-PD, 14
  ego psychologists (Hartmann, Kris,
    Lowenstein), B-PD, 19-20
    autonomous functions, B-PD, 20
    conflict-free, B-PD, 20
    erogenous zones, B-PD, 20
    maturation, B-PD, 19-20
    neutralized energy, B-PD, 20
    undifferentiated phase, B-PD, 20
  Erikson, B-PD, 20-21
    ego identity, B-PD, 20
    eliminative mode, B-PD, 20
    incorporation, B-PD, 20
    intrusive, B-PD, 20
    retentive mode, B-PD, 20
  Fromm, B-PD, 17-18
    authoritarian conscience, B-PD, 17
    character type, B-PD, 18
      exploitative, B-PD, 18
      hoarding, B-PD, 18
      marketing, B-PD, 18
      productive, B-PD, 18
      receptive, B-PD, 18
    humanistic conscience, B-PD, 18
  Horney, B-PD, 17
    aggressive type, B-PD, 17
    compliant type, B-PD, 17
    detached type, B-PD, 17
  Jung, B-PD, 14-16
    anima, B-PD, 15

Psychoanalytic Viewpoints (Other) (cont.)
  animus, B-PD, 15
  archetypes, B-PD, 15
  collective ideals, B-PD, 15
  collective unconscious, B-PD, 14
  complexes, B-PD, 55
  extraversion, B-PD, 15
  feeling type, B-PD, 15
  introversion, B-PD, 15
  intuitive type, B-PD, 15
  persona, B-PD, 15
  racial unconscious, M-HD, 1-2
  sensation type, B-PD, 15
  thinking type, B-PD, 15
Rank, B-PD, 16-17
  average type, B-PD, 16
  birth trauma, B-PD, 16, 31
  counterwill, B-PD, 16
  creative type, B-PD, 16, 18, 61
  neurotic type, B-PD, 16
  separations, B-PD, 16, 31
  will, B-PD, 16
Sullivan, B-PD, 18-19
  consensual validation, B-PD, 19
  empathy, B-PD, 18
  parataxic mode, B-PD, 19
  power motive, B-PD, 19
  prototaxic mode, B-PD, 19
  reflected appraisals, B-PD, 19
  syntaxic mode, B-PD, 19
Unconscious Influences upon
  action, B-PD, 62-66
    bizarre movement, B-PD, 62
    boredom, B-PD, 65-66
    catalepsy, B-PD, 62
    catatonia, B-PD, 62
    chronic fatigue, B-PD, 63
    compulsion, B-PD, 63
    hysterical mutism, B-PD, 62
    hysterical paralysis, B-PD, 62
    obsessive-compulsive reaction,
      B-PD, 63
    psychogenic tic, B-PD, 63
    psychosomatic, B-PD, 63
    sleepwalking, B-PD, 63
    spasms, B-PD, 63
    tremors, B-PD, 63
    voyeurism, B-PD, 49, 63
  perception, B-PD, 48-53
    blindness, B-PD, 43-44, 53
      hypnotic, B-PD, 43-44, 53
      hysterical, B-PD, 48-49, 53
      organic, B-PD, 49

Unconscious Influences Upon (cont.)
      simulated, B-PD, 49
    conversion reaction, B-PD, 49, 62-63
    defense, B-PD, 51-53
    distractibility, B-PD, 48-50
    fainting, B-PD, 48-49
    hallucinations, B-PD, 49
    inhibition, B-PD, 53
    needs and values, B-PD, 50
    resistance, B-PD, 51, 56
    sensory isolation, B-PD, 49
    size constancy, B-PD, 51
      field dependent, B-PD, 51
      field independent, B-PD, 51
    vigilance, B-PD, 51-52
    voyeurism, B-PD, 49, 63
  thought, B-PD, 53-61
    amnesia, B-PD, 54
    association
      controlled, B-PD, 55
      free, B-PD, 2, 21, 55-56
      of ideas, B-PD, 55-56
      principles of, B-PD, 57
    cognitive controls, B-PD, 59-60
      field articulation, B-PD, 60
      leveling-sharpening, B-PD, 59
      scanning, B-PD, 60
      style, B-PD, 59
    disorganization of, B-PD, 54
    dreams
      condensation, B-PD, 56-59
      day residue, B-PD, 56, 59
      displacement, B-PD, 57
      latent content, B-PD, 56, 63
      manifest content, B-PD, 56, 59, 63
      secondary elaboration, B-PD, 57, 61
      secondary process, B-PD, 61
      rapid eye movement, B-PD, 58-59
    forgetting, B-PD, 54-55
    fugue state, B-PD, 54
      multiple personality, B-PD, 54
    ideas
      association, B-PD, 55-56
      condensation of, B-PD, 56-59
      displacement, B-PD, 57, 59
    neologisms, B-PD, 54
    problem solving, B-PD, 60-61
      inspiration, B-PD, 61
    screen memory, B-PD, 55

§11 PSYCHOLOGICAL MEASUREMENT

Differences, H-QP, 9, 73-75; K-AHC, 4-5
  age, K-AHC, 5
  cultural, K-AHC, 4
  individual, H-QP, 60
  of performance, H-QP, 66
  physical, H-QP, 23-24
  physiological, K-AHC, 5
  qualitative, H-QP, 9
  race, K-AHC, 4
  of ratio, H-QP, 11-12
  relative, H-QP, 35-36
  sex, K-AHC, 4
  true, H-QP, 32, 35-36
  utility, H-QP, 48
Measurement, H-QP, 1-76; H-BS, 5-8,
  12-13, 18-19, 40-41; K-AHC, 4
  abstraction, H-QP, 8, 13
  basic operation, H-QP, 4-14, 20
  categorical, H-QP, 6-9, 22-55
  characteristics of subjects, H-QP, 58-76
  continuous, H-BS, 18-19
  derived, H-QP, 14-19, 23-29
  errors of, K-AHC, 39
  events, underlying psychological,
    H-QP, 16-17
  Mental Measurements Yearbook,
    K-AHC, 79
  nominal, H-QP, 7
  numerical, H-QP, 9-14, 20, 22
  and observations, H-QP, 4-6
  operations of, H-QP, 4-14, 20;
    K-AHC, 44
  ordinal, H-QP, 49-54, 71, 73
  physical, H-QP, 1-2, 5-6, 8, 11, 14-19, 74
  precision, K-AHC, 35, 43
  property
    extensive (fundamental), H-QP,
      15-17, 19
    implicit (latent), H-QP, 22
    intensive (derived), H-QP, 15-17, 19
  of psychological entities, H-QP, 1, 21
  psychometrics, H-QP, 23, 58-76 (See
    Scaling); K-AHC, 35, 100
  psychophysics, H-QP, 18-20, 22, 55,
    58, 71, 74; WW-P, 8 (See Scaling)
  pure psychological, H-QP, 29-55
  reliability of, H-QP, 75-76; K-AHC,
    35-43

Measurement (cont.)
  by scaling, H-QP, 22-76
  in science, H-QP, 1-2
  in sensation and perception
    hearing, ALW-SP, 65-101
    perception, WW-P, 76-92
    smell, ALW-SP, 103-113
    taste, ALW-SP, 113-123
    touch and kinesthesis, ALW-SP,
      124-125, 129, 143-144
    vision, ALW-SP, 19, 22-57
  standards, H-QP, 5, 13-14, 17-19, 24-25,
    32-33, 35, 39-40, 44-45, 60-61
  standard error of, K-AHC, 39
  stimulus characteristics, H-QP, 22-55
  stimulus scaling, H-QP, 22-55
    theoretical and empirical basis,
      H-QP, 12, 14-15, 18-20, 22-55, 58,
      64-68, 75-76
  traditional psychological, H-QP, 58
  units of, H-BS, 12-13, 40-41
Scaling, H-QP, 22-76
  attitude, H-QP, 53, 68-74
  attribute, H-QP, 8, 68; K-AHC, 1, 2, 93
  bipolar traits, K-AHC, 20-21
  category (interval), H-QP, 6-13, 16,
    20, 38-45, 48-51, 53-54, 58, 69-72
    boundary, H-QP, 40, 44-45, 53
    classification scheme of, H-QP, 6-8,
      13, 58
    equal-appearing, H-QP, 50-51, 53
    proportion, cumulative, H-QP, 40
  constant, H-QP, 11, 26-28, 58, 71-72
    mathematical, H-QP, 11, 26-28, 71-72
    stimulus (situation), H-QP, 58-59
    subject, H-QP, 58-59
  continuum, K-AHC, 20
  Coombs, C. H., H-QP, 23, 75
  Guilford, J. P., H-QP, 23, 34, 55
  Guttman, L., H-QP, 70, 75
    scalogram analysis, H-QP, 70-71
  interval, H-QP, 10-13, 20, 39, 43-46,
    48-49, 71-72; K-AHC, 21
    equal, K-AHC, 21
  joint, H-QP, 75
  nominal, H-QP, 7-8, 12
  norms, Z-SP, 89-91
    support for, Z-SP, 90
    transmission of, 89-91
  numerical rating, H-QP, 42, 49-55
  ordinal, H-QP, 10, 12, 71, 73
  position, true, H-QP, 30, 43; K-AHC,
    36, 39-40

Scaling (cont.)
  boundary, H-QP, 43
  category, H-QP, 43
  scale, H-QP, 30
  postulates, H-QP, 18
  preference, H-QP, 46-49
  equal, H-QP, 47-49
  psychometrics, H-QP, 23, 58-76;
    K-AHC, 35
  psychophysics, H-QP, 22-55, 58,
    71-74; WW-P, 8
  Fechner, G. T., H-QP, 25-29
    assumptions of, H-QP, 26-27
    method of, H-QP, 25-27
    results of, H-QP, 29
    theory of, H-QP, 28
  just noticeably different (jnd), H-QP,
    24-26
  limen, H-QP, 26, 71-72
  psychological and physical, H-QP,
    18-20, 22-24, 27, 29
  pure, H-QP, 29-55
  sensation, H-QP, 22-23, 25-30,
    71-72
  zero, H-QP, 71
  Stevens, S. S., H-QP, 27-29
    power law, B-NP, 77, 79; H-QP,
      28-29
    results, H-QP, 29
    scaling method of, H-QP, 27-28
    theory, H-QP, 28
  Weber, E. H., H-QP, 24-25, 27
    Weber's law, H-QP, 24-25, 27
  rank order, H-QP, 35-39
  rating, H-QP, 49, 53-54, 62; K-AHC,
    53-54, 63-64, 67, 78
    peer-evaluations, K-AHC, 54, 63-64
    self-evaluation, H-QP, 53-54, 62;
      K-AHC, 64, 67
    score, H-QP, 49
  ratio, H-QP, 11-12, 28-29, 71-73;
    K-AHC, 21
    differences, H-QP, 11-12
    numerical, H-QP, 28
    physical magnitude, H-QP, 28-29
    subjective magnitude, H-QP, 28-29
  successive intervals, H-QP, 39-42, 53,
    65, 69-70
  theoretical and empirical basis, H-QP,
    12, 14-15, 18-20, 22-55, 58, 64-68,
    75-76
  Thurstone, L. L., H-QP, 29-34, 38,
    42-49, 54, 58, 65, 69, 72-73

Scaling (cont.)
  Case V solution, H-QP, 32-33
  comparative judgment, law of,
    H-QP, 30-34, 38, 42-45, 54, 69, 72
  pair comparison, method of, H-QP,
    29-32, 34, 38, 45, 65, 69, 73
    lottery, H-QP, 46-49, 58
  unipolar traits, K-AHC, 20-21
  utility, H-QP, 46-49, 58
    difference, H-QP, 48
    equality of, H-QP, 49
    expected, H-QP, 47
    indifference, H-QP, 47-49
    option, H-QP, 46-49
  value, H-QP, 62 (See Value)
  weighting, H-QP, 62-66, 71; K-AHC,
    76, 78
  zero point, H-QP, 11, 39, 41, 71-72
    absolute, K-AHC, 21
Scores, H-QP, 4, 35-36, 60, 63, 72-73
  error factor of, H-QP, 5-6, 30-31, 66-67
  fallible, K-AHC, 41-42, 79
  intelligence quotient, H-QP, 8, 61
  obtained, H-QP, 66
  rating, H-QP, 49
  z, H-QP, 36, 53
Stimulus, H-QP, 63-66
  characteristic measurement, H-QP,
    22-55
  characteristics, H-QP, 1-30, 33-35, 49,
    53-55, 58-59, 65-67, 75
    physical, H-QP, 14-16, 23-24, 29-30
    psychological, H-QP, 1-20, 22, 26-28,
      30, 33-35, 49, 53-55, 58-59, 65,
      67, 75
  difficulty, H-QP, 64
  discriminating, H-QP, 65
  heterogeneous, H-QP, 65
  highly correlated, H-QP, 65
  homogeneous, H-QP, 63-64
  intensity, H-QP, 24, 27-29, 71-72
    increment, H-QP, 24
    physical, H-QP, 24, 27, 71
  magnitude, H-QP, 28-29, 33, 35, 75
  marker, H-QP, 51-52
  probability, H-QP, 47-48, 71
  -response, H-QP, 19, 23-26, 29, 74
  selection and evaluation of, H-QP,
    65-66
  situation, H-QP, 16, 60, 74
Values, H-QP, 9, 12-13, 30-54, 58-59,
  67-75
  category-boundary, H-QP, 44-45

Values (cont.)
density, H-QP, 41, 53-54
directly interpretable, H-QP, 12
distribution, H-QP, 31
error, H-QP, 30-31
expected, H-QP, 47
idealized, H-QP, 50
interval scale, H-QP, 35-36, 53
invariant, H-QP, 71-72
loading of traits, K-AHC, 21
mean, H-QP, 39-43, 53-54, 67, 72
median, H-QP, 50-52
numbers, H-QP,
    cardinal, H-QP, 12
    concatenation, H-QP, 59
    labeling, H-QP, 9, 12-13
    ordinal, H-QP, 9, 12-13
    physical addition, H-QP, 59
physical, H-QP, 58
rank, relation to, H-QP, 35
scale, H-QP, 32-34, 37-40, 42, 51,
    53-54, 58, 69-70, 73, 75
true, H-QP, 30-31, 39-40, 42, 51, 53-54,
    58, 69-70, 73, 75
utility (personal), H-QP, 46-49
z, H-QP, 32-33, 35, 38, 40-41, 44, 64

§12   SENSORY

GENERAL

Measurement (See also §11)
just noticeable difference (jnd), H-QP,
    24-26
psychophysics, H-QP, 22-55, 58, 71-74
    psychological and physical, H-QP,
        18-20, 22-24, 27, 29
    pure, H-QP, 29-55
Weber's Law, H-QP, 24-25, 27
Psychological Properties
adaptation, ALW-SP, 4-11, 121
sensory
    cells, B-NP, 137
    cues, B-NP, 161
    deprivation, M-HD, 46-47

Psychological Properties (cont.)
discrimination, B-NP, 160-163
feedback, B-NP, 66, 116, 146
    amplifier, B-NP, 116
    error comparator, B-NP, 116-117
    error detector, B-NP, 116
    negative, B-NP, 102, 126-127
    prime mover, B-NP, 116
    sensory, B-NP, 146
function, ALW-SP, 1-11; M-HD,
    13-15
information, B-NP, 25, 30-31, 37-39,
    123, 138, 151
    coding, B-NP, 118, 127
    processing, B-NP, 162
isolation, B-PD, 49
limitations, ALW-SP, 11
messages, B-NP, 171
modality, B-NP, 123
organs, B-NP, 2-3, 39
phylogenetic development, ALW-SP,
    4-11
selectivity, ALW-SP, 1-2, 4-11
sensation, ALW-SP, 4; H-QP, 22-23,
    25-30, 71-72
    mouth, B-PD, 149
    negative, B-PD, 1
    stomach, ALW-SP, 149
    zero, H-QP, 71
sensitivity, ALW-SP, 4-11
signal, B-NP, 137
somatic senses, B-NP, 70
stimulation, B-NP, 120, 122-123, 130
structure, ALW-SP, 1-11
systems, B-NP, 38, 157
Receptors, ALW-SP, 1-3, 6-11; B-NP, 6,
    8, 10, 25, 38-94, 104, 108, 142
electrophysiology of, B-NP, 93
exteroceptors, B-NP, 6, 107
glucose-sensitive cells, B-NP, 148
hypothalamic, B-NP, 148
organs, M-HD, 13
osmoreceptor, B-NP, 145-146
peripheral, B-NP, 144, 146
potential, B-NP, 38, 61, 76, 88, 93
sense organs, B-NP, 29, 38-39
sensitivity, B-NP, 89
sensory, B-NP, 157
    cells, B-NP, 108
specificity, B-NP, 93
Response Systems and Properties
investigation, B-NP, 38
selective attention, B-NP, 39

Response Systems and Properties (cont.)
  sniffing, B-NP, 38
Stimuli
  adequate, B-NP, 100
  classification of, ALW-SP, 3-4
  definition of, ALW-SP, 3-4
  detection, B-NP, 118, 137
  frequency, ALW-SP, 9-11
  input, B-NP, 116
  intensity differences, ALW-SP, 6-11
  temporal summation, ALW-SP, 6-11

BODILY ORIENTATION, ALW-SP, 127-133; B-NP, 70-86

Anatomy (Non-neural)
  structure, ALW-SP, 127-133
    saccule, ALW-SP, 60; B-NP, 108
    semicircular canals, ALW-SP, 60;
      B-NP, 60, 108; WW-P, 71
    utricle, ALW-SP, 60; B-NP, 108
    vestibular organs, B-NP, 107-108
Measurement
  slow rotation room, WW-P, 71
Psychological Properties
  canal sickness, WW-P, 71
  oculogravic illusion, WW-P, 72
  sensation, ALW-SP, 127-133
  spatial orientation, B-NP, 83
  vestibular coriolis reaction, WW-P, 73
Receptors
  function, ALW-SP, 127-133
  vestibular organ, B-NP, 99
Response Systems and Properties
  ataxia, B-NP, 117
  disequilibrium, B-NP, 117
  postural reactions, B-NP, 107
Stimuli
  angular acceleration of head, B-NP, 99
  body movements, B-NP, 108
  gravity, B-NP, 99, 102, 108
  linear acceleration of the head, B-NP,
    108
    deceleration, B-NP, 99
  position of head, B-NP, 99
  rotary acceleration of the head, B-NP,
    108
  vestibular stimulation, B-NP, 117

HEARING, ALW-SP, 65-101; B-NP, 58-69

Anatomy (Non-neural), ALW-SP, 85-100;
  B-NP, 58-69
  area vasicularis, B-NP, 60
  basilar membrane, ALW-SP, 88;
    B-NP, 60-65
  cochlea, ALW-SP, 85; B-NP, 60-61,
    67, 69, 108
  cochlear duct, B-NP, 60-61
  columella, ALW-SP, 90
  ears, B-NP, 58, 66-69
  endolymphatic fluid, B-NP, 61
  eustachian tube, ALW-SP, 85
  external ear, B-NP, 60
  external meatus, B-NP, 59-60
  external spiral sulcus, B-NP, 60
  head, B-NP, 66, 83
  incus, ALW-SP, 85; B-NP, 60
  inner ear, ALW-SP, 86; B-NP, 60
  lever action, B-NP, 60
  malleus, ALW-SP, 74, 85; B-NP, 60
  middle ear, B-NP, 59-60
    muscle, B-NP, 69
    ossicles, B-NP, 69
  organ of Corti, ALW-SP, 86
  ossicles, ALW-SP, 69; B-NP, 59-60, 69
  oval window, ALW-SP, 85; B-NP, 60-61
  petrous bone, ALW-SP, 86
  reticular lamina, B-NP, 60
  round window, ALW-SP, 85; B-NP, 60
  scala tympani, B-NP, 60
  scala vestibuli, B-NP, 60
  semicircular canals, ALW-SP, 85;
    B-NP, 60
  spiral ligament, B-NP, 60
  stapedius, ALW-SP, 86
  stapes, ALW-SP, 85; B-NP, 60, 62
  tectorial membrane, ALW-SP, 88;
    B-NP, 60-61
  tensor tympani, ALW-SP, 86
  tympanic membrane, ALW-SP, 69, 73,
    85; B-NP, 59-60
  vestibular membrane, B-NP, 60

Measurement
  discrimination, B-NP, 58, 160
    of temporal patterns, B-NP, 69
  free field method, ALW-SP, 77
  sensitivity, ALW-SP, 65, 72-78, 99
  threshold, ALW-SP, 67, 74-76, 82

Measurement (cont.)
    difference limen (DL), ALW-SP,
      83, 100
    increment, ALW-SP, 67, 82
    intensity, ALW-SP, 67, 82
    just noticeable difference (jnd),
      ALW-SP, 82, 84
Psychological Properties
    attention, ALW-SP, 76
    audition, B-NP, 58
    auditory information, B-NP, 70
    auditory stimuli, B-NP, 123
    chord, B-NP, 69
    combination tones, ALW-SP, 81
    consonance, ALW-SP, 67, 81
    cultural effects, ALW-SP, 79-80
    diplacusis, ALW-SP, 72
    dissonance, ALW-SP, 67, 81
    equal loudness contours, ALW-SP, 79
    expectation, ALW-SP, 76
    frequency discrimination, B-NP, 69
    isomorphic contours, ALW-SP, 78
    just noticeable difference (jnd),
      ALW-SP, 82
    loudness, ALW-SP, 73, 79; B-NP, 58
    motivation, ALW-SP, 76
    noise, ALW-SP, 71, 81
      white, M-HD, 15
    perceptual aspects, ALW-SP, 71-79
      of auditory space, B-NP, 69
    phon, ALW-SP, 78-79
    phonemes, B-NP, 69
    pitch, ALW-SP, 71-72, 81, 84; B-NP, 58
    qualitative composition, ALW-SP,
      66-67
    selection of auditory information,
      B-NP, 65
    sensation, ALW-SP, 65, 75-76
      level (SL), ALW-SP, 75-76
    signals of, B-NP, 58
      food, B-NP, 58
      predator, B-NP, 58
      prey, B-NP, 58
    sound localization, ALW-SP, 99-101;
      B-NP, 66-70
    sounds, B-NP, 3, 58, 61, 70, 172-173
    timbre, ALW-SP, 66-67, 79, 81-85;
      B-NP, 61, 64, 69
    tonal pattern analysis, B-NP, 69-70
    tones, ALW-SP, 66-67, 79, 81-85;
      B-NP, 61, 64, 69, 169-170
      pure, B-NP, 58, 66
    transduction, B-NP, 61

Psychological Properties (cont.)
    tremolo, ALW-SP, 67
    vibrato, ALW-SP, 67
Receptors, ALW-SP, 65, 85-100; B-NP,
    69-71
    auditory nerve, B-NP, 70
      fibers, B-NP, 61, 63-65, 67, 70
    central auditory pathways, B-NP, 64-65
      anatomy of, B-NP, 64-65
        nucleus, B-NP, 64
        olivocochlear bundle, B-NP, 65,
          67, 69
        subcortical nuclei, B-NP, 64-65
    cochlear nucleus, B-NP, 65-67, 69-70
    cochlear potential, B-NP, 61
    defects, ALW-SP, 72, 93-94
      presbycusis, ALW-SP, 72
      Wittmaack's observation, ALW-SP,
        93-94
    function, ALW-SP, 72, 85-99
    hair cell, B-NP, 60-61, 63, 65, 70
    organ of Corti, B-NP, 60-61
    organ of hearing, B-NP, 58
    place principle, B-NP, 65
    reception
      auditory, B-NP, 59, 61
      conduction of vibrations, B-NP,
        59-61
      of sound waves, B-NP, 59
    sensory processes of, ALW-SP, 65-101
    spiral ganglion, B-NP, 60-61
    tonotopic organization, B-NP, 65-66
    vestibular nerve, B-NP, 60
Response Systems and Properties
    attention, B-NP, 70
    conversation, B-NP, 70
    head movements, B-NP, 70
    orientation, B-NP, 70
    response areas (auditory, neural),
      B-NP, 63-64, 66
    selective listening, B-NP, 70
    sleeping, B-NP, 70
Stimuli
    acoustic combination, ALW-SP, 80
    amplitude, ALW-SP, 66-67, 74, 79,
      81-85; B-NP, 58
    anechoic chamber, ALW-SP, 76-77
    beats, ALW-SP, 80, 84-85; B-NP, 69
    binaural stimulation, B-NP, 67
    binaural time difference, B-NP, 67
      head, B-NP, 66, 83
      latency difference, B-NP, 66
      sound shadow, B-NP, 66

Stimuli (cont.)
  body effects, ALW-SP, 76
  click, B-NP, 67
  complexities of, ALW-SP, 65
  complex tones, B-NP, 69
  complex waves, ALW-SP, 70
  compression-rarefaction, ALW-SP,
    99-100
  decibel, (db), ALW-SP, 74-75, 79
    power, ALW-SP, 74
    ratio expression, ALW-SP, 75
  displacement of basilar membrane,
    B-NP, 62
  dynes, ALW-SP, 79
  frequency, ALW-SP, 67, 71-72, 81-82,
    84, 91, 93, 95-97, 99-100; B-NP,
    58-59, 62-65
  funneling, ALW-SP, 98
  general, B-NP, 123
  intensity, B-NP, 58, 62-64, 69
  language, B-NP, 58, 69
  phase difference, ALW-SP, 70
  physical character, ALW-SP, 67-71
  pressure, B-NP, 60, 76
    air, B-NP, 58-59
    water, B-NP, 58
    waves, B-NP, 58, 61, 64, 69
  random noise, ALW-SP, 71
  resonance principle, ALW-SP, 90-91
  sine wave, ALW-SP, 70-71, 73, 79,
    81, 93
  sound pressure level (SPL), ALW-SP,
    75
  sound wave, B-NP, 60-61
  spectrogram, B-NP, 59
  transmittivity, ALW-SP, 88-99
  vibration, ALW-SP, 65, 87-88, 90, 94-97
  voice, B-NP, 58
  wavelength, ALW-SP, 69-71, 95, 99
  white noise, ALW-SP, 71

Theories
  atomic, ALW-SP, 68
  Békésy, ALW-SP, 92-99
  DuVerney, ALW-SP, 92, 95-97
  Helmholtz, ALW-SP, 91-92, 95-97
  resonance, ALW-SP, 90-97
  Rutherford, ALW-SP, 97
  standing wave, ALW-SP, 92, 95-97
  statistical decision, ALW-SP, 76
  telephone, ALW-SP, 91, 97
  traveling wave, ALW-SP, 92-98
  volley, ALW-SP, 92

Theories (cont.)
  Wever-Bray, ALW-SP, 92
    effect, ALW-SP, 98

SMELL, ALW-SP, 102-113; B-NP, 86-90

Anatomy (Non-neural)
  nasal cavity, B-NP, 87-88, 90
  nose, ALW-SP, 102-113
Measurement
  electro-olfactogram (EOG), B-NP, 88
  olfactory discrimination, B-NP, 87, 90
  selectivity, ALW-SP, 109-111
  sensation, ALW-SP, 103-112
  sensitivity, ALW-SP, 103-112
    chemical, ALW-SP, 103-112
  threshold, ALW-SP, 106-107
    absolute, B-NP, 88
    differential, B-NP, 88
Psychological Characteristics
  anosmia, B-NP, 86
  chemical sense, B-NP, 86
  interspecies comparisons, B-NP, 86-87
  microsmic, B-NP, 86, 90, 95
    affective value, B-NP, 86, 91
    biological drives, B-NP, 86
    evaluative reaction, B-NP, 86
    reinforcement, B-NP, 86
  odors, ALW-SP, 102-113; B-NP, 88-90
    burnt, B-NP, 88
    characteristics, ALW-SP, 103
    chemistry of, ALW-SP, 102-113
    flowery, B-NP, 88
    foul, B-NP, 88
    fruity, B-NP, 88
    mixed, ALW-SP, 107
    pure, ALW-SP, 107
    quality, B-NP, 147
    resinous, B-NP, 88
    spicy, B-NP, 88
  olfaction, B-NP, 34
  olfactory sense, B-NP, 86
    sensitivity, B-NP, 87
  sense of smell, B-NP, 87, 152
Receptors (Nose), ALW-SP, 102-113
  function, ALW-SP, 106-113
  olfaction, ALW-SP, 102-112
  olfactory morality, ALW-SP, 102
  sensory processes of, ALW-SP, 102-113
  structure, ALW-SP, 104-113; B-NP, 88

Receptors (Nose) (cont.)
olfactory epithelium, ALW-SP, 114;
B-NP, 87-89
Response Systems and Properties
alerting behavior, B-NP, 90
arousal, B-NP, 86, 90, 95
maternal behavior, B-NP, 86
sexual behavior, B-NP, 86, 95
social behavior, B-NP, 86
chewing, B-NP, 90
feeding, B-NP, 86, 95
heart rate, B-NP, 90
licking, B-NP, 90
pupillary dilation, B-NP, 90
salivation, B-NP, 90
Stimuli
acetone, B-NP, 90
absorption, B-NP, 88
amylacetate, B-NP, 90
atomic bonds, B-NP, 88
breathing, B-NP, 87
eddy currents, B-NP, 87
inspiration, B-NP, 87
sniffing, B-NP, 87, 90
chemistry, ALW-SP, 102-113
odiferous elements, ALW-SP, 103
electrical stimulation, B-NP, 90
enzyme systems, B-NP, 88
fat, B-NP, 88
glandular substances, B-NP, 90
infrared absorption, B-NP, 88
mercaptan, B-NP, 88
musk, B-NP, 88
odorous particles, B-NP, 87-88
olfactory stimuli, B-NP, 161
soluble, B-NP, 88
water, B-NP, 88

TASTE, ALW-SP, 113-123; B-NP, 91-97

Anatomy (Non-neural)
epiglottis, B-NP, 95
oral cavity, B-NP, 91
rat tongue, B-NP, 94, 96
stomach, B-NP, 94
throat, B-NP, 91
tongue, B-NP, 91, 93-95
Measurement
discrimination, B-NP, 95-96
sensation, ALW-SP, 113-123
thresholds, ALW-SP, 114, 119

Measurement (cont.)
aversion, B-NP, 95
preference, B-NP, 95
Psychological Characteristics
adaptation, B-NP, 92
cross-adaptation, B-NP, 92-93
affective value of taste, B-NP, 91
appetitive behavior, B-NP, 91
aversions, B-NP, 91, 96
for salt, B-NP, 95-96
bitter, B-NP, 91-93
learning, B-NP, 91
motivation, B-NP, 86, 90, 95
affective value, B-NP, 86, 91
biological drives, B-NP, 86
bodily needs, B-NP, 91
evaluative reactions, B-NP, 86
hunger, B-NP, 91
reinforcement, B-NP, 86
NaCl, B-NP, 94
nutritional value, B-NP, 91
perceived intensity, B-NP, 92
preferences, B-NP, 91, 96
food, B-NP, 96
salt, B-NP, 95-96
quinine, B-NP, 95
saltiness, B-NP, 92
sensations from
mouth, B-NP, 149
stomach, B-NP, 149
sense of taste, B-NP, 91
sensory qualities, B-NP, 91-92
sourness, B-NP, 92
sugar, B-NP, 93, 174
sweetness, B-NP, 92
taste, ALW-SP, 113-123
basic, ALW-SP, 113
qualities, B-NP, 91, 93, 147

Receptors, ALW-SP, 114-122; B-NP, 91-93
chemoreceptors, B-NP, 91
cilia, B-NP, 87
coding, B-NP, 93
functions, ALW-SP, 114-122
gustatory pore, B-NP, 91-92
microvilli, B-NP, 92
papillae, ALW-SP, 114; B-NP, 91
taste buds, ALW-SP, 114; B-NP, 91-93
taste cells, B-NP, 93
taste receptors, B-NP, 91-93, 95

Response Systems and Properties
arousal, B-NP, 86, 90, 95
maternal behavior, B-NP, 86

Response Systems and Properties (cont.)
sexual behavior, B-NP, 86, 95
social behavior, B-NP, 86
fear, B-NP, 96
feeding, B-NP, 86-95
predator, B-NP, 86
prey, B-NP, 86
sexual behavior, B-NP, 95
Stimuli, ALW-SP, 113-122; B-NP, 91-93
acidity, B-NP, 92
amino acids, B-NP, 92
beryllium salt, B-NP, 92
chemical sensitivity, ALW-SP, 113-120
chemistry of, ALW-SP, 113-122
chloride ion, B-NP, 92
citric acid, B-NP, 92
glucose, B-NP, 92
hydrogen ion, B-NP, 92
organic acid, B-NP, 92
saccharine, B-NP, 91-92
salt, B-NP, 93, 95
sodium chloride, B-NP, 92
sodium ion, B-NP, 92
stomach distension, B-NP, 94
balloon, B-NP, 94
sucrose, B-NP, 92, 95
taste stimuli, B-NP, 91-93
water, B-NP, 96
Theory, ALW-SP, 115-118
Davis, ALW-SP, 115-118

Anatomy (Non-neural) (cont.)
prepuce, B-NP, 74
skin, B-NP, 72, 74, 77, 79, 81
smooth muscle, B-NP, 73
soles, feet, B-NP, 74
subcutaneous fat, B-NP, 73
tongue, B-NP, 72
trunk, B-NP, 79
uvula, B-NP, 72
Measurement
conditioned reflex method, ALW-SP, 143-144
discrimination, B-NP, 160
esthesiometer, B-NP, 72
power function, B-NP, 77, 79
sensation, ALW-SP, 124-125
sensitivity, ALW-SP, 124-125; B-NP, 72, 74-75
threshold, ALW-SP, 129; B-NP, 78-83
two-point, B-NP, 72
vibratory, B-NP, 72
mechanical vibratory, B-NP, 72
verbal report of human subjects, B-NP, 72
Psychological Properties
adaptation, B-NP, 76-78
thermal, B-NP, 78
behavior, ALW-SP, 124-125, 130-133, 144-145
milieu intérieur concept, ALW-SP, 140
muscular cues of depth perception, WW-P, 38
kinesthesis, B-NP, 71, 79, 83; WW-P, 21
sensations of accommodation, WW-P, 21, 33
sensations of convergence, WW-P, 21, 33
proprioceptive feedback, M-CP, 37, 44, 59-60
psychotic states, B-NP, 86
sensations
burning, B-NP, 77
hollow feeling, B-NP, 71
human pin cushion, B-NP, 72
inflammation, B-NP, 71
noxious stimulation, B-NP, 77, 79, 84, 86, 138
perceived magnitude of stimulus, B-NP, 77
pressure spots, B-NP, 72
pricking, B-NP, 77

TOUCH AND KINESTHESIS, ALW-SP, 124-145, B-NP, 70-86

Anatomy (Non-neural)
arm, B-NP, 81
body, B-NP, 70, 81, 83
cat tongue, B-NP, 77-78
conjunctiva, B-NP, 74
cornea, B-NP, 75
dermis, B-NP, 73
epidermis, B-NP, 73
face, B-NP, 72, 84
finger, B-NP, 71-72, 81, 83
hair, B-NP, 73
follicles, B-NP, 74
hand, B-NP, 71, 78, 83
joint, B-NP, 71, 79
leg, B-NP, 72
limb, B-NP, 71, 79, 83
palm, hand, B-NP, 72-74

Psychological Properties (cont.)
    satin, B-NP, 71
    sensitivity (cutaneous, sensibility,
        senses), B-NP, 78
        cold, ALW-SP, 134; B-NP, 71-72,
            74, 78
        heat ,warm., ALW-SP, 134; B-NP,
            71-72, 74, 78, 100
        kinesthetic, B-NP, 85
        pain, ALW-SP, 134; B-NP, 70-72,
            74, 77, 83, 85-86, 100, 103, 105,
            138; B-PD, 5-6
        tactile (touch), B-NP, 74, 84-85;
            ALW-SP, 134
        thermal, B-NP, 75, 77, 84; ALW-SP,
            134
    sensory information, B-NP, 83
    somatosensory information, B-NP, 79
Receptors, ALW-SP, 124-146
    classification, ALW-SP, 124-129, 134-144
        extero, ALW-SP, 124-129, 134-144;
            B-NP, 71
        intero, ALW-SP, 124-129, 134-144;
            B-NP, 71
    cutaneous, B-NP, 73-75, 77
        nerve endings, B-NP, 105
    dermatome, B-NP, 79
    encapsulated endings, B-NP, 74, 77
    end organs, B-NP, 77
    free nerve endings, B-NP, 10, 73-74,
        77, 79
    function, ALW-SP, 124-145
    internal environment, ALW-SP, 124-146
        behavioral effects, ALW-SP, 130-133
        bodily orientation, ALW-SP, 127-133
    joint, B-NP, 79
    Krause end bulbs, B-NP, 73-74
    mechanical filter, B-NP, 76
    Meissner's corpuscle, ALW-SP, 134;
        B-NP, 73-74
    Merkle's disks, B-NP, 73-74
    Pacinian corpuscle, ALW-SP, 134;
        B-NP, 73-76
    physiological response, B-NP, 75-76
    proprioceptor, B-NP, 56, 71, 99, 101,
        107-108; M-CP, 37
    Ruffini cylinder (endings), ALW-SP,
        134; B-NP, 73-74
    sensory spots, B-NP, 72-74
    somatic, B-NP, 71-72, 79
    sebaceous gland, B-NP, 73
    tactile, B-NP, 38, 77, 79
    thermal, B-NP, 143

Receptors (cont.)
    transduction, B-NP, 71
Response Systems and Properties
    movement, B-NP, 83
        apraxia, B-NP, 83
        sensory guidance of, B-NP, 99
        skilled, B-NP, 83
    muscles, B-NP, 83
    spatial orientation, B-NP, 83
Stimuli
    cutaneous, B-NP, 86
    displacement, B-NP, 74-76
        of hairs, B-NP, 74
        of skin, B-NP, 71
    intensity, B-NP, 77
    mechanical stimulation, B-NP, 75
    movement, B-NP, 71
    muscle stretch, B-NP, 103
    object quality
        composition, B-NP, 71
        shape, B-NP, 71
        size, B-NP, 71
        texture, B-NP, 71, 80-81
            sandpaper, B-NP, 81
    pressure against skin, B-NP, 99
    somatic, B-NP, 71
    tactile, B-NP, 77, 81, 83-84, 100, 104,
        123, 161
        light touch, B-NP, 76-77
        pressure, B-NP, 99
    temperature, B-NP, 72
    heat, B-NP, 77-78, 100
    radiant energy, B-NP, 72

VISION, ALW-SP, 13-64; B-NP, 39-58

Anatomy (Non-neural)
    anterior chamber, B-NP, 41
    chorioid, B-NP, 41
    ciliary muscle, B-NP, 41-42
    cornea, B-NP, 41-42
    eye, B-NP, 100, 131, 163
    eyeball, B-NP, 56
    eye muscle, B-NP, 56
    extraocular muscle, B-NP, 42
    extrinsic muscles, B-NP, 42, 56
    iris, B-NP, 41-42
    lens, B-NP, 40-41
    orbit, B-NP, 42
    pigmented epithelium, B-NP, 43
    pupil, B-NP, 42

Anatomy (Non-neural) (cont.)
  sclera, B-NP, 41
  sphincter muscle, B-NP, 42
  tendon, B-NP, 56
  vitreous humor, B-NP, 41
  zonule fibers, B-NP, 41-42

Measurement
  acuity, ALW-SP, 22, 55-59; B-NP, 44
    Snellen fraction, ALW-SP, 56
    Arago phenomenon, ALW-SP, 22
  densitometry, ALW-SP, 32
  difference spectrum, ALW-SP, 34
  discrimination, B-NP, 159-160, 162-164
  microspectrophotometry, ALW-SP,
    36-37, 39
  psychophysical, ALW-SP, 19
  resolution, ALW-SP, 56-57
    acuity, ALW-SP, 56
    capacity, ALW-SP, 57
  sensitivity, ALW-SP, 14-17, 20-55
    visual, ALW-SP, 14-17, 22-55, 56
  threshold, ALW-SP, 23, 37, 39, 49-50,
    52, 56
    increment, ALW-SP, 23, 49-50, 52
    intensity, ALW-SP, 23, 49-50, 52
    separable, ALW, 56

Psychological Properties
  achromatic, ALW-SP, 19, 23-48
    Arago phenomenon, ALW-SP, 22
    brightness, ALW-SP, 18-19, 22,
      24-25, 32, 37-38, 41, 44-45, 47,
      49, 52, 55, 57; B-NP, 39-40,
      45-46, 49
      constancy, B-NP, 40; WW-P, 56ff
    attention, B-NP, 52
    binocular fusion, B-NP, 53
    contrast phenomena, ALW-SP, 44,
      WW-P, 64-65
    simultaneous brightness, ALW-SP,
      44; B-NP, 49; WW-P, 65
    simultaneous color, ALW-SP, 44;
      WW-P, 65
    successive, WW-P, 64
      adaptation level theory, WW-P, 64
      temporal induction, ALW-SP, 44

  chromatic
    adaptation, WW-P, 63-64
    anomalies, ALW-SP, 17-18, 22-24,
      27-48
      dichromatism, ALW-SP, 27-48
      monochromatism, ALW-SP, 18,
        27-48

Psychological Properties (cont.)
    trichromatism, ALW-SP, 17, 22-24,
      27-48
    chromaticity, ALW-SP, 17-19, 22-24,
      27-28; B-NP, 46, 48
    color code, B-NP, 46
      component system, B-NP, 47
      opponent system, B-NP, 48
    color vision theories, ALW-SP, 36,
      48; B-NP, 44
    differential excitation, ALW-SP, 37
    hue, ALW-SP, 18-19, 23; B-NP, 39,
      48; WW-P, 52ff
      primary, B-NP, 44
      spectral, B-NP, 44
    saturation, ALW-SP, 18-19; B-NP,
      39; WW-P, 52ff
      supersaturation, WW-P, 65
    spectral sensitivity, B-NP, 46
  learning, discrimination, B-NP, 52, 55
  photopic
    sensitivity, B-NP, 45
    system, B-NP, 46
    vision, B-NP, 44
  prey, B-NP, 51
  scotopic
    sensitivity, B-NP, 45
    system, B-NP, 46
    vision, B-NP, 44
  stability (of visual world), B-NP, 40
  visual field, B-NP, 56-57
Receptors (Eye), ALW-SP, 16-62; B-NP,
  39-58; WW-P, 20-21, 81ff
  adjustment mechanisms
    accommodation, ALW-SP, 19-21,
      61-62; B-NP, 42
    adaptation, ALW-SP, 19-62
      dark, ALW-SP, 20-21, 24-37,
        49-54; WW-P, 82
      night vision, WW-P, 81ff
    conjugate movement, B-NP, 42
    convergence, B-NP, 42
    photo-pupil motility, ALW-SP, 20-21
    photoreceivers, ALW-SP, 16-62
    pupillary dilation, B-NP, 118
    saccadic movement, ALW-SP, 60
    vergences, ALW-SP, 60
    versions, ALW-SP, 60
  chemistry of vision, ALW-SP, 27-36, 53
    chlorolabe, ALW-SP, 33
    cyanolabe, ALW-SP, 35
    erythrolabe, ALW-SP, 33
    iodopsin, ALW-SP, 33

Receptors (Eye) (cont.)
  opsin, B-NP, 43
  pigments, ALW-SP, 27-55; B-NP, 46
    absorption spectrum, B-NP, 44-45
  protein, B-NP, 43
  retinene, B-NP, 43
  rhodopsin, ALW-SP, 29; B-NP, 43-45
  vitamin A, B-NP, 43
 chromaticity response, B-NP, 48
 defects, ALW-SP, 33-34, 39-40, 57,
  60-61, 132-133
  color, ALW-SP, 33-34, 39-40
  deuteranomalous, ALW-SP, 40
  diplopia, ALW-SP, 61
  hyperopia, ALW-SP, 57
  nystagmus, ALW-SP, 60, 132-133
  protanomalous, ALW-SP, 40
  retinal, ALW-SP, 57
  tritanomalous, ALW-SP, 40
 function, ALW-SP, 19-62
 sensory processes of, ALW-SP, 13-64
 structure, ALW-SP, 19-62; B-NP, 41-48,
  51-53, 56; WW-P, 20-21
  cones, ALW-SP, 21ff; B-NP, 43-46
  fovea, ALW-SP, 21; B-NP, 41, 44, 46
  retina, ALW-SP, 20ff, B-NP, 40-48,
   51-53, 56, 125-126
   anatomical organization, B-NP,
    45-50, 53, 56
Response Systems and Properties
 eye movements, B-NP, 38, 42, 52,
  56-57, 132-134
 light reflex, B-NP, 42
 orienting, B-NP, 52
 pupillary dilation, B-NP, 118
 rapid eye movements, B-PD, 58-59
Stimuli
 absorption, ALW-SP, 14-15, 21,
  27-37, 39
 bar, B-NP, 53
 border, B-NP, 53
 dominant wavelength, ALW-SP, 18-19,
  47
 edge, B-NP, 53
 frequency, ALW-SP, 13-14, 53-54, 57-58
  critical fusion (c.f.f.), ALW-SP, 53;
   WW-P, 61
   plateau law (Talbot), ALW-SP, 53
 illumination, B-NP, 40, 44-45, 49, 51
 intensity, B-NP, 39-40, 46, 49
 light, ALW-SP, 13-62; B-NP, 39-40,
  125, 169; WW-P, 52
  definition of, WW-P, 52

Stimuli (cont.)
  flashes, B-NP, 125
  offset, B-NP, 51
  rays, B-NP, 40-42
  scattering, B-NP, 43
 luminance, ALW-SP, 14, 16, 18-19, 37;
  B-NP, 39, 44, 46, 48
 luminosity curve, ALW-SP, 16
 movement (head), B-NP, 52, 56
 movement (passive), B-NP, 56
 patterns, B-NP, 55, 69
 pressure, B-NP, 99
 purity, ALW-SP, 18-19
 quantum theory, ALW-SP, 14
 radiant energy, ALW-SP, 13-14
 reflectance, B-NP, 49
 refraction, B-NP, 40-42
 retinal image, B-NP, 40, 42-43;
  WW-P, 10, 39
  focus, B-NP, 40, 42
  geometry of size, WW-P, 39
  homologous points, B-NP, 42
  image points, B-NP, 40-41
  inversion, WW-P, 10
  object points, B-NP, 40-41
  orientation, WW-P, 10
 sine wave, ALW-SP, 53-55, 57-59
 spectrum, B-NP, 40, 44
 useful dimensions of, B-NP, 40
 visual field, B-NP, 56-57
 visual stimulus, B-NP, 99, 123, 161
 wavelength, ALW-SP, 13-47; B-NP,
  39, 48
  purity, B-NP, 39
Theories, ALW-SP, 36-48
 color, ALW-SP, 36-48
 component theory (Young), ALW-SP,
  36-43, 48; B-NP, 47
 duplicity theory, ALW-SP, 21-22
 opponent (Helmholtz), ALW-SP, 43,
  46-47; B-NP, 48

§13 SOCIAL

Attitude, H-QP, 19, 58; M-HD, 23; Z-SP,
  5, 62-64
  change, Z-SP, 5, 45-48, 65-66
  logic, M-CP, 102
  measurement, H-QP, 53, 68-74
  memory, M-CP, 32
  message interpretation, M-CP, 72-79
  scaling, H-QP, 53, 68-74
Audience Effects, Z-SP, 10-15
  dominant responses, Z-SP, 14
  monitoring tasks, Z-SP, 11-12
  multiplication, Z-SP, 12
  nonsense syllable learning, Z-SP, 12
  pursuit rotor performance, Z-SP, 10-11
  relearning, Z-SP, 13
  word association, Z-SP, 12
Coaction Effects, Z-SP, 16-28
  ants, Z-SP, 17-18
  avoidance learning, Z-SP, 24-28
  birds, Z-SP, 18
  chain associations, Z-SP, 20
  cockroaches, Z-SP, 18-19
  discrimination learning, Z-SP, 18-19
  dominant responses, Z-SP, 21
  drinking, Z-SP, 25
  eating, Z-SP, 25
  fish, Z-SP, 21-22
  judgments, Z-SP, 20
  maze learning, Z-SP, 18-19, 21-24
  multiplication, Z-SP, 20
  nest building, Z-SP, 17-18
  problem solving, Z-SP, 20
  reversible perspective, Z-SP, 20
  stress tolerance, Z-SP, 16, 24-28
  vowel cancelation, Z-SP, 20
Communication, M-HD, 34-36, 66-67;
  Z-SP, 52, 53-66
  co-linearity, Z-SP, 63-64
  consummatory, Z-SP, 58, 64-65
  incidental, Z-SP, 58, 65-66
  instrumental, Z-SP, 58, 60-64
  persuasion, Z-SP, 55, 66
  rumor, Z-SP, 61-62
  selective factors, Z-SP, 60-63
  uniformity, Z-SP, 58-60
Competition, Z-SP, 2, 53
  choice to compete, Z-SP, 72-78
  dominance, Z-SP, 78-81, 93
  population density, Z-SP, 93

Competition (cont.)
  love, Z-SP, 93-95
Conflict, Z-SP, 53
  conventionalization, Z-SP, 81
  dominance, Z-SP, 79-80
Conformity, Z-SP, 37-40, 87-88
  adaptive function of, Z-SP, 39-40
  judgment difficulty, Z-SP, 38-39
Cooperation, Z-SP, 53
  choice to cooperate, Z-SP, 72-78
  development of, Z-SP, 68-72
  with a simulated partner, Z-SP, 76-77
Group, Z-SP, 99-108
  decision, Z-SP, 101-103
  division of labor, Z-SP, 102-108
  individual products, combined, Z-SP,
    102-108
  performance, Z-SP, 99-108
  coordination, Z-SP, 103
  individual performance, Z-SP, 99-102
Imitation, Z-SP, 29-40
  false judgments, Z-SP, 37-40
  instinct, Z-SP, 29-30
  low probability responses, Z-SP, 40
  social reinforcement, Z-SP, 48-50
Learning, Z-SP, 5, 7-8, 12-13, 16, 18,
  51-82 (See LEARNING)
  audience effects
    relearning, Z-SP, 13
    nonsense syllable learning, Z-SP, 12
  coaction effects
    avoidance learning, Z-SP, 24-28
    discrimination learning, Z-SP, 18
    maze learning, Z-SP, 18-19, 21-24
  reinforcement, Z-SP, 43-53
    behavior control, Z-SP, 42-43
    facilitation, Z-SP, 16
    imitation, Z-SP, 48-50
    instincts, Z-SP, 7-8
    interaction, Z-SP, 5, 51-82
    reciprocity, Z-SP, 53
    tantrums, Z-SP, 41-43
    verbal, Z-SP, 43-48
      opinions, Z-SP, 44-46
      self-acceptance, Z-SP, 48
Moral, Z-SP, 49-50
  development, Z-SP, 49
  judgment, Z-SP, 49-50
Motivation, Z-SP, 14-15, 51
  affiliation, Z-SP, 6
  aggression, Z-SP, 6
  aggressiveness, Z-SP, 79
  dominance, Z-SP, 79-80

Motivation (cont.)
  eating, Z-SP, 25
  stress tolerance, Z-SP, 16, 24-48
  cognitive dissonance, M-CP, 102-104;
    Z-SP, 6
  conflict, Z-SP, 53, 79-81
  dominance, Z-SP, 93
  interdependence (motivational),
    Z-SP, 52
  presence of others as arousal, Z-SP,
    13-15
Opinions, Z-SP, 5, 45-48, 62-66
  authoritarianism, Z-SP, 45-46
  co-linearity, Z-SP, 63-64
  E-scale (ethnocentrism), Z-SP, 46-48
  F-scale (fascism), Z-SP, 46-48
  self-acceptance, Z-SP, 48
Presence of Others, Z-SP, 2, 10-28
  adrenocortical activity, Z-SP, 14
  arousal, Z-SP, 13-15
  hydrocortisone secretion, Z-SP, 14
  performance, Z-SP, 2, 10-28
  source of cues, Z-SP, 23
Social (General)
  aspects of behavior, Z-SP, 7-8
  behavior, Z-SP, 5-50
    perception, M-CP, 86
  characteristics and perception,
    M-CP, 75
  differentiation, Z-SP, 83, 92-98
    antireciprocity bias, Z-SP, 98
    balance, Z-SP, 97-98
    reciprocity bias, Z-SP, 95
    sociometric bias, Z-SP, 95
    sociometry, Z-SP, 94-95
  ills, Z-SP, 6
    industrial conflict, Z-SP, 6
    juvenile delinquency, Z-SP, 6
    prejudice, Z-SP, 6
    race relations, Z-SP, 6
    war, Z-SP, 6
  man as a social animal, Z-SP, 7-8
  psychology, Z-SP, 1-5
    definition, Z-SP, 1
    development of, Z-SP, 2-5
    topics, Z-SP, 5-6
      attitude, Z-SP, 5
      attitude change, Z-SP, 5
      group cohesiveness, Z-SP, 5
      individual processes, Z-SP, 6
      leadership, Z-SP, 5
      persuasion, Z-SP, 5
      role relations, Z-SP, 5

Social (General) (cont.)
    self, Z-SP, 5
    socialization, Z-SP, 5
  schemata, Z-SP, 97
  situation (minimal), Z-SP, 67-72
  uniformity, Z-SP, 4, 58-60, 83-92
    autokinetic effect, Z-SP, 88
    beliefs, Z-SP, 89-90
    cohesiveness, Z-SP, 5, 60
    communication, Z-SP, 58-60
    conventions, Z-SP, 81, 89
    culture, Z-SP, 89
    animals, Z-SP, 91-92
    development of, Z-SP, 85-92
    maintenance of, Z-SP, 87-91
    norms, Z-SP, 89-91
      support for, Z-SP, 90
      transmission of, Z-SP, 89-91
    pressures toward, Z-SP, 58-60

§14 STATISTICS

Association, H-BS, 88-106
  bivariate frequency distributions,
    H-BS, 27-30
    and statistical association, H-BS, 91ff
    scatter plots, H-BS, 28-30
  contingency tables, H-BS, 28-30,
    91-96, 104
    departures from independence,
      H-BS, 91
  indices of relationship between
    variables, H-BS, 59, 66, 91-106
  C^2, H-BS, 94-96
  chi-square, H-BS, 94-96, 104-105,
    113
    expected frequency, H-BS, 94
    obtained frequency, H-BS, 94
    tables of, H-BS, 113
    test significance, H-BS, 104
  correlation coefficient, H-BS, 96-106;
    K-AHC, 3, 38
    curvilinear relation, H-BS, 97-98;
      K-AHC, 38
    linear association, H-BS, 97-105

Association (cont.)
    qualitative variables, H-BS, 96
    regression, "r," K-AHC, 3, 91
    significance of correlation
      coefficient, H-BS, 104
    significant values of r for various
      degrees of freedom, H-BS, 114
    standard error of estimate, H-BS,
      102-3
Central Tendency, H-BS,
  measures of, H-BS, 32
    mean, H-BS, 33-43
      as central tendency measure,
        H-BS, 33-38
      in computing standardized scores,
        H-BS, 41-43
      in computing variance, H-BS, 39
      of a grouped distribution, H-BS,
        34-36
      of probability distribution,
        H-BS, 55
      of a random variable, H-BS, 55-58
      sampling distribution of, H-BS,
        70-86
    mode, H-BS, 32-33, 38
    and shapes of distributions, H-BS, 36
Characteristics and Properties, H-BS,
  1-5, 20
  descriptive, H-BS, 1-2, 5, 20
  inferential, H-BS, 2
  methods, K-AHC, 3, 69, 99
  problems, H-BS, 4, 30-31, 43-44,
    64-65, 86-87, 106-107
  in psychology, H-BS, 1
  uses of, H-BS, 3; K-AHC, 95
Data and Variables
  abstraction (loss of information), H-BS,
    8-10
  data, H-BS, 1, 17, 23, 28, 45
    events, H-BS, 45
    numerical, H-BS, 1, 17, 23, 28
    qualitative, H-BS, 28
  induction, H-BS, 2
  scores, H-BS, 41-43, 62
    raw, H-BS, 41-42
    standardized, H-BS, 41-43, 62
    true, K-AHC, 36, 40
    value, H-BS, 24, 32-33, 40
  standardized, H-BS, 41-43, 62
    scores, H-BS, 41-43, 62
    values, H-BS, 41
  variables, H-BS, 27, 88
    cluster of, K-AHC, 91

Data and Variables (cont.)
  dependent, H-BS, 88, 91
  dimensions, K-AHC, 91-93
  independent, H-BS, 88, 92
  nuisance, H-BS, 89-91
  random, H-BS, 50-61
    continuous, H-BS, 54-55
    discrete, H-BS, 52-54
    mean of, H-BS, 55-58
    standard deviation of, H-BS, 56-57
    variance of, H-BS, 56-57

Distributions
  defined, H-BS, 5
    attribute, H-BS, 5-6
  frequency, H-BS, 5-31, 55, 61; H-QP, 52
    bivariate, H-BS, 27-30, 91ff
    cumulative, H-BS, 23-27, 71
      relative, H-BS, 24-27
    dispersion, discriminable, H-QP, 31
    marginal, H-BS, 28-29
    relative, H-BS, 14-15, 19, 54-55, 92
    and sampling, H-BS, 70-71
    univariate, H-BS, 27
    value, H-QP, 31
  graphs of distributions, H-BS, 6, 15-31
    frequency polygons, H-BS, 17-19
      cumulative-relative, H-BS, 26-27
    histogram, H-BS, 16-17
    shape, H-BS, 20-23
      and central tendency, H-BS, 36-38
      multimodal, H-BS, 20-23
      symmetrical, H-BS, 23
      unimodal, H-BS, 20-23
    of variable relationships, H-BS, 96-97
  intervals
    class, H-BS, 9-14
      size, H-BS, 9-13
    grouped distribution, H-BS, 9-13
      means of, H-BS, 34-36, 40, 55
    limits of, H-BS, 9, 11-12
      apparent, H-BS, 12
      of confidence, H-BS, 73
      real, H-BS, 12
    midpoints of, H-BS, 13
      in computing mean, H-BS, 35
      in computing variance, H-BS, 40
      in graphing, H-BS, 17
    percentiles, H-BS, 24-26
  pairings, H-BS, 5-6, K-AHC, 6
  probability (density) distributions and
    functions, H-BS, 3, 5, 45-64
    basic rules of, H-BS, 46-47

Distributions (cont.)
  cumulative distribution function,
    H-BS, 51-54
  density function, H-BS, 54-55, 59-61
    normal, H-BS, 59-64
    standardized normal, H-BS, 62-64
  elementary event, H-BS, 45-50
  event, H-BS, 45-50
  numerical event, H-BS, 50-51
  probabilities (basic), H-BS, 46
  random samples, H-BS, 49-50, 66-73
    how drawn, H-BS, 68
    importance, H-BS, 67
  random variables, H-BS, 55-57
    mean of, H-BS, 55
    sums and differences of, H-BS, 57
  normal, H-BS, 54-64, 73, 108; H-QP,
    31-64, 53-54, 64-67
  parameters of distribution, H-BS, 61
  probability and density, H-BS, 108
  standardized, H-BS, 62-64

Experimental Design, K-AHC, 90
  classical, K-AHC, 90
  multivariate, K-AHC, 90

Inference, H-BS, 3, 57, 60, 66-86
  central-limit theorem, H-BS, 73
  confidence interval, H-BS, 73-78
  confidence limits of means, H-BS, 74
  errors in measurement, H-BS, 61
  errors in sampling, H-BS, 69-70, 73
  estimate principle, H-BS, 69, 72-73
  hypothesis testing, H-BS, 80-86, 104-105
    use of chi-square, H-BS, 104

Inference (cont.)
  and correlation coefficient, H-BS,
    104-105
  of differences between means, H-BS,
    83-86
  null hypothesis, H-BS, 60, 80-82, 105
  means, sums and differences of, H-BS,
    78-80
  population distribution, H-BS, 67,
    70-71
  random number tables, H-BS, 68
  samples, H-BS, 66, 70-86
    independent, H-BS, 78-80
    random, H-BS, 66
    sampling distribution, H-BS, 70-86
Variability, H-BS, 14, 26, 31, 32, 39-43,
  51-57, 61-62, 67, 71-75, 79-80, 84,
  102-103; K-AHC, 3, 11, 93
  scatter, H-BS, 14, 26
  source of, K-AHC, 93
  standard deviation, H-BS, 39, 41-43,
    56-57, 61-62; H-QP, 33, 39, 45;
    K-AHC, 39
    in linear association, H-BS, 102-103
    of a random variable, H-BS, 56-57
    of a sampling distribution, H-BS,
      71-72, 74, 79-80, 84
  variance, H-BS, 39-41, 56-57; H-QP,
    31-32, 51-54, 67, 75; K-AHC, 88
    covariance, H-QP, 31-32
    in linear association, H-BS, 102-103
    of a random variable, H-BS, 56-57
    of a sampling distribution, H-BS,
      71-72